POSTCARD HISTORY SERIES

Sanibel and Captiva Islands

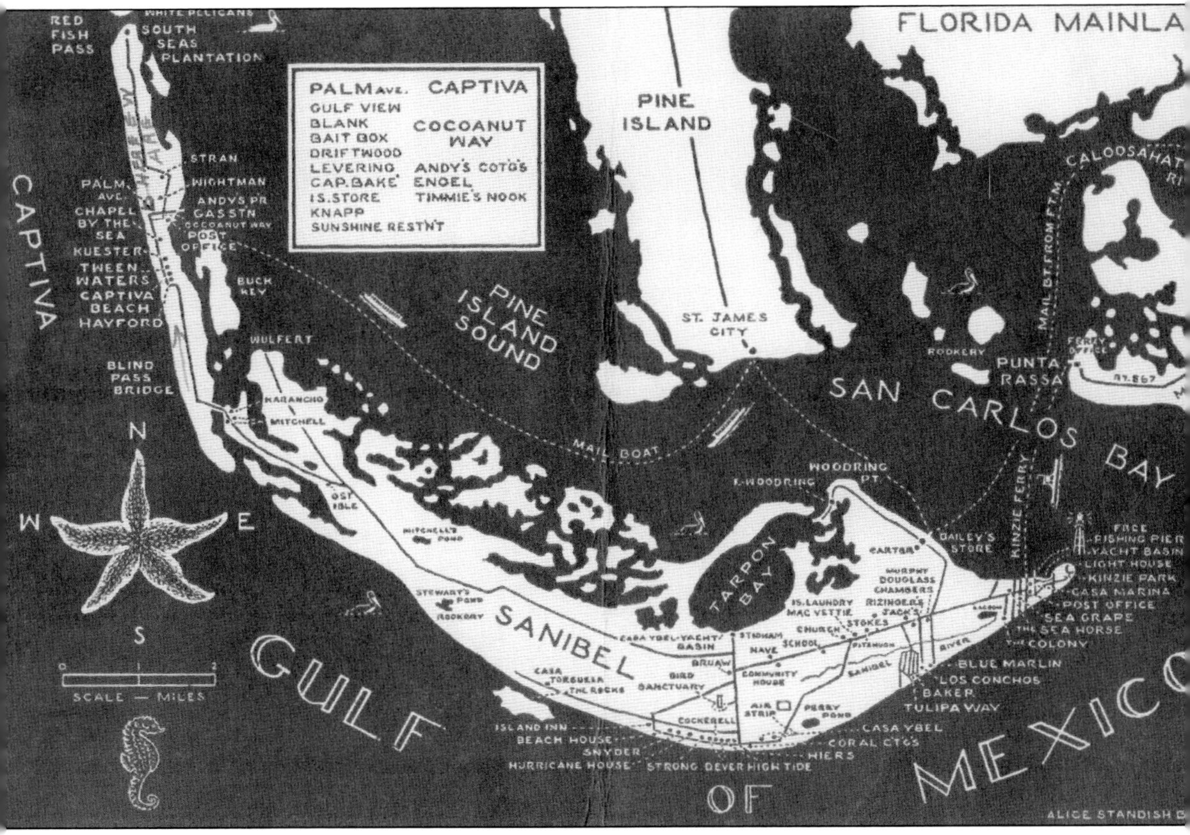

This Sanibel and Captiva Islands map was rendered as an oversize c. 1956 postcard. Although this card bears no prominent advertising, it was probably the brainchild of Priscilla Murphy, a realtor. At that time, the communities on each island were tiny, with a total population of around 200 full-time residents, so few there was room for both businesses and personal residences on this unique island directory. (Courtesy of Islander Trading Post.)

On the Front Cover: The steel-hulled, 78-gross-ton *Yankee Clipper* was built by Blount Boats Inc. of Warren, Rhode Island, for the Kinzie Brothers Steamer Line in 1952. Her sister, the *Rebel*, was built at the same shipyard in 1957 but was smaller and displaced 73 gross tons. Both ferries plied San Carlos Bay, carrying vehicles, passengers, and necessities of all kinds from Punta Rassa to Sanibel and Captiva Islands until 1963. (Courtesy of Islander Trading Post.)

On the Back Cover: The first Blind Pass Bridge was wooden and spanned the pass in 1918, replacing a barge-like ferry. This postcard illustrates the second bridge, built after a 1926 hurricane destroyed the original. The one-lane bridge has angled trusses over the deepest part of the pass, which was closer to Sanibel. These supported the span to provide a wider horizontal clearance for the passage of small boats. (Courtesy of Islander Trading Post.)

POSTCARD HISTORY SERIES

Sanibel and Captiva Islands

Deborah Gleason and Charles LeBuff

ARCADIA PUBLISHING

ISBN 978-0-7385-9087-5

Published by Arcadia Publishing
Charleston, South Carolina

Printed in the United States of America

Library of Congress Control Number: 2012944277

For all general information contact Arcadia Publishing at:
Telephone 843-853-2070
Fax 843-853-0044
E-mail sales@arcadiapublishing.com
For customer service and orders:
Toll-Free 1-888-313-2665

Visit us on the Internet at www.arcadiapublishing.com

To all islanders and soon-to-be-islanders who may read our book and share a memory or learn a bit about the past that has shaped (with the help of numerous hurricanes) our present-day islands.

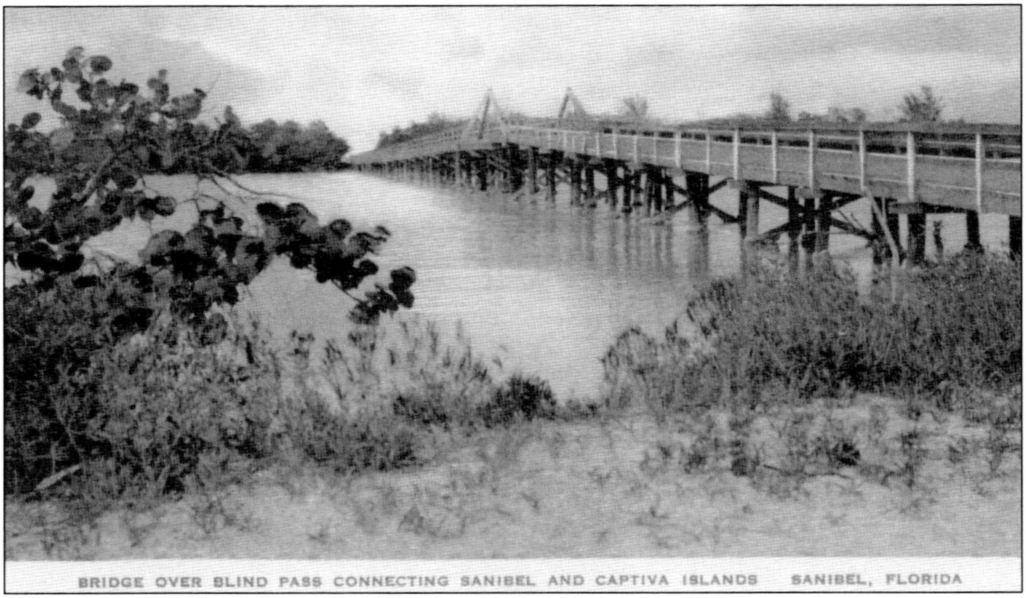

Captiva and Sanibel Islands were socially and economically integrated until 1974. That year, the communities divided politically when Sanibel chose to curtail rampant development and become a city. Captiva residents voted to not join their neighbor's efforts in self-preservation and remained under the direct political jurisdiction of Lee County. Today, most residents of these "sister islands" are united to preserve their common natural environments and values. (Courtesy of Islander Trading Post.)

Contents

Acknowledgments

We the authors, Deb Gleason and Charles LeBuff, each moved to Sanibel Island in 1958 and began leading our quaint, unhurried island lives, now more than 55 years ago. Never did we imagine we would have a future as deltiologists. That is because we only recently found out that the study and collection of postcards (something we have done independently for decades) is called deltiology. We are in good company though because worldwide, postcard collecting is the third largest hobby after stamp collecting and coin or money collecting. (We both also like to collect money, too, but in the bank.)

Postcard collections range from family albums to extensive library or genealogical society collections. There are postcard clubs to join, shows to attend, and antique shops and flea markets to visit. The interest is not only the subject matter on the front of the card but the wealth of information to be gleaned from the back of a postmarked, mailed card from long ago. Many of the postcards reproduced in this book are early photochrome cards, but we also feature a number of RPPC, or real-photo postcards, and vintage linen cards.

In compiling this book, we had several exceptional sources of postcards to select from, including our own collections. Without the generous contributions and consent from fellow collectors, we could not have nearly achieved such a vast inventory of postcard images. We extend our heartfelt thanks to contributors who have shared many outstanding old cards from their collections, including Bob Averill, owner of the Islander Trading Post; Sanibel Historical Museum and Village; Captiva Island Historical Society and Ty Christoff; the Sanibel Public Library and Betty Anholt; Ralph Curtis; Tom Hoopes; Alvin Lederer; Gerri Much; and Jim Pickens. We also want to thank the Bailey family and Sanibel Packing Company for decades of producing and selling Sanibel Island postcards in their island-essential general store, where the motto was "If we don't have it you don't need it."

Introduction

Those who sailed aboard the three-vessel fleet led by Castilian adventurer Juan Ponce (Juan Ponce de León) and master pilot António (Antón) Alaminos were the first known Europeans to visit Sanibel and Captiva Islands in 1513. Postcards were not in vogue—they had not been invented yet—appearing almost another four centuries later. Had souvenir cards been around, Juan Ponce certainly would have posted a few back home. He and his mariners were the first non-native people to become enraptured with these islands, and Ponce dared to return a few years later, even after being repulsed and driven away the first time by the Calusa Indians shortly after their team "discovered" Florida.

Alaminos and Ponce could not shake memories of what centuries later would be called Captiva and Sanibel by other settlers and visitors. Alaminos joined another expedition in 1517 and returned to Southwest Florida. He was the first of the Florida discoverers to revisit the peninsula, but his and Ponce's independent returns did not end well for either. Alaminos joined Francisco Hernández (Francisco Hernández de Córdoba) to explore the coast of the Gulf of Mexico. Along the way, Hernández planned to capture Native Americans for the Caribbean slave trade. Alaminos described the alluring islands to his conquistador commander with such fervor that the expedition changed their priorities and course. They sailed directly from a position near the coast of Yucatan to Southwest Florida, to find what would be described by a future Spanish historian as a group of "islands that make out to the sea." Among these cays would be the islands described by Alaminos, and the largest of them, Sanibel, would later be known among Spanish seafarers of the period as "Juan Ponce's watering place."

Hernández told Alaminos that he would apply for a land grant from King Carlos I of Spain for title to this island if it turned out to be as perfect as his trusted pilot claimed. If this island had a deep natural and protected harbor, luxuriant vegetation, excellent climate, and abundant natural resources, the most important of which was the availability of firewood and freshwater, he would reward him well. After landfall, this expedition was confronted by the Calusa. Unrelenting savage attacks by the natives resulted in Hernández being wounded 20 times by chert and shark tooth projectiles. He would later die in Cuba, killed by the fierce-fighting Calusa. Alaminos himself was struck 16 times by their arrows and darts but miraculously survived.

Four years later, in 1521, Ponce did not fare any better when he returned to the Bay of Calos (San Carlos Bay). Once again, the Calusa attacked in overwhelming force, and he had no choice but to withdraw would-be colonists from Florida after suffering a serious leg wound from a Calusa projectile. In about 10 days, Ponce would also die in Cuba as a result of this injury. The "special islands" were later named Puerto Sur Nivel and Cautivo by early-18th-century cartographers.

The once-powerful Calusa were essentially gone from Southwest Florida by 1700. Many had fallen victim to the new and virulent diseases introduced to the western hemisphere by the Europeans. The remaining Calusa had been Christianized and chose to migrate to Cuba with the Spanish when England took control of Florida. The Calusa were replaced by the Seminoles, a loosely connected group of Native Americans that were driven south out of Alabama and Georgia because of English and, later, American expansion. They occupied most of the peninsula of Florida by the mid-1800s.

Europeans rarely visited these isolated islands during Spain's rule because they feared the natives. Over time, the Spanish name for the larger island corrupted to the English, Sanybel, and the place name of its neighbor was Anglicized to Captiva. In 1833, a group of New York investors acquired a shady title to Sanybel Island. The islands were part of a Spanish land grant, which the US legal system had recently invalidated. The New Yorkers subdivided Sanybel Island and began to sell land for homesites and farmland. The Second Seminole War (1835–1842) interrupted sales, and the region became so dangerous it was virtually abandoned by civilization. Severe hurricanes and unbearable populations of salt marsh mosquitoes played a role, too.

In 1883, the federal government established the Sanibel Island Light Station Reservation, and all land on Sanibel was included in its boundary. The Sanibel Lighthouse became operational in August 1884, and the only permanent residents on the island were the two lighthouse keepers and their families. By 1888, much of the land to the west of the lighthouse was declared surplus to lighthouse needs and became available as provided by the Homestead Act of 1862. The land was released from the public domain, and hardy settlers swarmed to the islands to take possession of their "free" land.

Near the end of the 19th century, word leaked out, and the world became aware of the islands' beautiful, white, shell-strewn beaches. In the wintertime, northern visitors converged in Punta Gorda and Fort Myers. Profitable excursion vessels transported day-trippers to the barrier islands for seashell collecting and sport fishing, and Sanibel and Captiva Islands were "rediscovered." Entrepreneurs saw the need for on-island accommodations and small resorts like The Sisters, The Matthews, The Sanibel House, The Palms, and Fisherman's Lodge soon appeared on the waterfront. The wetland interior of Sanibel abounded with birds and other wildlife, but land that was dry enough remained dedicated to farming. Over time, other hotels and inns supported this growing tourist destination. These facilities adopted the new postcard fad, giving their own cards away free to their patrons for advertising. The Sanibel Packing Company, established in 1899, published a fine series of postcards and sold them to customers at Bailey's General Store.

In recent years, the circulation of postcards has waned. The paper card has been replaced by smartphones and iPads. These devices transmit photographs and messages from visitors to loved ones back home, and they have mostly replaced published nostalgic postcards. Postcards were important because they documented changes to these islands, conveyed their history, and recorded a writer's personal adventures. We have selected some of the best to include in this book.

Welcome to Juan Ponce's watering place!

One

The Sanibel Island Light Station

The first lighthouse built in the New World was the Boston Harbor Lighthouse, erected by the Massachusetts Bay Colony in 1716. Thereafter, manned lighthouses were placed along seacoasts and in the Great Lakes. For more than two centuries, these beacons were state-of-the-art aids to navigation and provided safety and positioning benefits to seamen. Today, they are often referred to as "America's castles," and like the castles of Europe, many are inactive and have fallen into disrepair.

For mariners in the mid-1800s, the entrance to the Gulf of Mexico was marked by the Loggerhead Key Lighthouse in Florida's Dry Tortugas. After passing that landmark, seamen sailing north hoped to find the Egmont Key Lighthouse at the entrance of Tampa Bay. After the Civil War, Punta Rassa (near the Causeway tollbooth) was a hub for cattle shipments between Florida and Cuba. The economy of the area was inextricably connected to shipping volumes and justified a lighthouse. Petitions requesting the construction of a light station were submitted to the US Lighthouse Establishment. In 1883, the US Congress approved funding for a coastal light between the Keys and Tampa Bay. Sanibel Island was selected for this new installation, and the lighthouse was lit on August 20, 1884.

Sanibel's lighthouse would differ from the older light towers. The latter were constructed of brick and mortar, but Sanibel is fabricated from wrought iron and is a pyramidal, skeletal structure, designed to withstand hurricane-force winds. The Sanibel light was equipped with a third-order Fresnel lens, the lantern was fueled by kerosene, and its light reached 16 miles offshore. Each lighthouse had its own characteristic (the coding of the frequency of the light's flashing) to aid navigators, and in the case of the Sanibel installation, to act as a guidepost for vessels entering San Carlos Harbor aiming to reach Port Punta Rassa. The Sanibel Lighthouse remains lit and functional. Over the years, the fuel it has used, the lenses in its lantern room, and the ownership of the land have all changed.

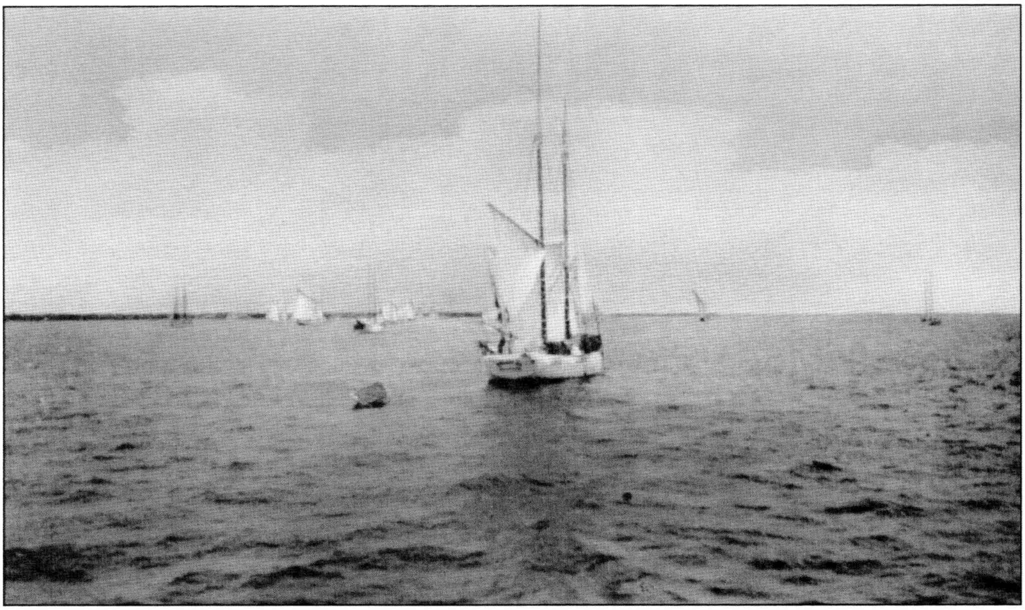

The deep water of San Carlos Bay was often used as an anchorage for Cuban fishing smacks. These sailboats sought protection that the bay provided during storm events. Commercial tonnage processed at Punta Rassa increased after erection of the Sanibel Lighthouse. Cattle boats (about 300 feet long) passed by the Sanibel Lighthouse to reach the port. Over 25,000 head of cattle were shipped to Cuba from Punta Rassa each year. (Courtesy of Islander Trading Post.)

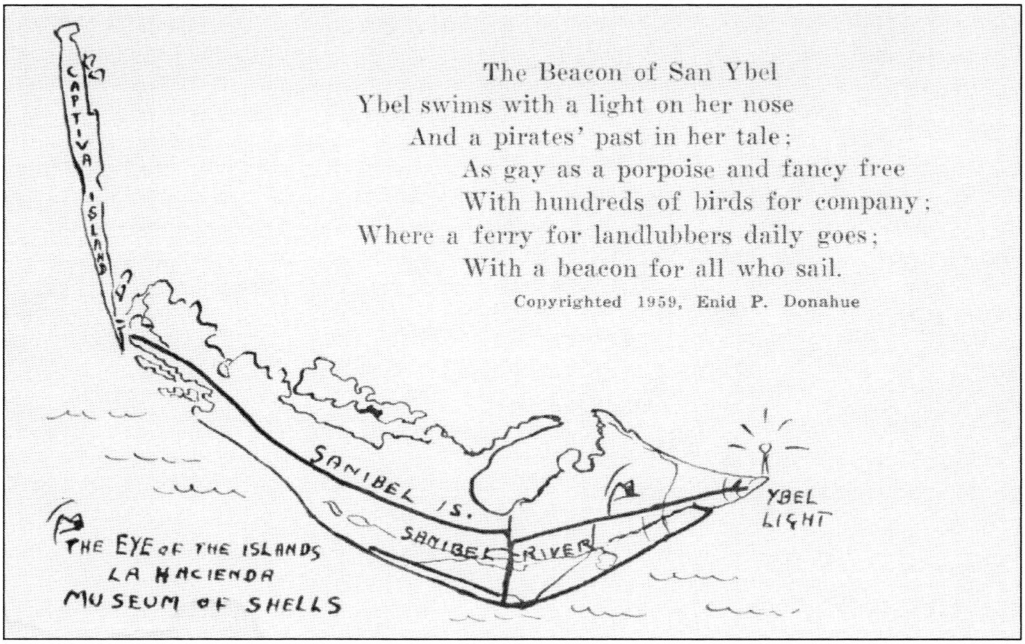

This postcard, "Beacon of San Ybel," was the brainchild of Enid Donahue. Donahue's mother, Lillias Cockerill, owned the La Hacienda Museum of Shells on Main Street, Sanibel, in the 1950s. This postcard demonstrates the connection that islanders have always had with the lighthouse and how this has been used for business and advertising purposes. The "eye" of Sanibel marks the location of this early, often cluttered shell shop. (Courtesy of Islander Trading Post.)

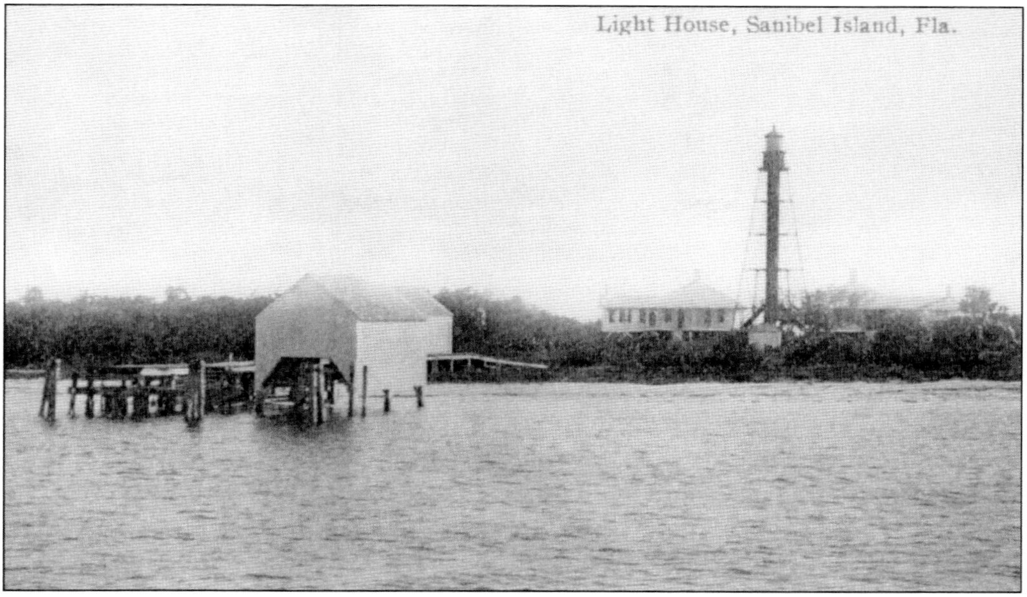

Soon after its construction, the Sanibel Lighthouse started appearing on postcards. This c. 1915 postcard shows the bay-side of the light station, complete with covered pier and boathouse. The curtains are in place in the lantern room to protect the Fresnel lens from sunlight. These shrouds were removed each evening at dusk when the light was activated. At this time, the third-order lens rotated around a kerosene lamp. (Courtesy of Sanibel Historical Museum and Village.)

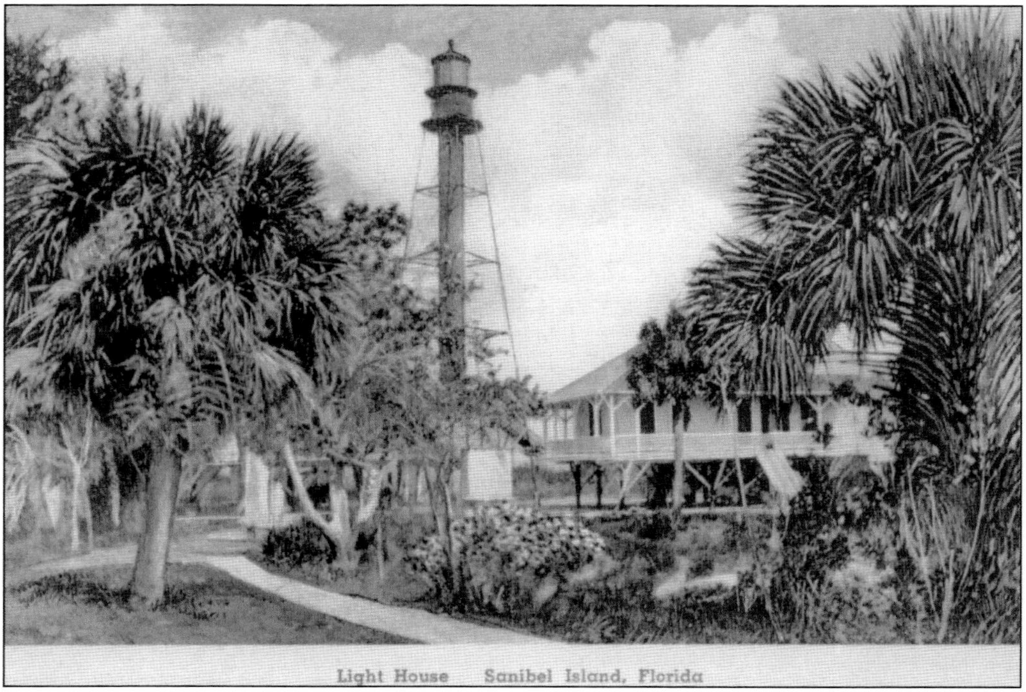

The lighthouse compound appeared much different by 1930. The manicured grounds featured gardens and pathways. Even a ball field was located on the Gulf side as early as 1917. Slowly, encroaching erosion whittled away at the beach, and by 1960, the waters of the Gulf of Mexico were rushing under Quarters No. 2, the easternmost building. (Courtesy of Charles LeBuff collection.)

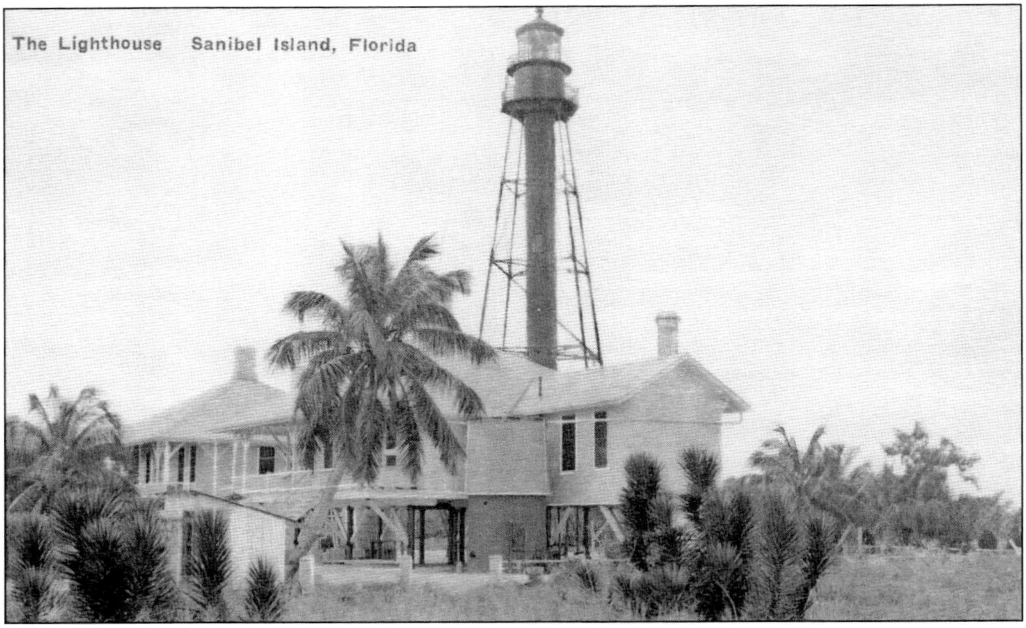

This c. 1935 postcard shows the uncovered lens. This is the second Fresnel lens used in the tower. It did not rotate and was fueled by acetylene gas. The lens change occurred in 1923, the same time indoor plumbing was installed in the residences. At this time, the station was still administered by the US Lighthouse Establishment, often referred to as the US Lighthouse Service. (Courtesy of Charles LeBuff collection.)

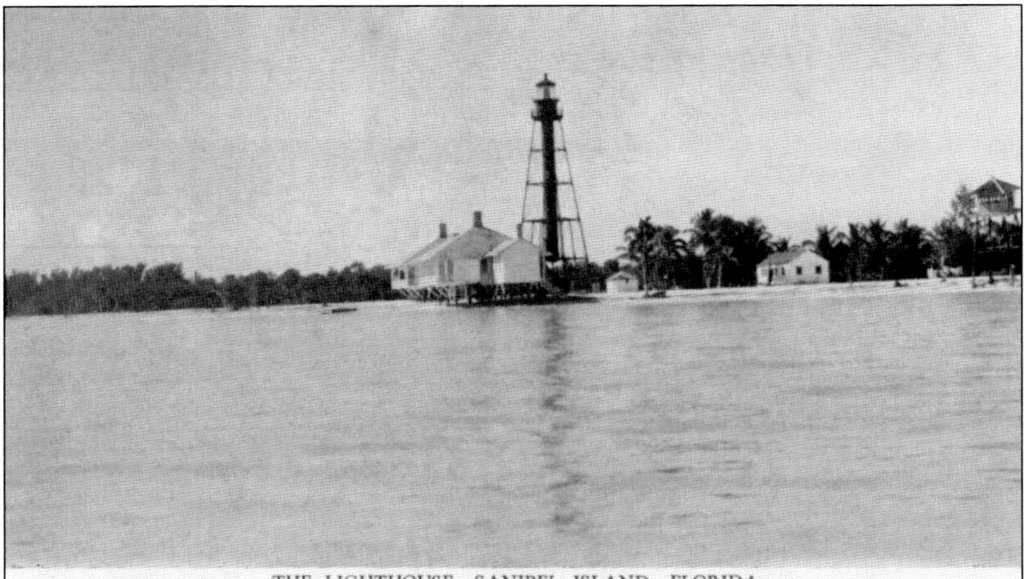

Dudley Richardson was the first keeper of the Sanibel Lighthouse. In 1939, the US Coast Guard was given responsibility for lighthouses, and in 1949, the Sanibel Lighthouse was automated and decommissioned. W.R. "Bob" England was the last resident keeper. The small cottage and tower to the right were built during World War II; the tower was a submarine lookout station, and the cottage housed their enlisted personnel. (Courtesy of Sanibel Historical Museum and Village.)

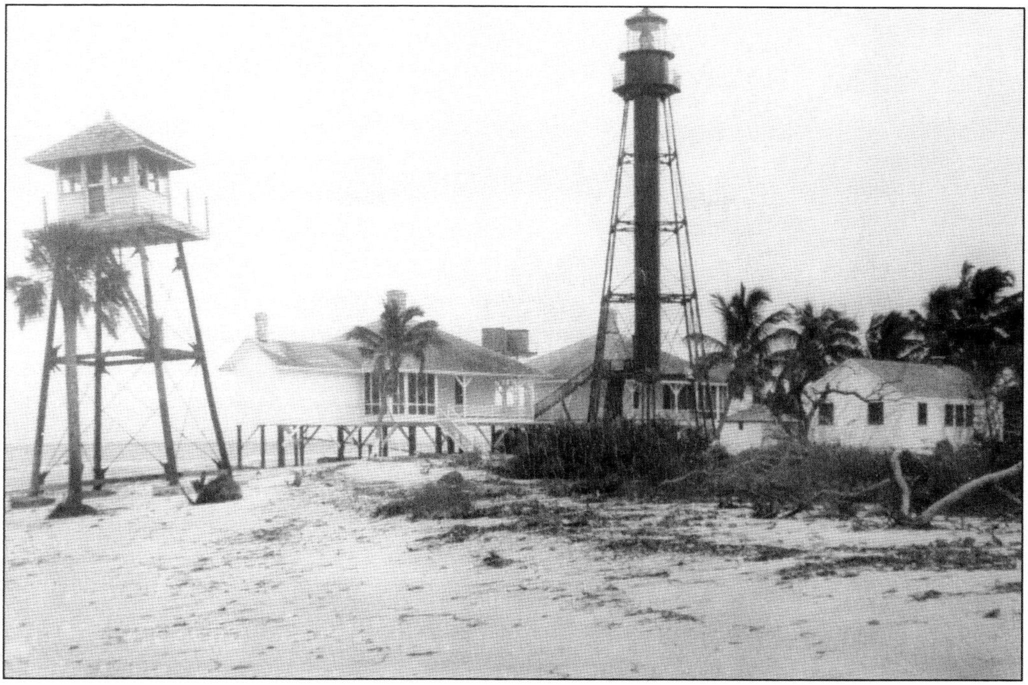

This 1949 postcard reveals a close-up of the U-boat tower and cottage. At this time, the US Fish and Wildlife Service managed Point Ybel, and the lighthouse property became the headquarters for the national wildlife refuge until 1982. Note the stairways leading from the porches to the tower's entrance for access during floods. Coauthor Charles LeBuff and his family lived in the left-hand quarters for 22 years. (Courtesy of Sanibel Historical Museum and Village.)

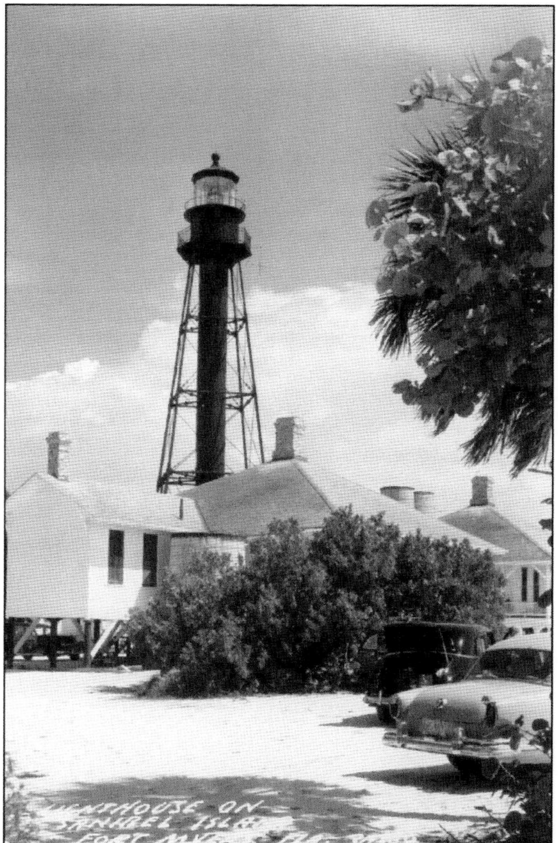

The light station is pictured here in the late 1950s. Drinking water for occupants still fell onto the asbestos-shingled roofs and flowed into a cistern. The top of that cypress tank is visible in the center of the card. Two elevated water tanks that supplied gravity-pressurized water to the three dwellings are visible between the quarters. After the Coast Guard left, the lantern room curtains were never hung again. (Courtesy of Sanibel Historical Museum and Village.)

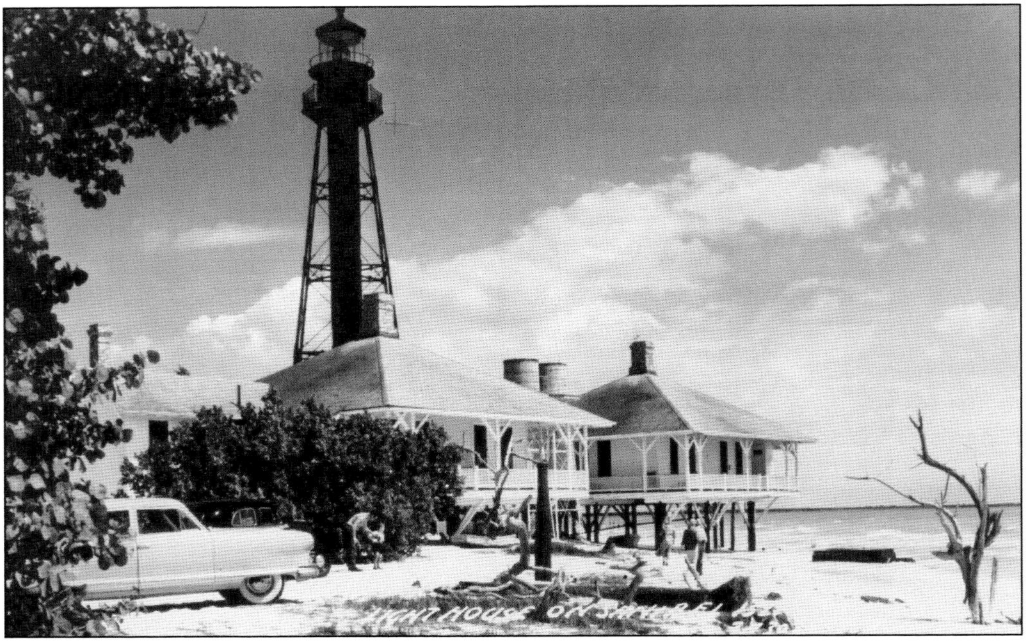

Erosion accelerated in the 1960s at Point Ybel; its effect is visible on this postcard. During spring tides, a lure could be cast from the waterfront porch of Quarters No. 2 (right) to catch snook, or a cast net could be thrown and filled with mullet. The rectangle on the beach to the right is the station's septic tank, uncovered because of erosion and put on exhibit. (Courtesy of Sanibel Historical Museum and Village.)

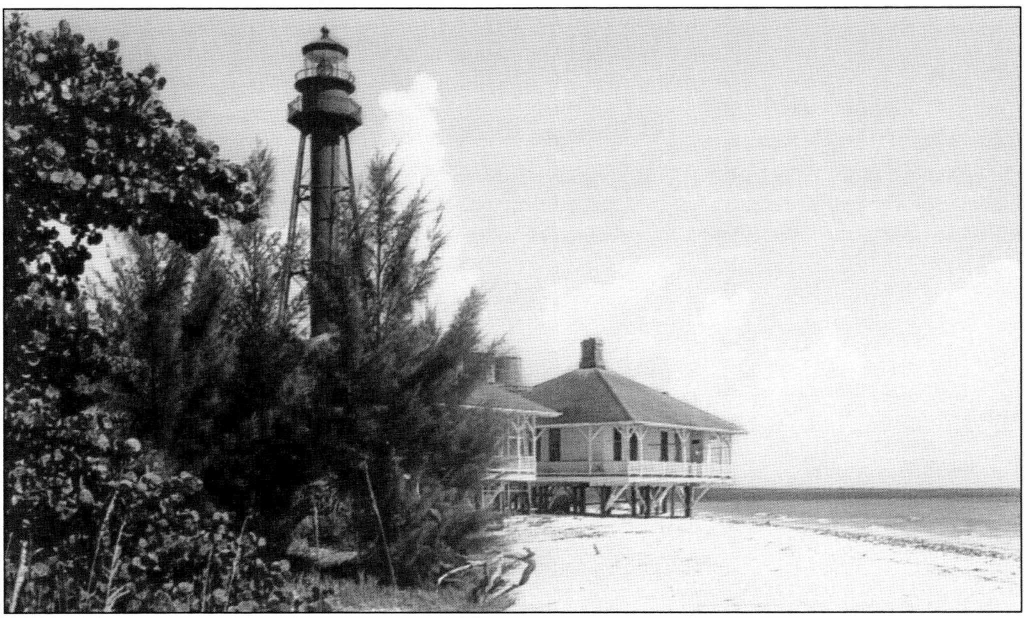

In the foreground are sapling Australian pines. After Hurricane Donna in 1960, the seeds of this invasive plant were dispersed by the tidal surge. They germinated and impacted the beaches for decades until it could be brought under control on public lands. At the lighthouse, these trees were first grown as landscape hedges; no one had a clue how much environmental damage could be caused by Australian pines. (Courtesy of Charles LeBuff collection.)

This 1963 postcard shows the cistern still intact at Quarters No. 1, but the second Fresnel lens was replaced by a drum lens in 1962 when the light was electrified. This third lens was replaced about 1982 with the present airport-style beacon. (The drum lens is currently on exhibit at the Sanibel Historical Village and Museum.) The cypress tank collapsed in 1976, but its brick base remains. (Courtesy of Charles LeBuff collection.)

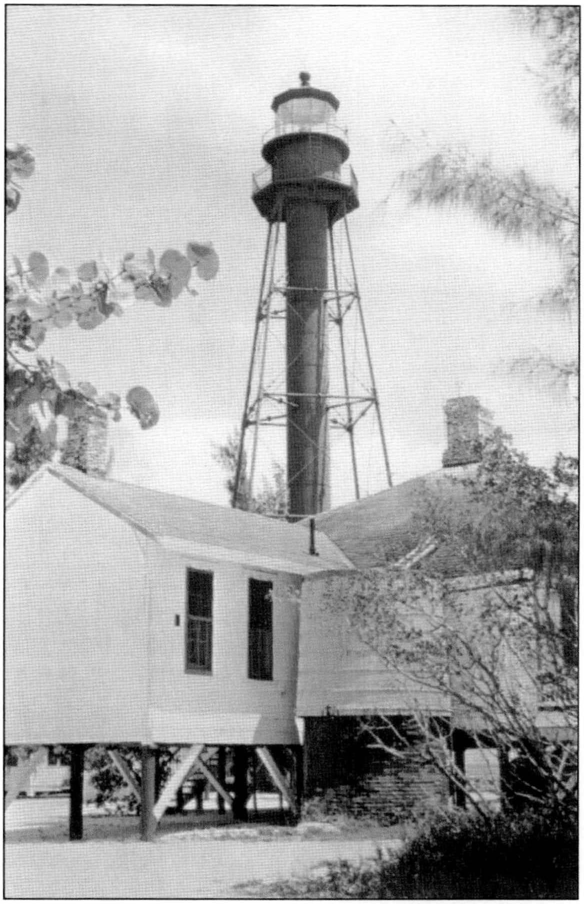

In 1890, a lighthouse was built on Gasparilla Island at the entrance of Port Boca Grande. Boca Grande Pass is famous for its fantastic tarpon fishing. This 1930s postcard captures a jumping silver king that is probably destined for a wall mount. Currently, tarpon fishing is restricted to catch and release. The lighthouse is part of the keeper's quarters, and the Boca Grande Light Station is open to the public. (Courtesy of Charles LeBuff collection.)

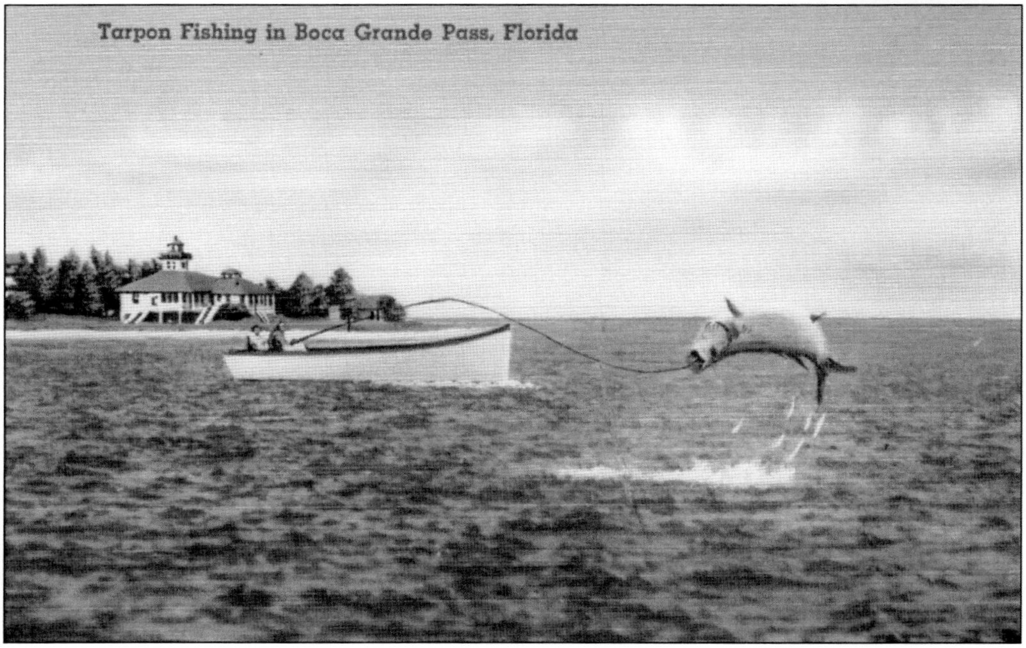

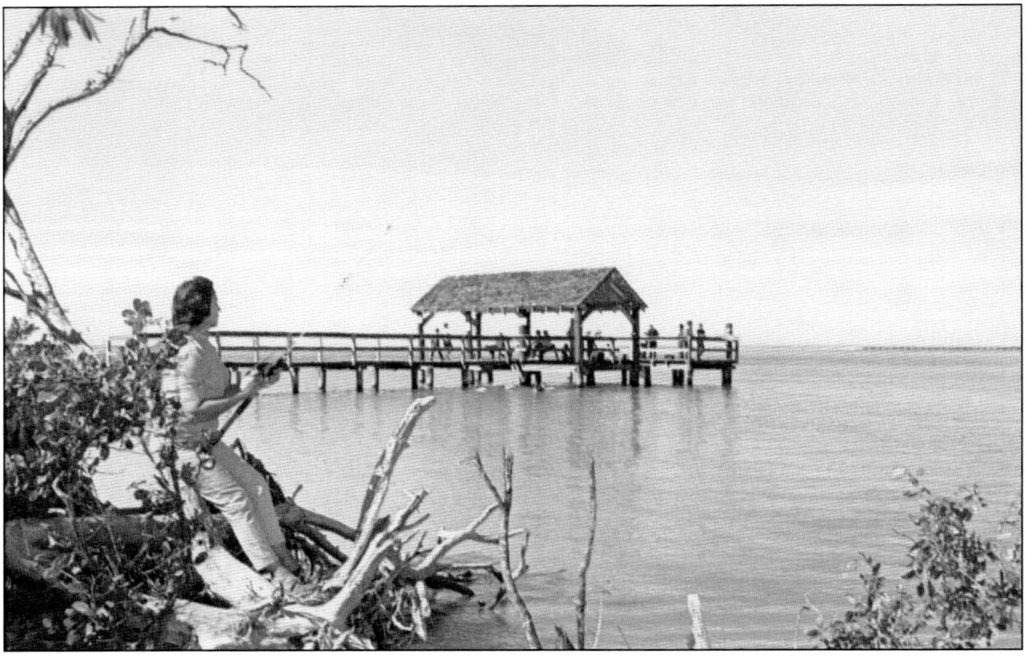

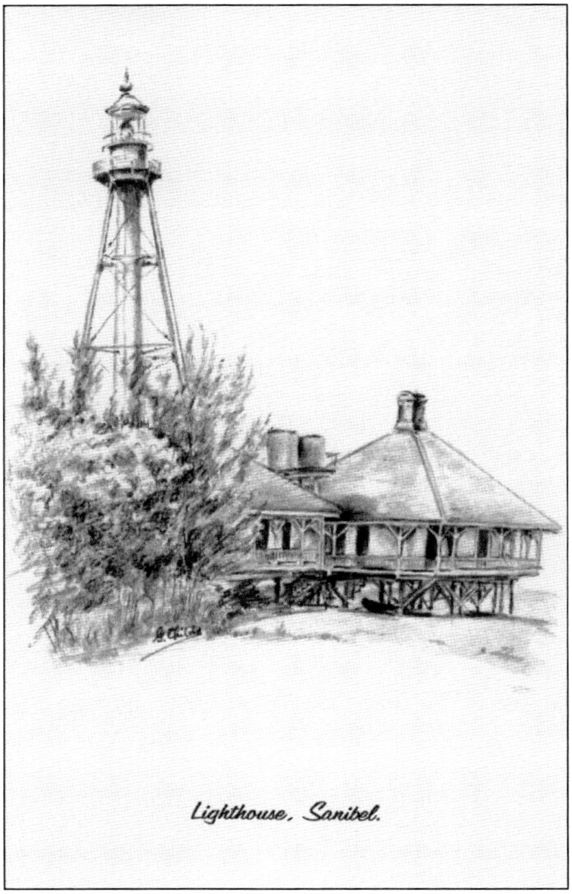

The US Coast Guard pier at the Sanibel Lighthouse is pictured on this 1958 postcard. The public fishing pier of today is located 300 feet west of this structure. In 1982, the City of Sanibel took over management of Point Ybel, and in 2010, they acquired the title to the lighthouse property for (believe it or not) $447.70 from the federal government. (Courtesy of Ralph Curtis.)

In the early 1960s, artist Gladys Childs was a Sanibel Island winter visitor, and during her annual stays, she produced an interesting series of postcards. Her art captured for posterity many elements of island life and community features that were present at that time. Gladys's postcard legacy is drawn upon throughout this book. Pictured is her rendition of the Sanibel Lighthouse. (Courtesy of Charles LeBuff collection.)

Two

The Island Ferries and Mail Boat

Geologically, Sanibel is younger than Captiva by about 5,000 years. The first known residents of the islands were the Calusa Indians. The Calusa left limited evidence of their 1,200-year occupation in the form of huge mounds, heaps of waste seashells that were in part the by-products of their shellfish diet. (To visit one, explore the Shell Mound Trail on "Ding" Darling Refuge.) The mollusks, from which these Indian mounds were built, were harvested from the rich and still-productive estuary. At their peak, 10,000 Calusa lived in Southwest Florida, and they plied the local waters in dugout canoes.

After Spanish "discovery" in 1513, sailing vessels occasionally anchored in San Carlos Bay. As maritime transportation evolved, paddle wheelers and steamships used local waters. Once the islands were opened up to homesteading, piers were soon in place; these were located along the Sanibel bay front at Wulfert Point and at vantage points along Captiva's inland shoreline. Homesteaders could then receive goods and send produce (vegetables and citrus) to off-island markets more easily. Steamers were soon regularly transporting machinery, automobiles, and the US mail to the barrier islands.

At first, most animal-drawn wagon traffic used the Gulf beach as the local highway. In 1926, an entrepreneur, W.E. Cogdell, introduced a short-lived ferry system so he could bring prospective buyers to the islands to inspect (and hopefully buy) lots in his two subdivided beachfront properties. Needless to say, unpaved mule and horse trails did not accommodate Model T and Model A Fords very well. In 1928, Kinzie Brothers Steamer Line was granted a Lee County franchise to ferry automobiles and passengers between Punta Rassa and Sanibel. Their fleet grew, and by the early 1960s, four ferryboats served the islands' residents and visitors. The Kinzie ferries operated until May 26, 1963, when the first Sanibel Causeway was opened and the real changes to these barrier islands started. That same day, after years of service, the islands' mail boat, *Santiva*, ended its six-day-a-week round-trip from Fort Myers to Sanibel, St. James City on Pine Island, and Captiva.

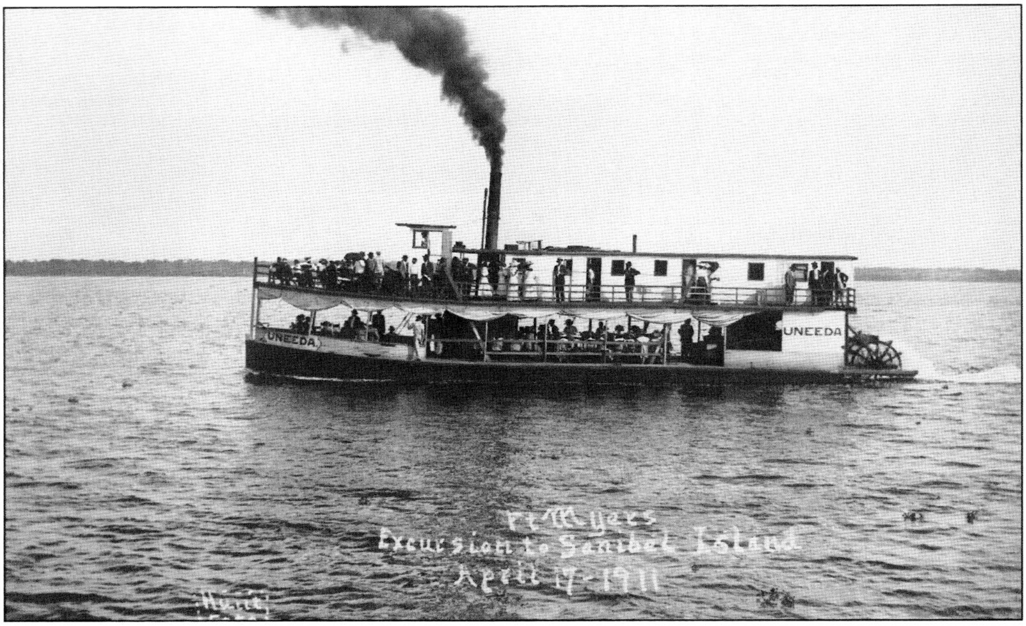

The stern paddle wheeler *Uneeda* crosses San Carlos Bay, bearing a large group of people on what appears to be a holiday excursion to Sanibel Island. Such vessels usually stopped at Matthews Wharf at the end of what is now Bailey Road. Passengers dispersed and walked across the island to the Gulf beach with their picnic baskets for a few hours of shelling and swimming. (State Archives of Florida, Florida Memory.)

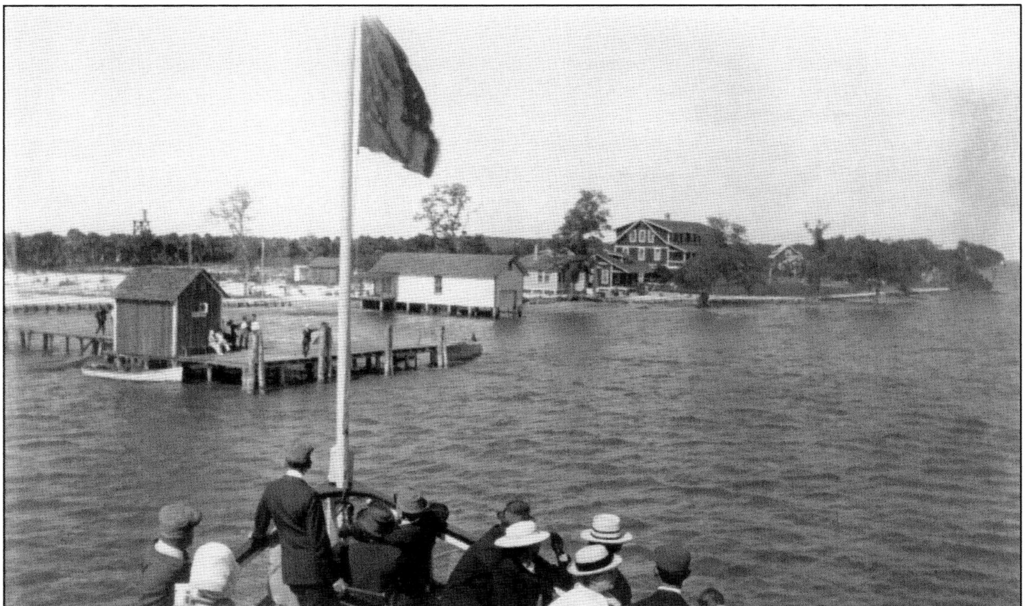
The steamer *Dixie* approaches Randall's Dock on Captiva in the early part of the 20th century. This pier extended out into Pine Island Sound from the eastern end of Palm Avenue (now named Andy Rosse Lane). Passengers disembarked to stay at early resorts or for a temporary visit for shell collecting. (Courtesy of Islander Trading Post.)

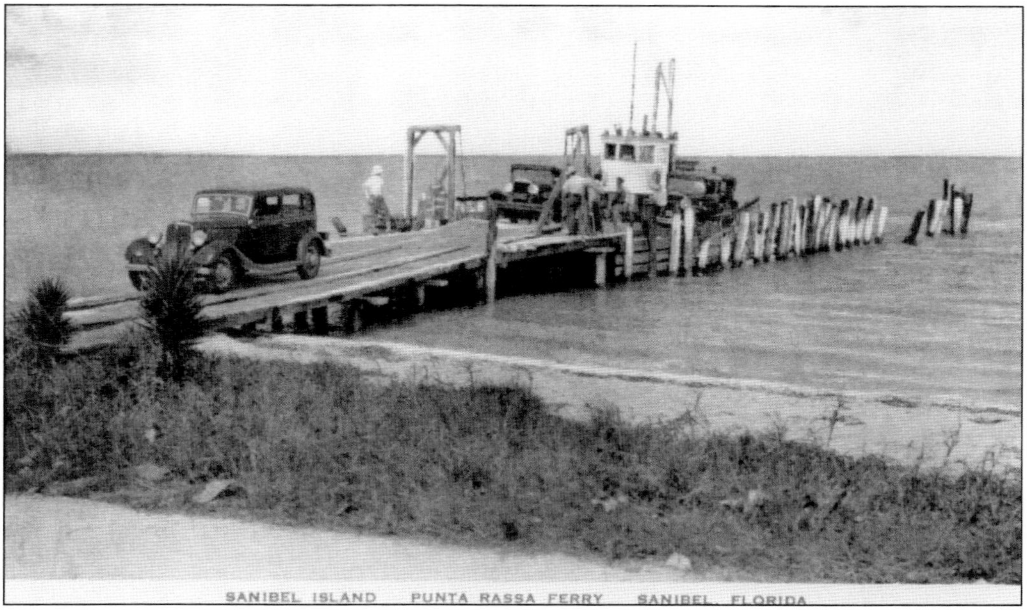

The *Best*, featured on this postcard, was the first of the Kinzie family ferries to go into service. The ferry landing was located near Bailey's General Store on the bay front, but eventually, Ernest Kinzie and his sister Charlotte Kinzie White leased a parcel from the US Lighthouse Board and moved the landing farther east. The Kinzies later purchased the ferry landing when the Lighthouse Reservation was downsized. (Courtesy of Charles LeBuff collection.)

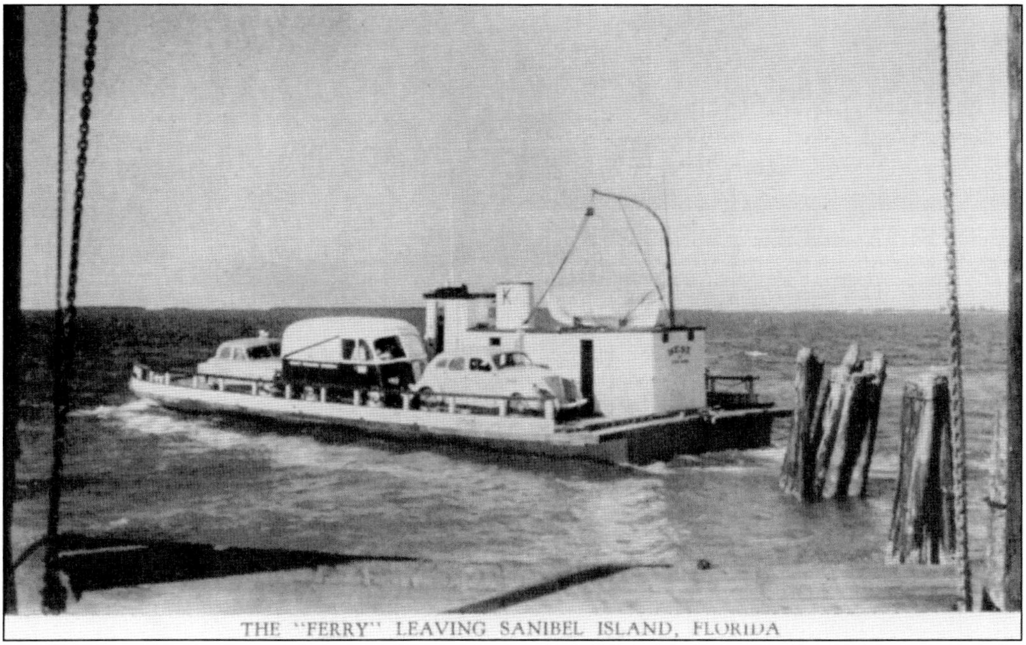

Almost everything and everybody that arrived on the islands came by ferry. The *Best*, on this postcard, was the smallest in the fleet and carried eight automobiles. The Volkswagen van was the Fort Myers Prather's Laundry delivery vehicle that serviced most island resorts. Occasionally, seaplanes delivered newspapers, but almost everything else, except the US mail, made the three-mile trip across the bay by ferryboat. (Courtesy of Charles LeBuff collection.)

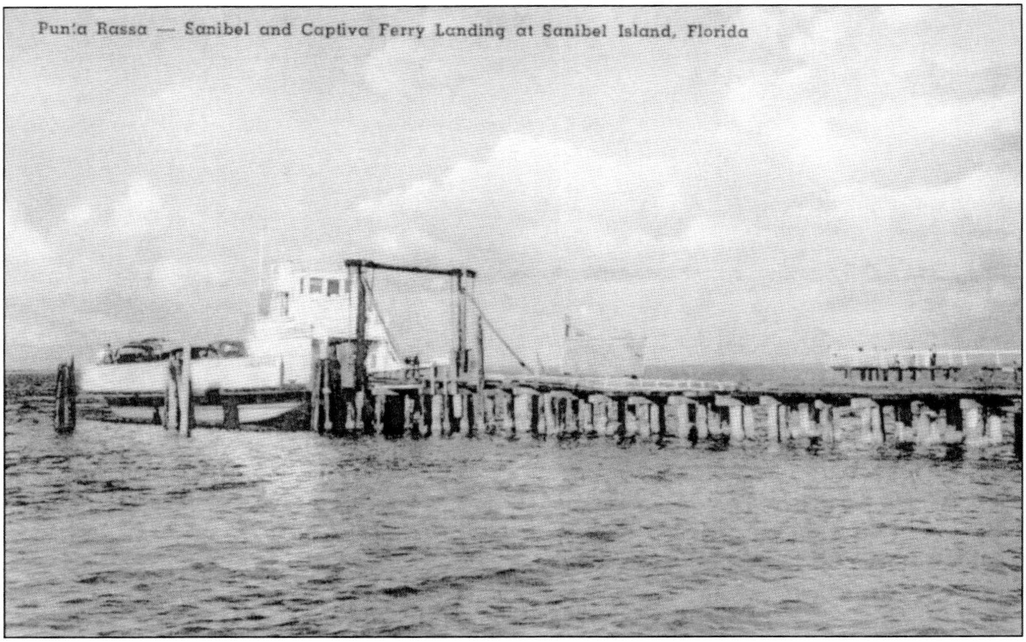

Over time, the Kinzie ferry landing on Sanibel changed. This postcard shows the Kinzie fishing pier, located just east of the ferry slip in the 1950s. Kinzie's property had other amenities, too, including a park on the Gulf side and a convenient restaurant, the Casa Marina. (Courtesy of Charles LeBuff collection.)

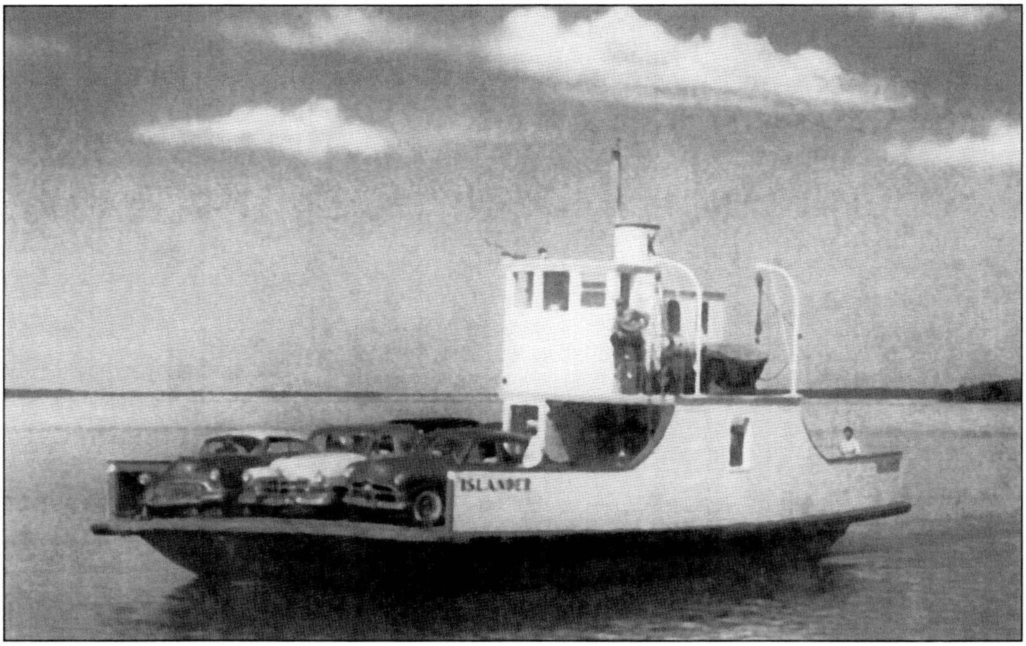

The *Islander* was the second of the Kinzie ferries. A larger, earlier vessel by this same name had been conscripted into the World War II effort and was replaced by the boat on this postcard. Like the *Best*, the *Islander* served for the duration of the Kinzie ferry franchise. The *Islander* was wooden-hulled and held nine automobiles. Capt. Leon Crumpler stands outside the wheelhouse, probably training a new captain. (Courtesy of Islander Trading Post.)

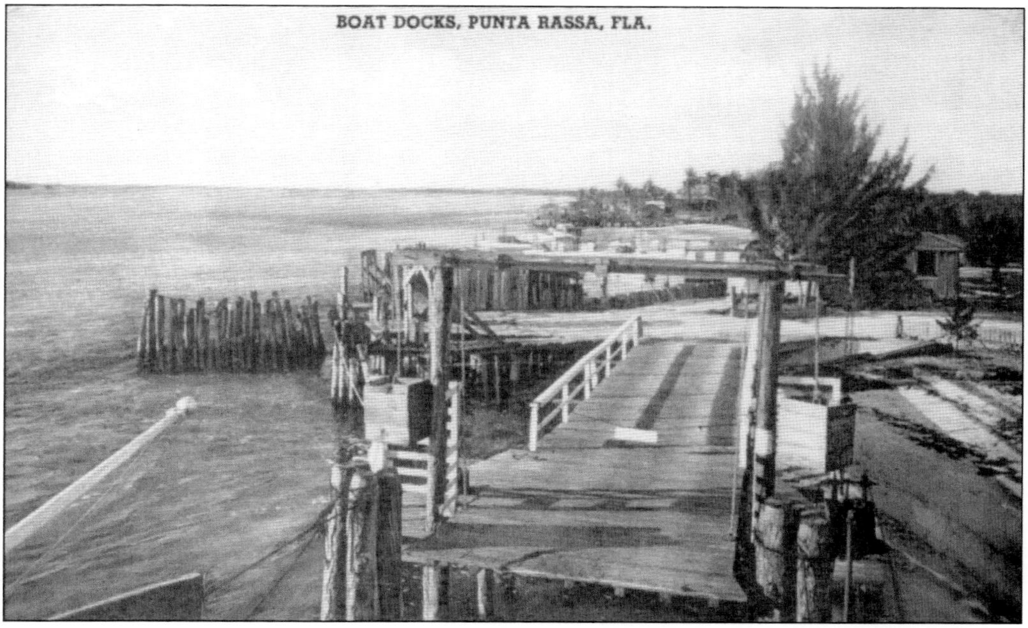

Before the ferries, Punta Rassa was a bustling seaport. During the Second Seminole War, the hamlet was the site of the US Army's Fort Dulaney. Cattle and vegetables were shipped to Key West, Cuba, and Punta Gorda to connect to the railhead. After the railroad reached Fort Myers in 1904, most island produce traveled there by boat and was distributed to major markets by rail. (Courtesy of Sanibel Historical Museum and Village.)

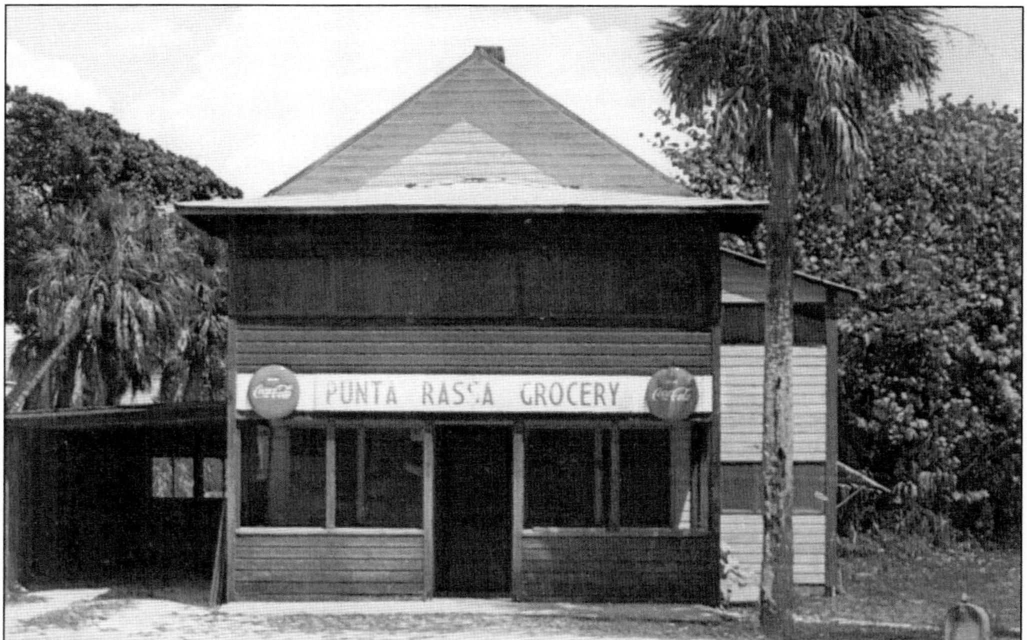

Leon Crumpler was the chief captain of the Kinzie brothers ferry system. He and his wife also owned and operated the Punta Rassa Grocery store on this postcard that was located next to the ferry landing. The Crumplers lived in an apartment above the store. Leon Crumpler was the sage of Punta Rassa, beloved by many. (Courtesy of Ralph Curtis.)

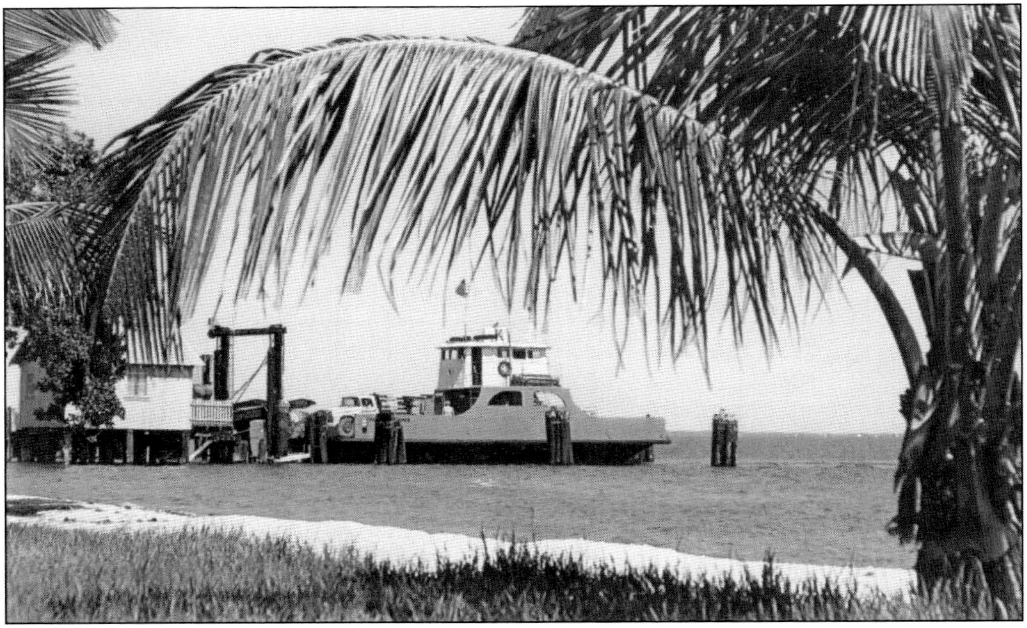

The *Yankee Clipper* unloads on Sanibel. This ferry and her sister ship, the *Rebel*, were steel-hulled and each carried nine vehicles. The truck belonged to J.P. Carter Co., a Sanibel-based freight company that transported everything to the islands except gasoline. Gas-hauling vehicles crossed alone because rules prohibited them sharing passage with other vehicles or passengers. Fuel costs on the islands have always been higher due to tolls. (Courtesy of Charles LeBuff collection.)

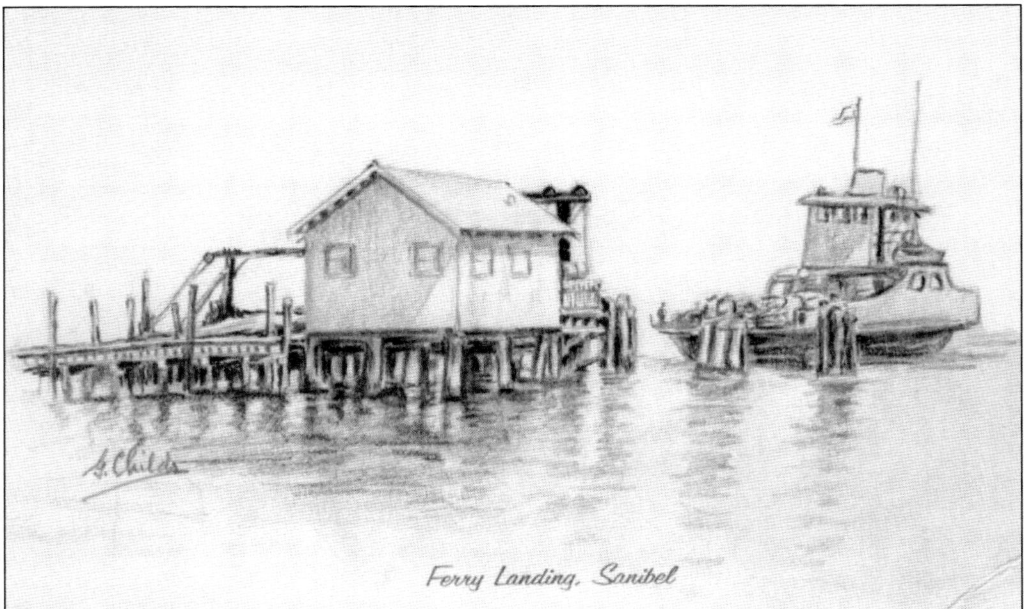

This is a Gladys Childs postcard of the *Rebel*. A crossing took about 20 minutes. The last ferry of the day left Sanibel at 5:30 p.m. unless cars were lined up, and in the winter season, they often reached around the corner to the Sea Horse Shop. In those cases, the ferries ran until all had crossed. To take a vehicle to Punta Rassa on an emergency nighttime ferry cost $25. (Courtesy of Charles LeBuff collection.)

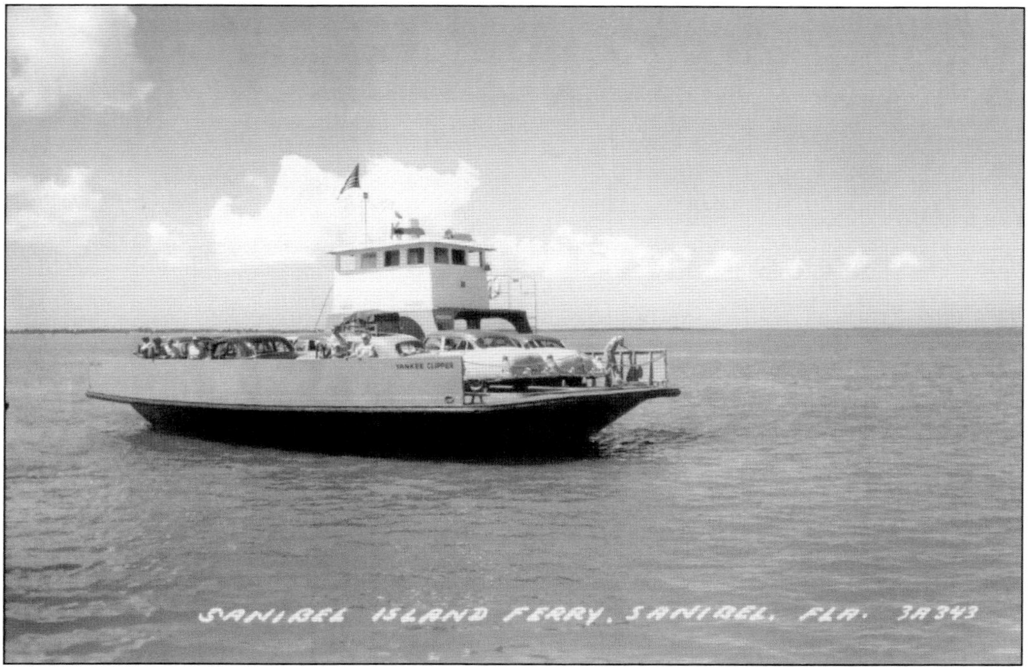

After motoring astern, the fully loaded *Yankee Clipper* turns at Punta Rassa to head for the islands. Crossings were not always uneventful. The authors remember when a hurried passenger put his Buick automobile in gear too soon and drove overboard a few yards short of the ramp at Punta Rassa before it could be lowered to the ferry's deck. (Courtesy of Islander Trading Post.)

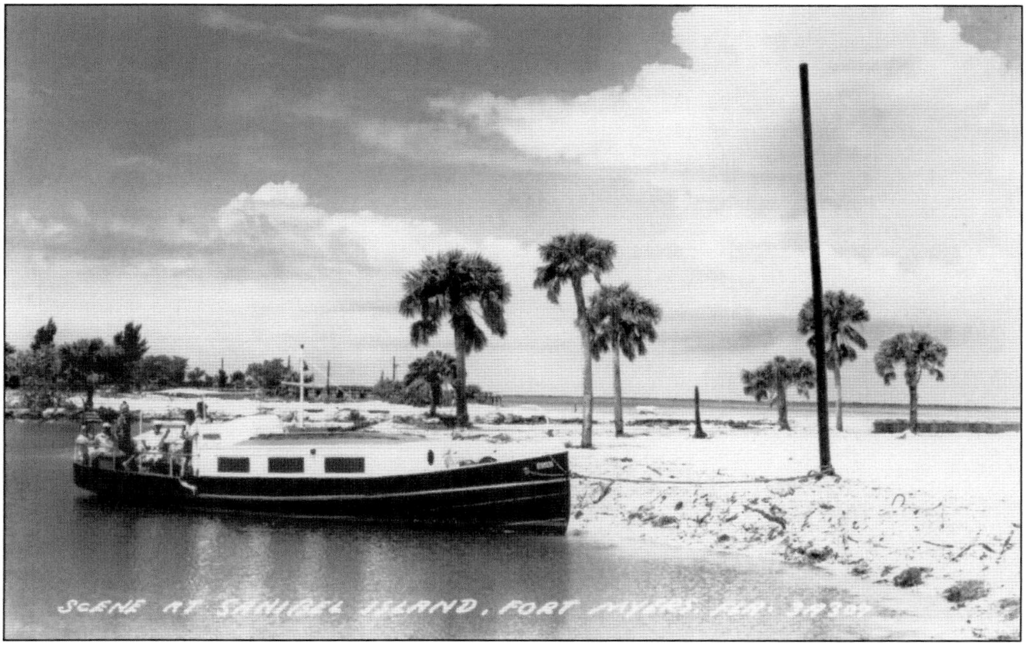

Ernest Kinzie dug a canal from the bay that led into this freshly excavated Kinzie Yacht Basin. Two concrete seawalls protected its entrance. It was later completed with a small dock and boathouse. This basin still exists as a landlocked, mangrove-bordered pool at Lighthouse Pointe Condominium next to the lighthouse property. (Courtesy of Sanibel Historical Museum and Village.)

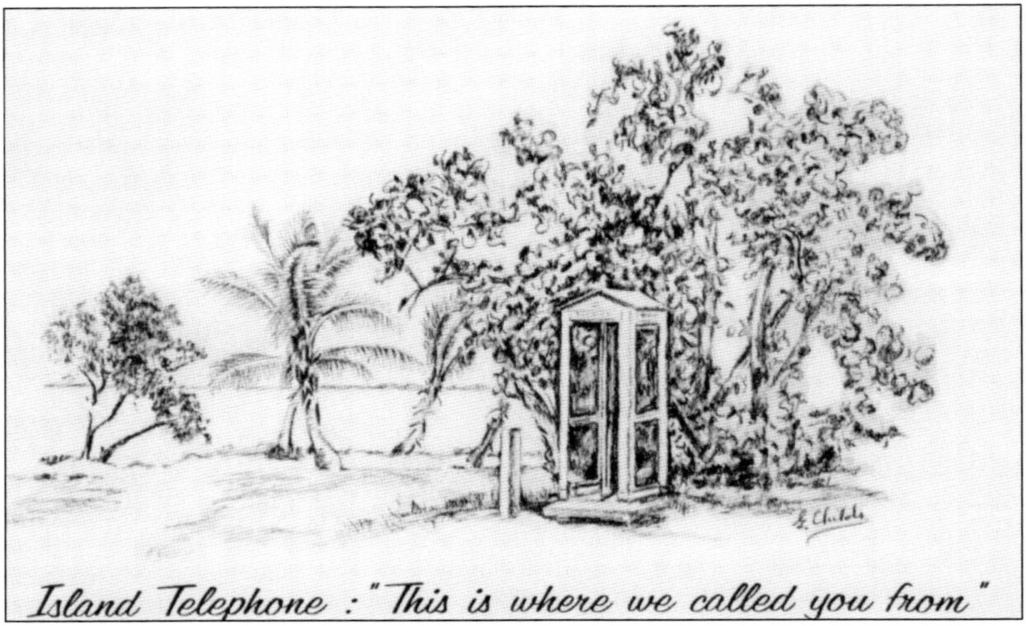

Gladys Childs preserved a piece of island history with this popular postcard. For years, the only public telephone on the islands was located at the ferry landing. To have to use this at night in the summer could be absolute torture due to the mosquitoes. The world record of salt marsh mosquitoes were attracted to a light trap placed here during one night in 1950—an astonishing 365,000 females. (Courtesy of Charles LeBuff collection.)

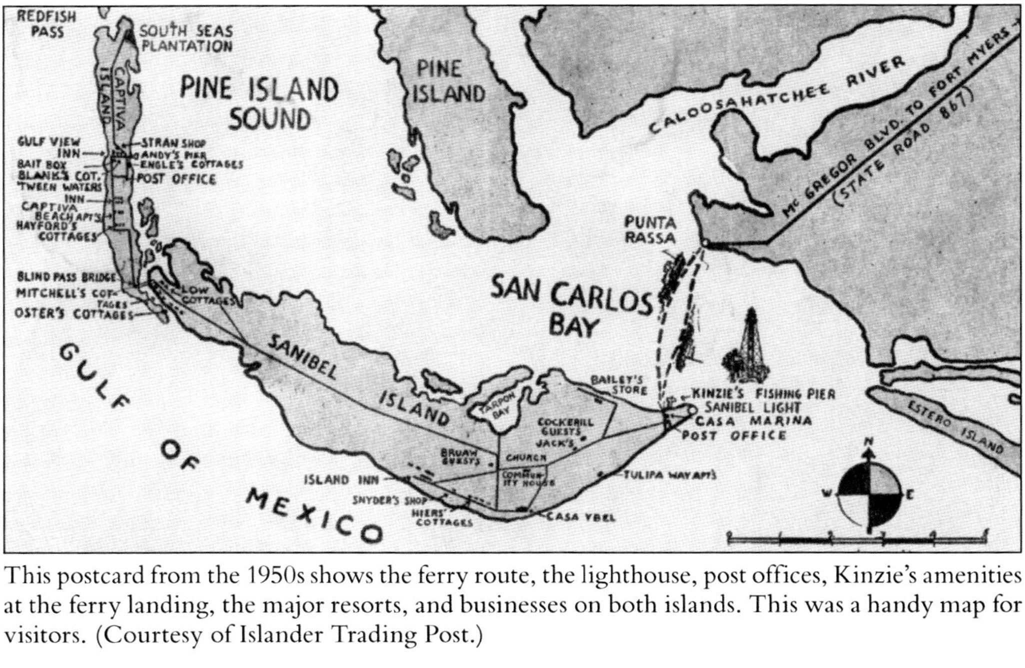

This postcard from the 1950s shows the ferry route, the lighthouse, post offices, Kinzie's amenities at the ferry landing, the major resorts, and businesses on both islands. This was a handy map for visitors. (Courtesy of Islander Trading Post.)

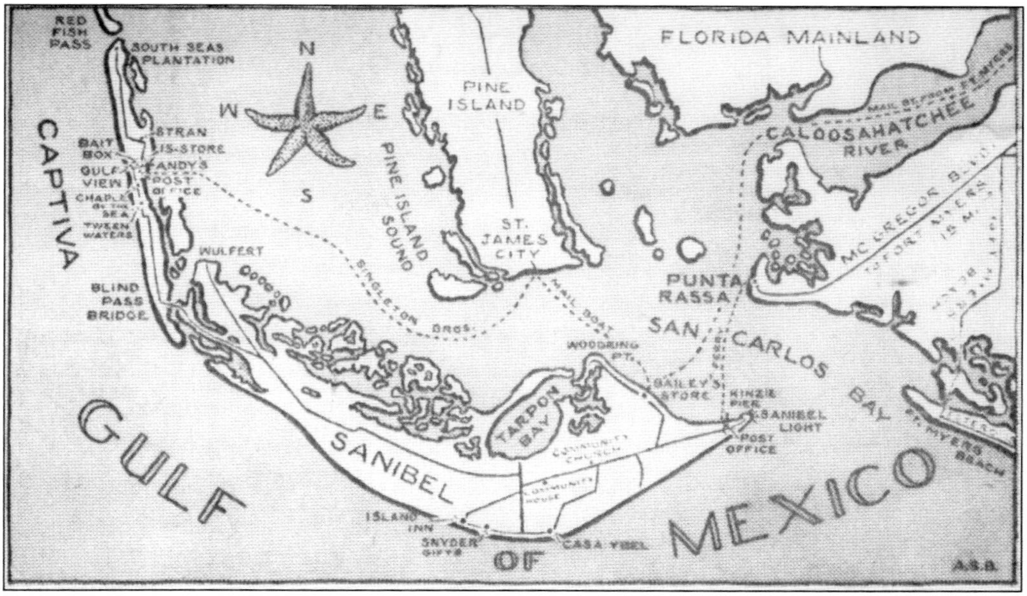

This postcard shows the ferry and mail boat routes. The mail boat left Fort Myers six mornings a week with mail and sightseers. The boat cruised down the Caloosahatchee and reached Bailey's General Store by late morning. The next stop was St. James City on Pine Island and then on to the landing to deliver Captiva's mail. It retraced its trip, picking up outgoing mail, and returned to Fort Myers late in the day. (Courtesy of Charles LeBuff collection.)

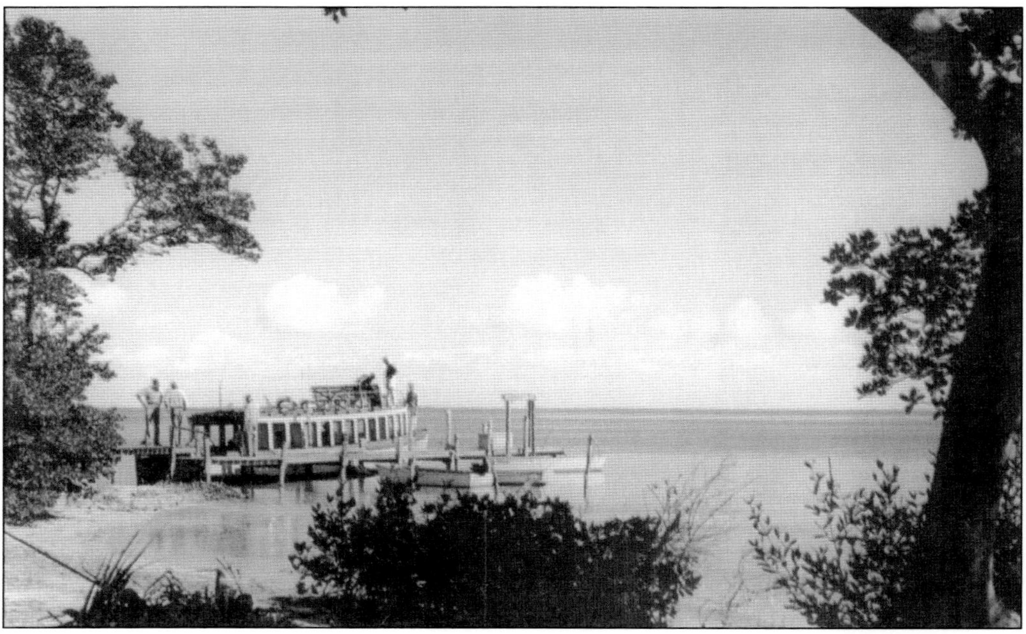

The mail boat *Santiva* waits at the Captiva Island dock for passengers to return from visiting friends or shelling on the beach, before retracing its route back to Fort Myers. More than once, passengers failed to get back in time and were marooned on Sanibel or Captiva overnight. (Courtesy of Charles LeBuff collection.)

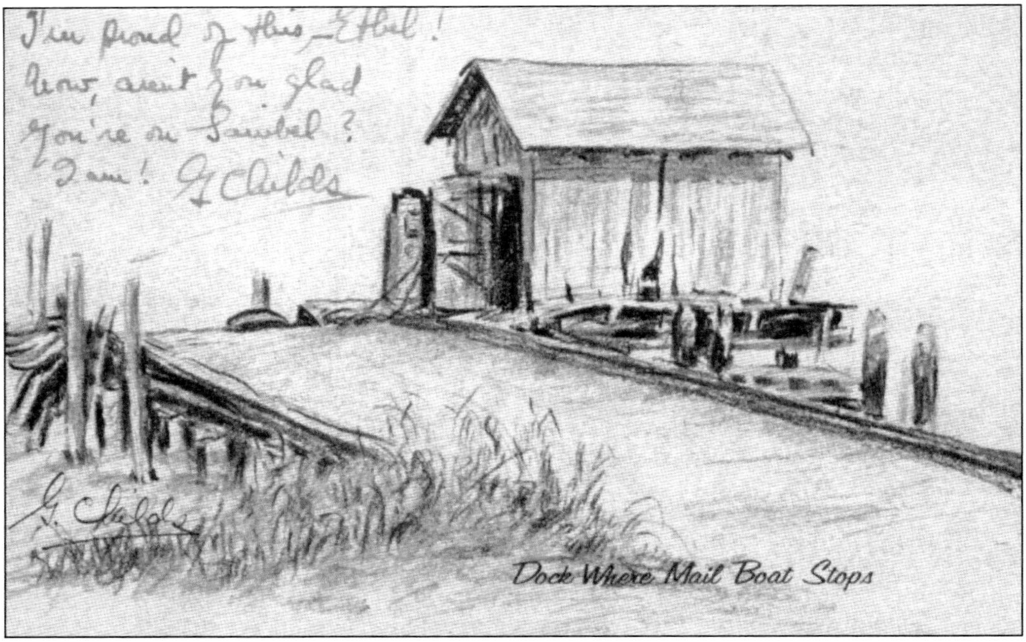

This postcard was sent by artist Gladys Childs to a Sanibel friend. It announces her pleasure at drawing this particular card of the mail boat dock at Bailey's General Store. This little building served as a high-diving platform for many island adults and children before it disappeared during Hurricane Donna in 1960. (Courtesy of Sanibel Historical Museum and Village.)

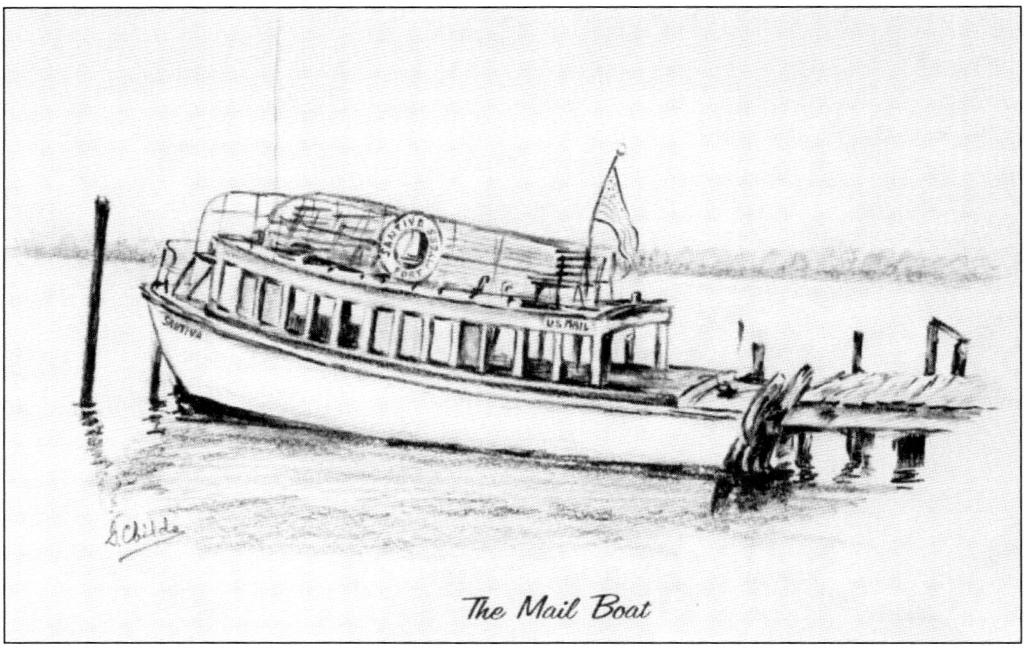

The *Santiva*, drawn by Gladys Childs, plied the Caloosahatchee and Pine Island Sound for decades until it became obsolete in 1963, when the causeway opened and mail was thereafter trucked to the islands by contractors. Joe Redinger (1921–1964) was the last Sanibel carrier to pick up mail from the *Santiva*. He carried it to the post office for sorting and later delivered it. He is buried at the Sanibel Cemetery. (Courtesy of Charles LeBuff collection.)

Three

LANDSCAPES

The Gulf and bay beaches of Sanibel and Captiva Islands are in constant flux. As barrier islands, they began as sandbars and may someday return to that simple state. But the beaches have made these islands dear to those visiting and living here. One only has to be an islander for a short time to witness the changes occurring, whether it is a strong thunderstorm or a major hurricane causing the erosion or accretion.

Man continues to make attempts to influence those changes, but in the end, Mother Nature can erase all evidence of those attempts in a matter of hours. It is also the interior of the islands that has shaped much of their future. The ancient ridges, shaped years ago by currents, were perfect for farming vegetables and citrus. The prairie grasslands, having relatively few trees, were easily converted to acres of farmland. Freshwater marshes lay between the dry ridges, keeping some areas irrigated.

It was not only the high ground that made the islands hospitable to humans, the mangrove forests were also of great importance, serving as nurseries to vast numbers of fish. The success of the Calusa Indians was largely due to the wealth of food available from the bays. For centuries, Cuban fishing smacks came here to fish, knowing they could quickly fill their hulls and return home. Early Native Americans, farmers, and fishermen were attracted to these desolate but bountiful islands that were once accessible only by boat.

Today, many work to conserve the original landscapes of Sanibel and Captiva. Organizations like Sanibel-Captiva Conservation Foundation, J.N. "Ding" Darling National Wildlife Refuge, and the City of Sanibel have retained and protected much of the remaining native landscape. With strict land use codes and an ongoing mission to preserve more undeveloped land, these organizations have saved not only the land, including upland grasslands, mangrove forests, and pristine beaches, but also the wildlife.

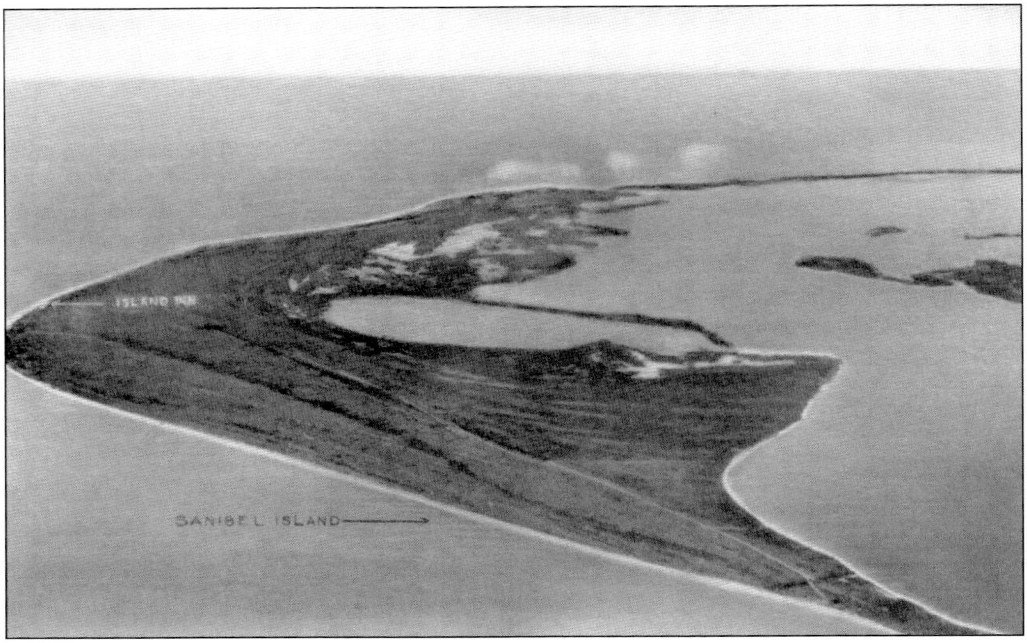

This c. 1937 aerial postcard of Sanibel Island was produced by the Island Inn to promote business and illustrate their Gulf-side location. At that time, there were approximately 100 inhabitants, some which had once farmed the inland ridges, visible even from this altitude. The natural freshwater slough, the Sanibel River, is visible as a dark line running along much of the island's midsection. (Courtesy of Charles LeBuff collection.)

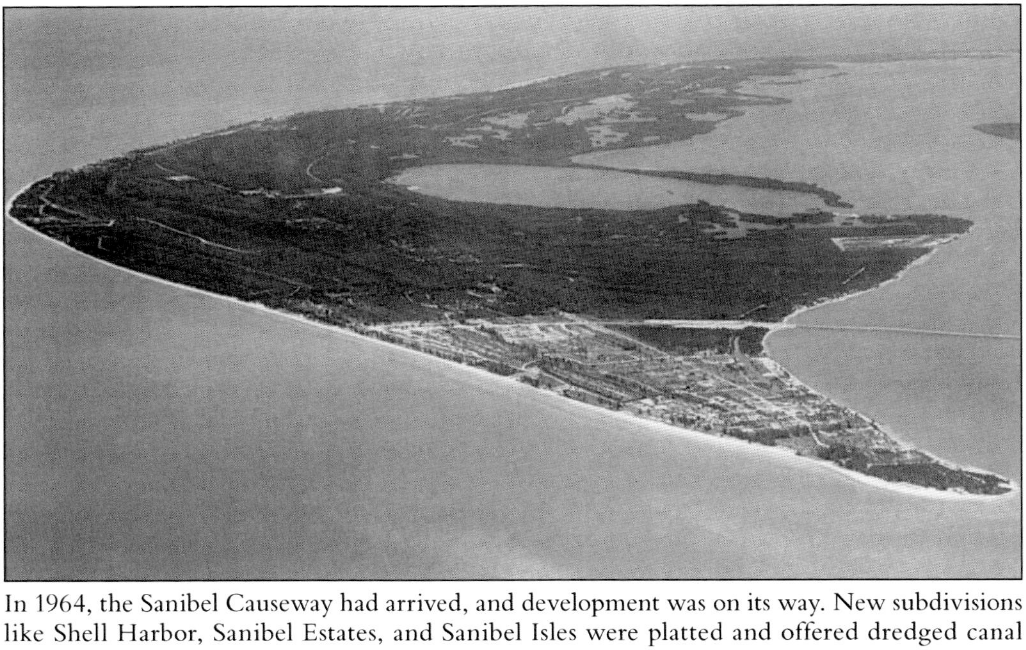

In 1964, the Sanibel Causeway had arrived, and development was on its way. New subdivisions like Shell Harbor, Sanibel Estates, and Sanibel Isles were platted and offered dredged canal homesites. Land that had once been vegetable fields or citrus groves became the new shopping centers or country clubs. The residents of Sanibel realized they had to slow the accelerating growth of Sanibel before they no longer recognized their island nature preserve. (Courtesy of Jim Pickens.)

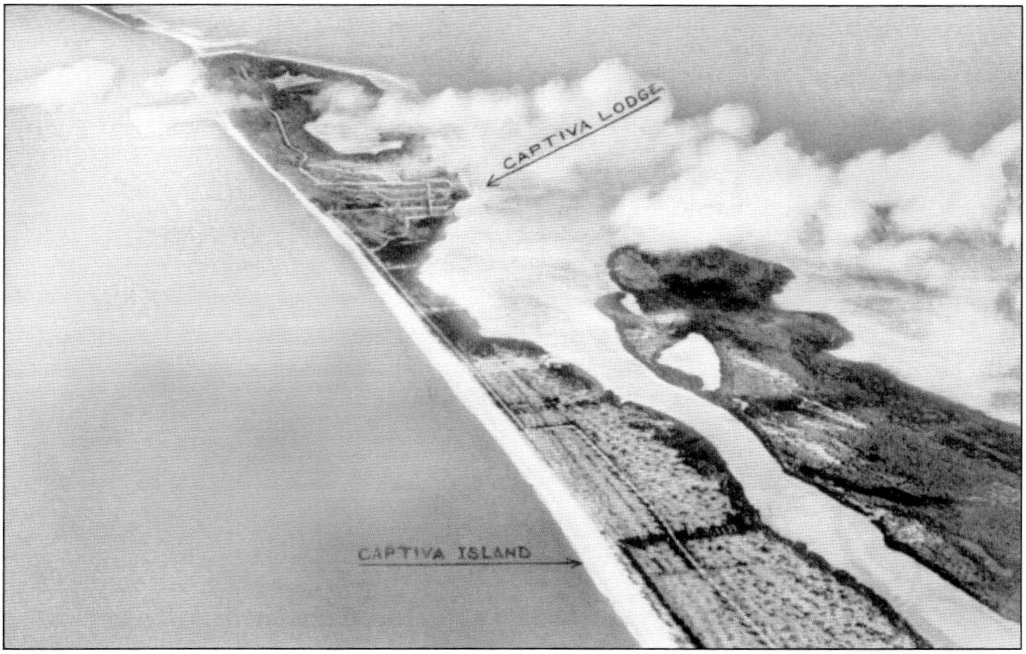

The farmlands of Captiva and Buck Key are still visible in this vintage aerial postcard. Unlike today, Captiva Road continued on the Gulf front until it veered east at the Gulfview Inn (now the Mucky Duck Restaurant). The Captiva Lodge was a bay-front hotel that was also known as the Bayview Hotel. Captiva has had decades of documented erosion, and at one time, before it was broken in two by a hurricane, it was longer than Sanibel. (Courtesy of Tom Hoopes.)

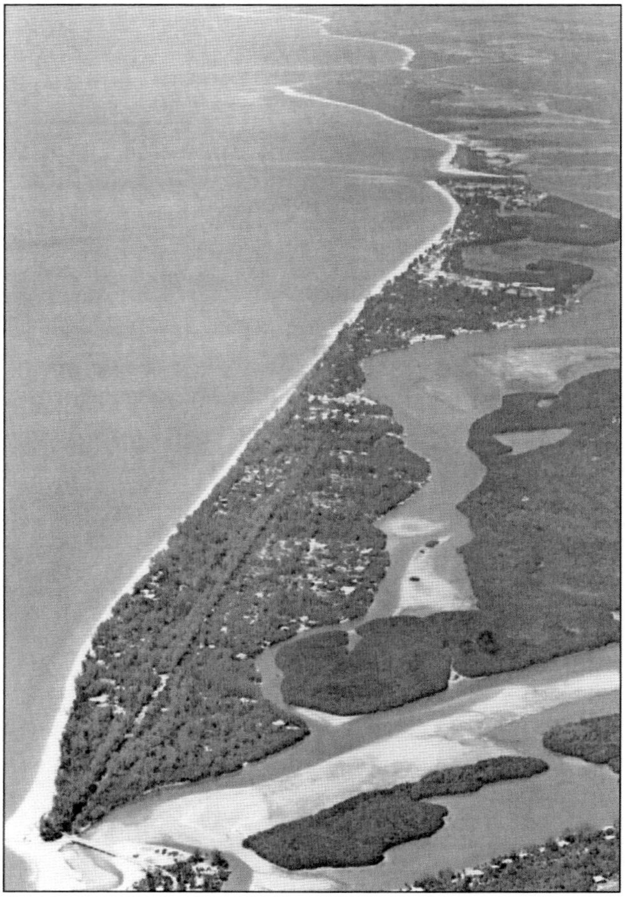

This 1995 aerial shows the Sanibel and Captiva Blind Pass Bridge with the pass closed by sand. The passes of Sanibel and Captiva are forever changing. Redfish Pass is well etched, while Blind Pass closes regularly, filling with sand from Captiva's beaches. Navigation in this area of Sunset Bay and Roosevelt Channel is possible but only with local knowledge and respect for changing tides. (Courtesy of Deborah Gleason collection.)

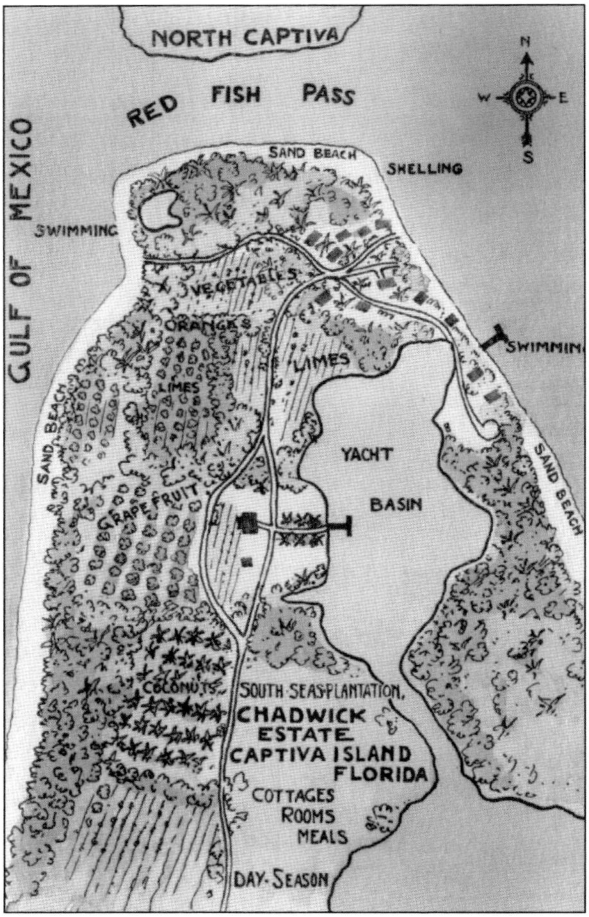

By the 1920s, after a series of hurricanes, many of the pioneer families of Captiva had retired from farming. Clarence and Rosamond Chadwick of Denver, Colorado, bought the northern end of Captiva from the Bryant and Carter families, starting the Chadwick Estate. They proceeded to create a southern plantation of coconut palms and citrus groves, eventually adding cottages. In 1945, the Chadwicks sold their plantation to American Hotels Corporation. (Courtesy of Ralph Curtis.)

Prior to 1921, Captiva and North Captiva islands were one. The Narrows, as it was called, was home to the Mickle family in 1909, until their departure to Fort Myers in 1916. The unoccupied home was destroyed by a hurricane in 1921 as the land was inundated, and Redfish Pass was born. North Captiva is home to adventurous residents who are content to rely on boat traffic for supplies and transport to the mainland. (Courtesy of Tom Hoopes.)

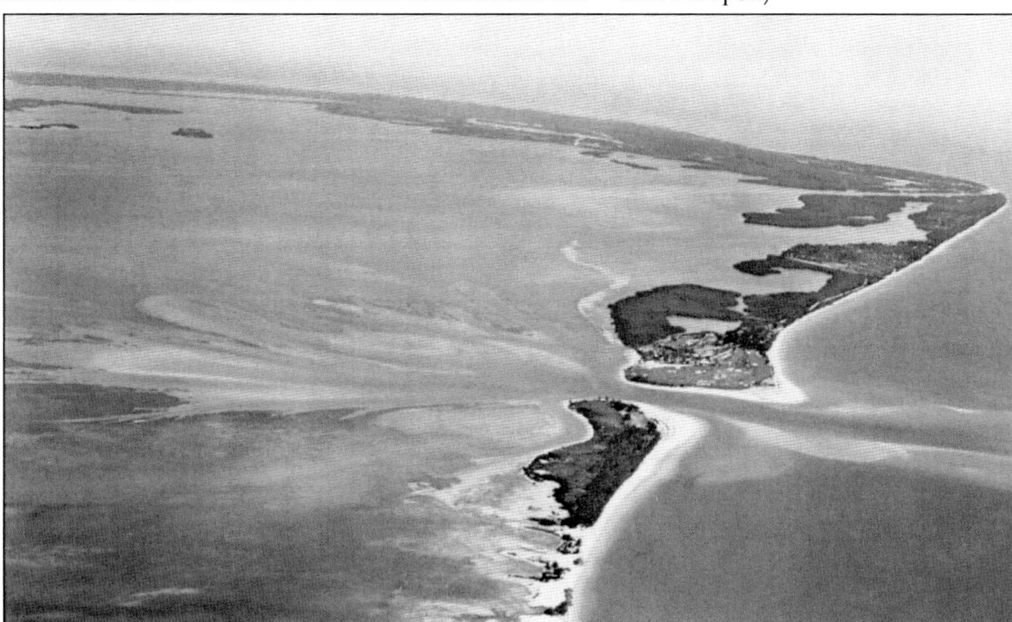

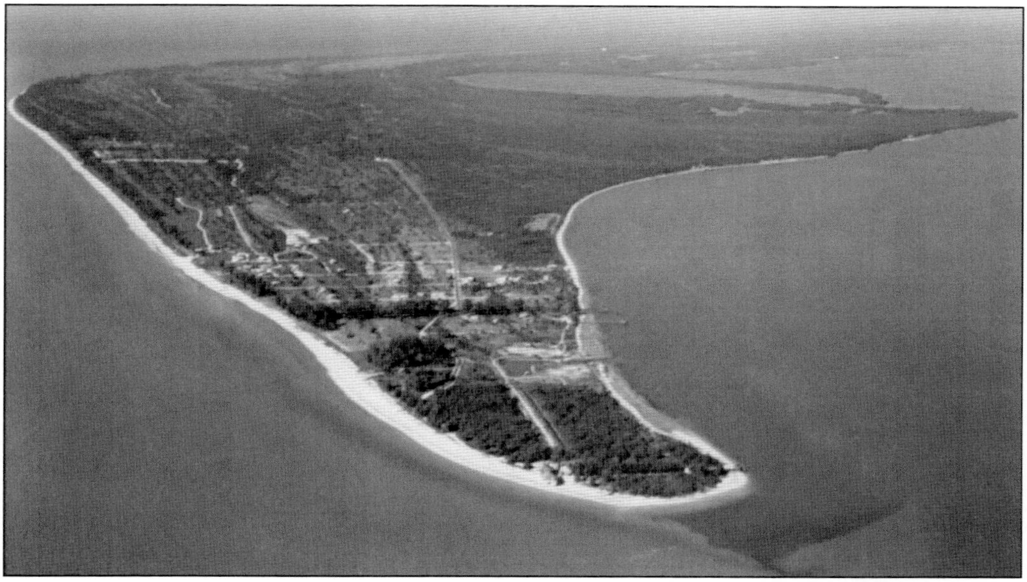

Australian pines did much to change the landscape of the barrier islands. The bay-side Ferry Road was lined with pines and the Gulf-side Kinzie Park was shaded with dozens of the non-native trees. Prior to the pine trees and the causeway, the grasslands of the east end had been used for a castor bean plantation, fishing ranches, Ocean Leather Company (a sharkskin factory), vegetable farming, and residences. (Courtesy of Charles LeBuff collection.)

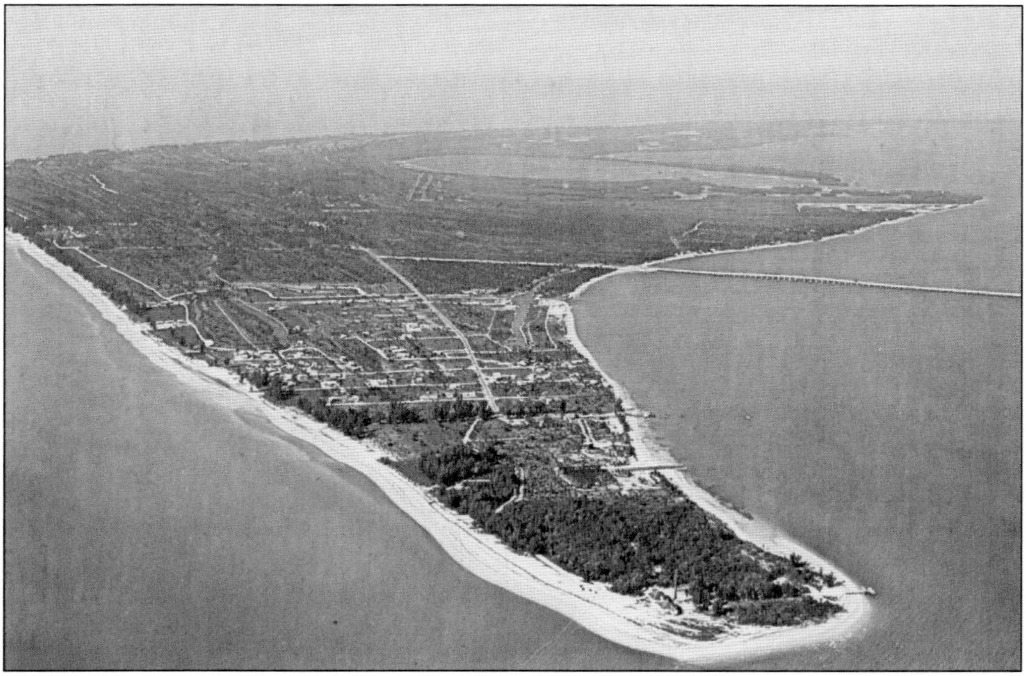

By the early 1960s, the causeway was being built, and Bill Way had created the Sanibel Marina. The Sanibel Marina, under the ownership of Myton Ireland, grew to include a restaurant and various boating services. The Kinzie family had dredged an inland harbor of their own, perhaps with thoughts of a future sea aquarium. Eventually, the inlet closed and the property became the Lighthouse Pointe Condominium. (Courtesy of Jim Pickens.)

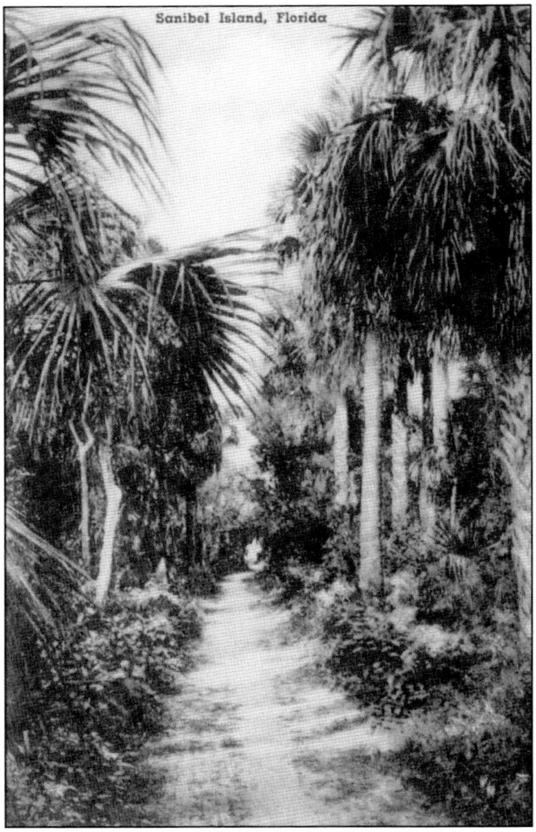

This Sanibel Packing Company card illustrates the simple roadways of Sanibel and Captiva. No power poles are visible, as electricity did not come to the islands until 1941. It is documented that many Calusa shell mounds were destroyed for the purpose of providing a shell base for local roadways. Periwinkle Way was not paved until later in the 1950s. (Courtesy of Islander Trading Post.)

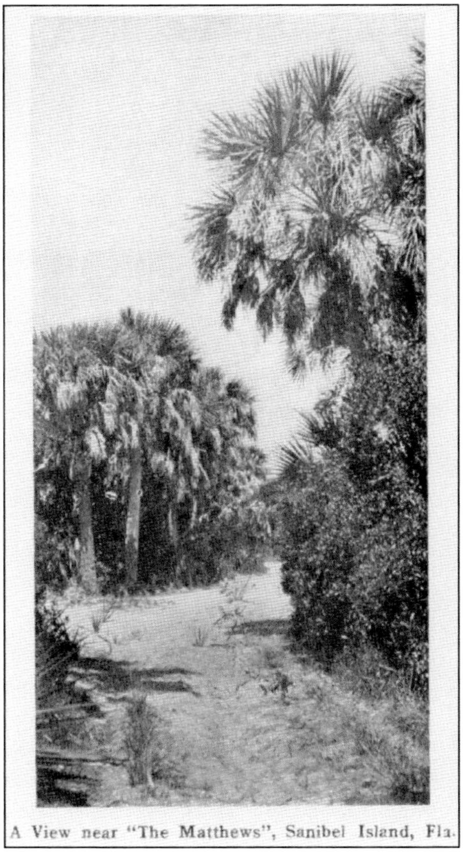

The palmetto-lined sand roads that lead to The Matthews crossed marshes and the grassland prairie between the bay and Gulf shores. Wagons carrying guests and provisions were drawn by a horse, or more commonly, a mule. With such effort to reach a remote island, guests often stayed for the entire winter. This card was also produced by Sanibel Packing Company. (Courtesy of Islander Trading Post.)

Sanibel's interior was mostly grassland with occasional sabal palm trees. Guests at The Matthews (later called the Island Inn) or The Sisters (later called Casa Ybel) would arrive by steamer at the bay-front dock and be transported several miles to their inn. Francis and Sam Bailey recall a time when they could stand at the Gulf-front Island Inn, look north, and see a passing schooner in the bay. (Courtesy of Ralph Curtis.)

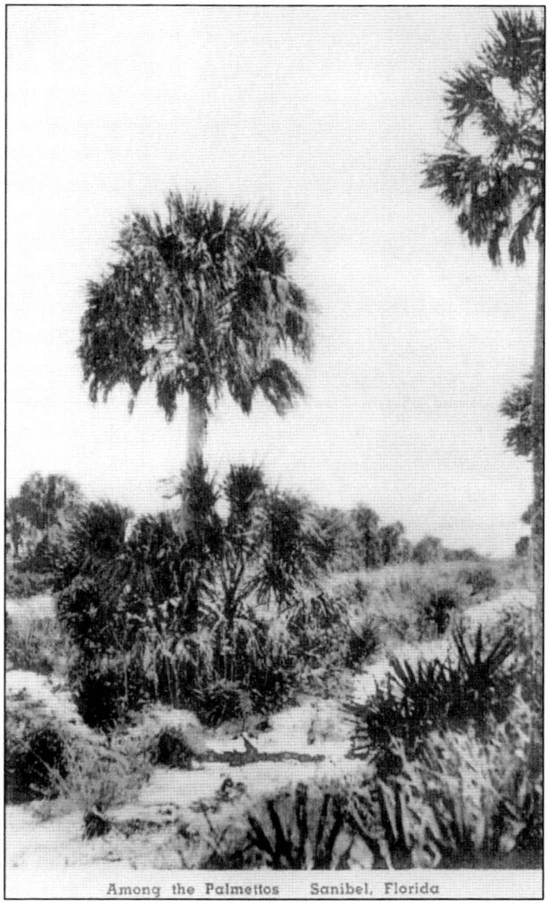

The Bailey family was known for their citrus groves of mostly grapefruit and limes. They also farmed tomatoes, eggplant, peppers, and watermelon. Soon after their arrival and the hardships of the Great Freeze, they replanted and were reported to be doing well by 1898. The sandy soil of Sanibel and Captiva was well suited to growing citrus and vegetable crops as long as storms did not bring saltwater over the land. (Courtesy of Sanibel Public Library.)

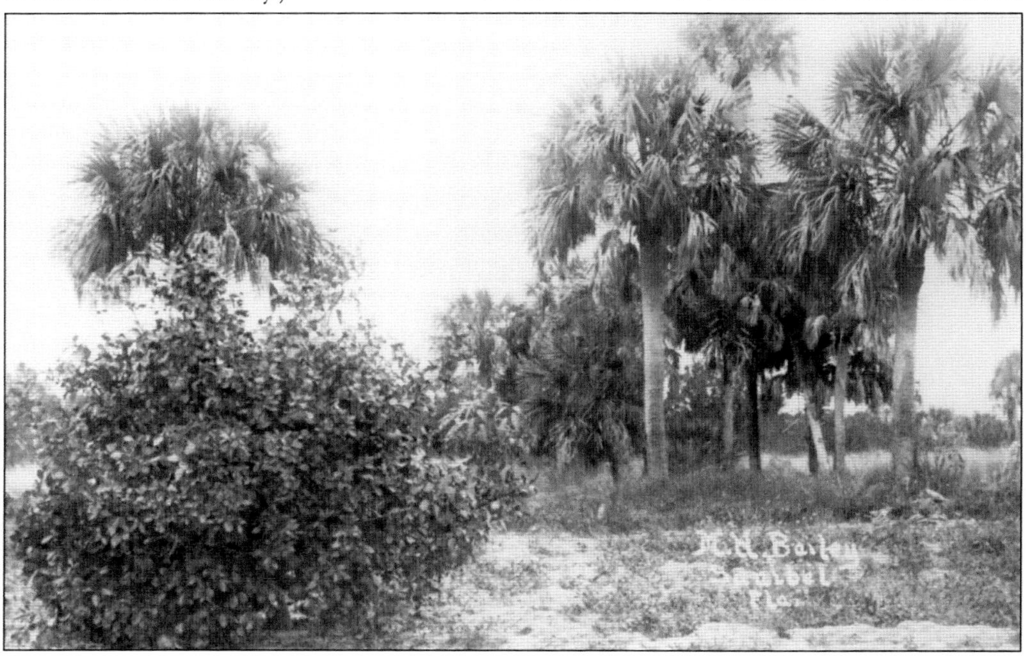

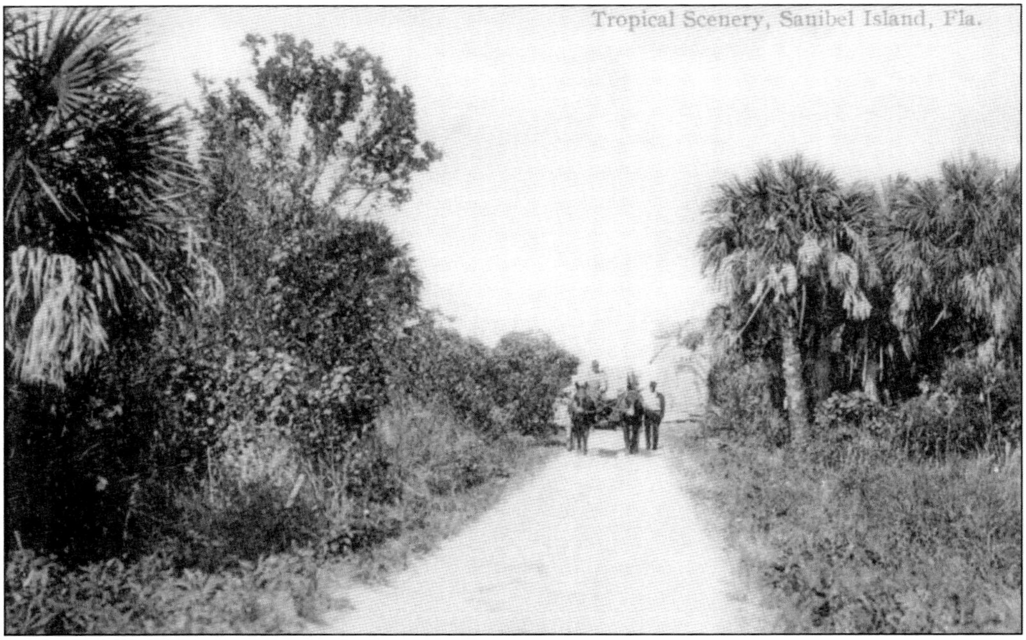

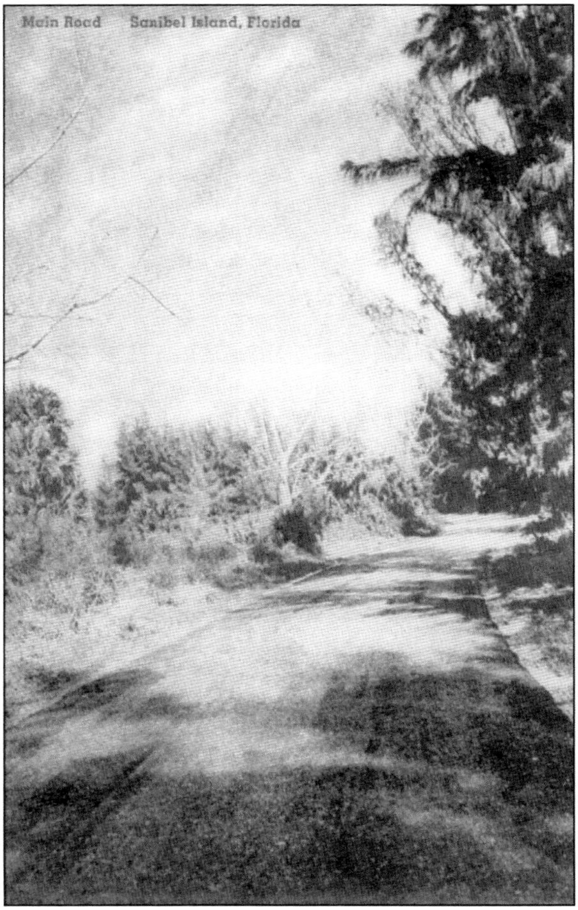

This postcard, produced by Sanibel Packing Company, may portray farmers returning from delivering crops to a packinghouse. Sanibel and Captiva had both white and black farmers and sharecroppers, and all relied on the strength of their mules. Most livestock did not survive the heat, mosquitoes, and other pests, but mules were known to be dependable and tough. (Courtesy of Islander Trading Post.)

The early maps of Sanibel show very few roads, mostly main arteries leading from landings, docks, or bulkheads. Sanibel's main road was not named Periwinkle Way until well after the early days of homesteading. It was finally upgraded with asphalt in the late 1950s, although it may have had an earlier treatment of oil, sprayed to keep the dust down. (Courtesy of Sanibel Public Library.)

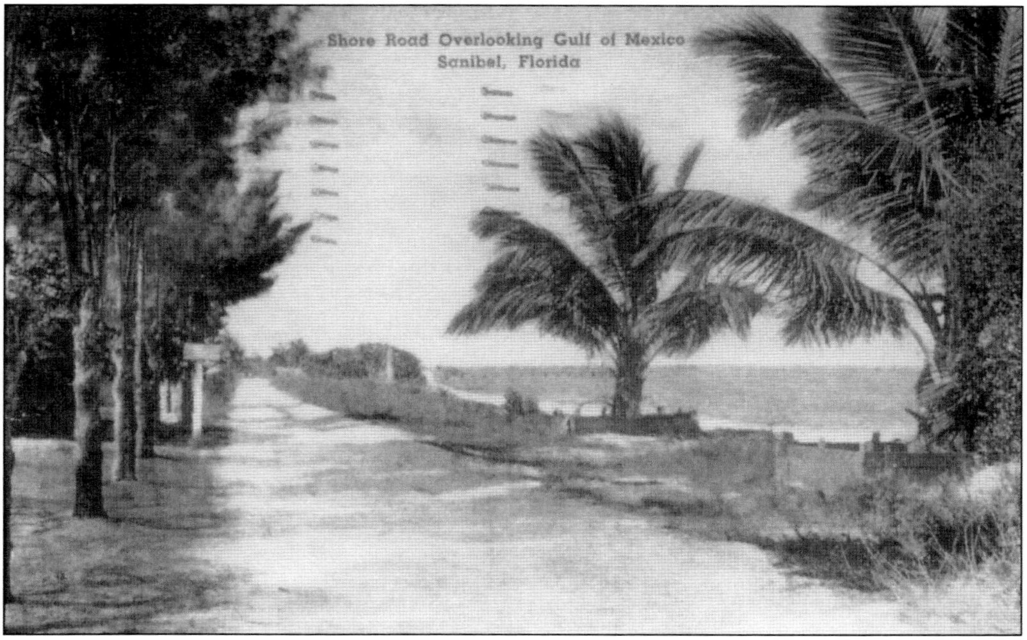

Contrary to the postcard, this was actually a bay-front road that in 1958 went from the end of Bailey Road, past the county dock, Bailey's General Store, and Miss Charlotta's Tea Room, and ended at the tip of Woodring Point. Because of years of erosion, use of this road was discontinued, and homes were accessed via a more southern road. (Courtesy of Sanibel Historical Museum and Village.)

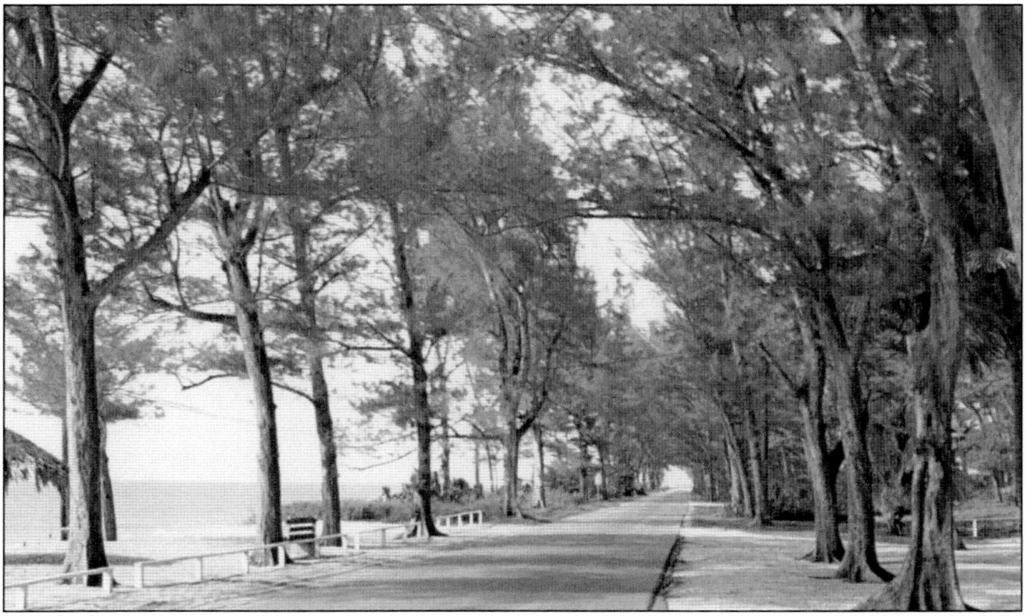

The main road through Captiva has been in constant change, thanks to nature's wind and waves. Years ago, it was not uncommon to detour to one lane after the beach had eroded under the west lane. The Captiva Erosion Prevention District now works to keep the beaches and roads safe. After the devastation of Hurricane Charley, islanders and visitors had to adjust to a roadway without the shade of the Australian pines. (Courtesy of Deborah Gleason collection.)

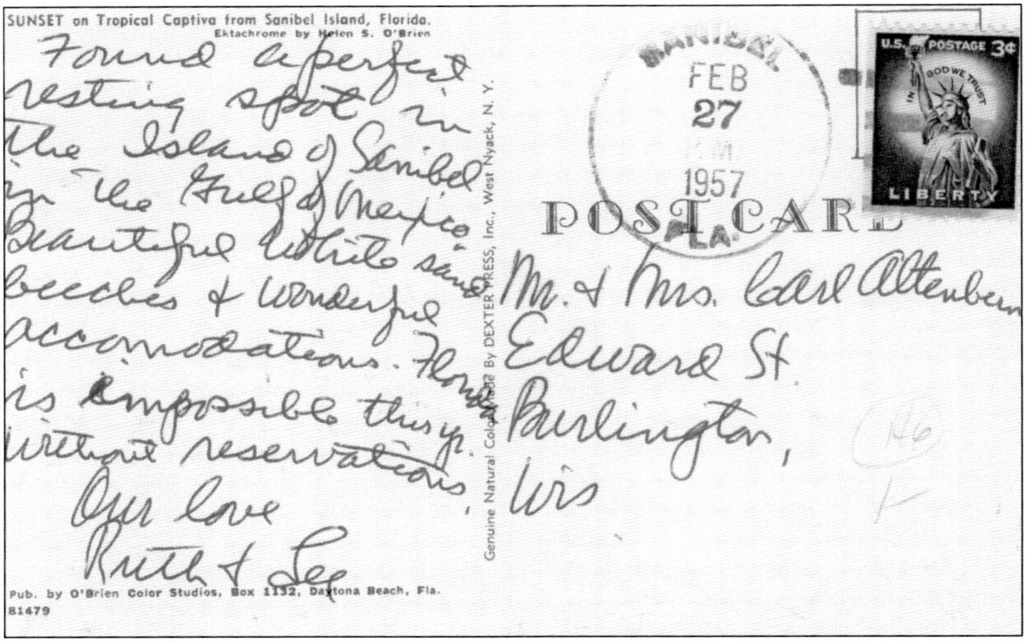

The 1950s were part of the rediscovery of Sanibel and Captiva. Dated February 27, 1957, this vacationer described a virtual paradise to the addressee in wintry Wisconsin. The local area of Santiva, the northern tip of Sanibel, was the setting for this happy message home. As relayed in the message, even before the causeway, motels and inns were often at full occupancy in the winter season. (Courtesy of Tom Hoopes.)

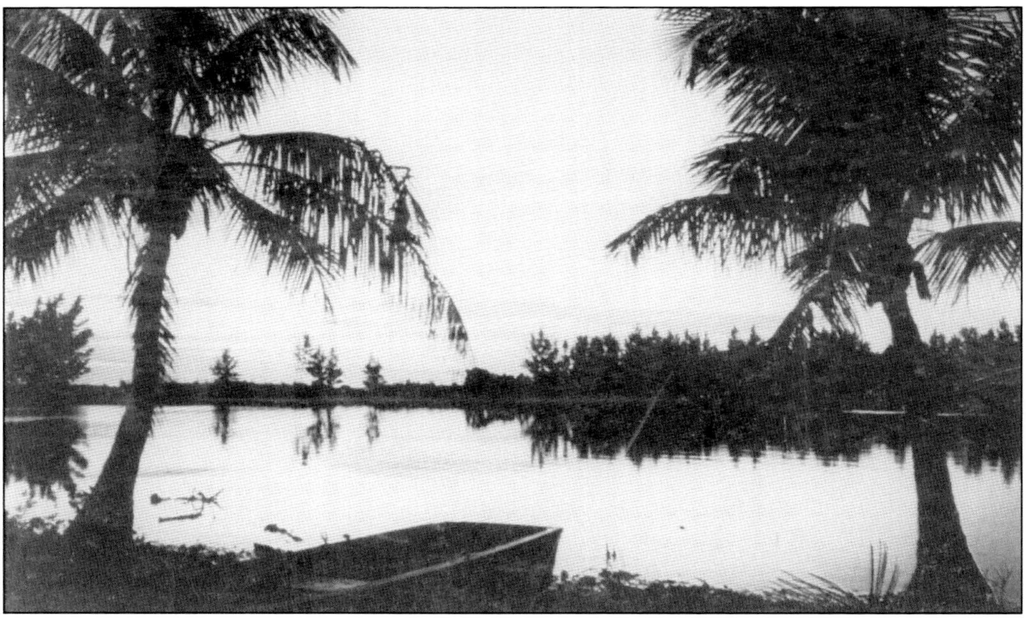

This is the postcard front of the previous written message. While standing on Sanibel, the photographer was viewing a sunset over a part of Captiva, Turner Beach, now largely removed by erosion. The waterway was Blind Pass, at a time when the pass emptied into the Gulf near Bowman's Beach. At this date, in 1957, a restaurant, docks, and cottages lined the Sanibel side of the pass. (Courtesy of Tom Hoopes.)

Four

The Famed Beaches

The unique alignment of Sanibel makes it the perfect depository for seashells. It is perhaps the one most common reason vacationers visit here, as the islands are known as one of the world's shelling meccas. To ensure that these islands continue to have healthy populations of shell species, there is a live shelling ban. But it would be a mistake to think only of seashells when the white sand beaches of Sanibel and Captiva offer so much more.

Dozens of species of shorebirds regularly hunt the waves and sand for crabs and other sea life important to their diet. Dolphins and manatees visit the shallows near the beach, and sea turtles search for the perfect place to crawl up and lay their eggs. Because of the presence of female turtles, summer shelling is discouraged at night.

Fishermen wait patiently on the shore for the reward of a snook, redfish, or sea trout on their lines. Wind surfers, skim boarders, sailors, kayakers, swimmers, and joggers visit the beach daily. And of course, families with beach chairs, umbrellas, buckets, and towels, are often out for a day of sunning, wading, splashing, and creating sandcastles. Many weddings have taken place on the beaches of Captiva and Sanibel, often because of precious memories of past family vacations.

An island sunrise or sunset is best appreciated while walking or sitting on the beach, with colors reflecting off the water and clouds. The quest to see the famous "Green Flash" at sunset is also a favorite beach activity. This optical phenomenon only lasts one to two seconds as the sun sets below the horizon, but it is still an experience to pursue.

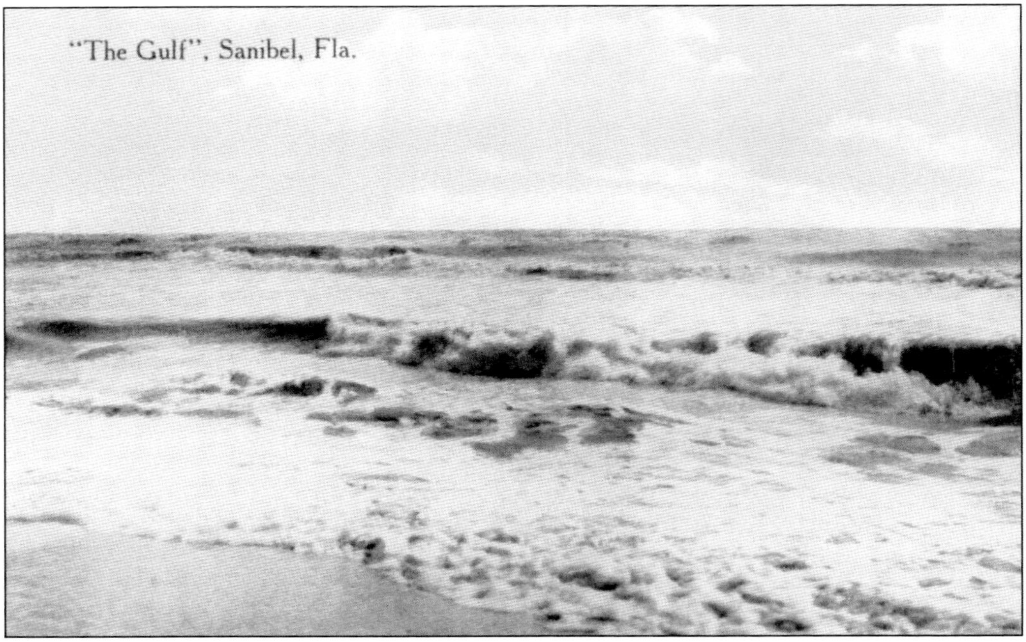

Yet another of the Sanibel Packing Company postcards shows a day when the Gulf waters are unsettled by a storm. Blustery days like this one are a sheller's delight. This card was produced and sold sometime before World War II. (Courtesy of Islander Trading Post.)

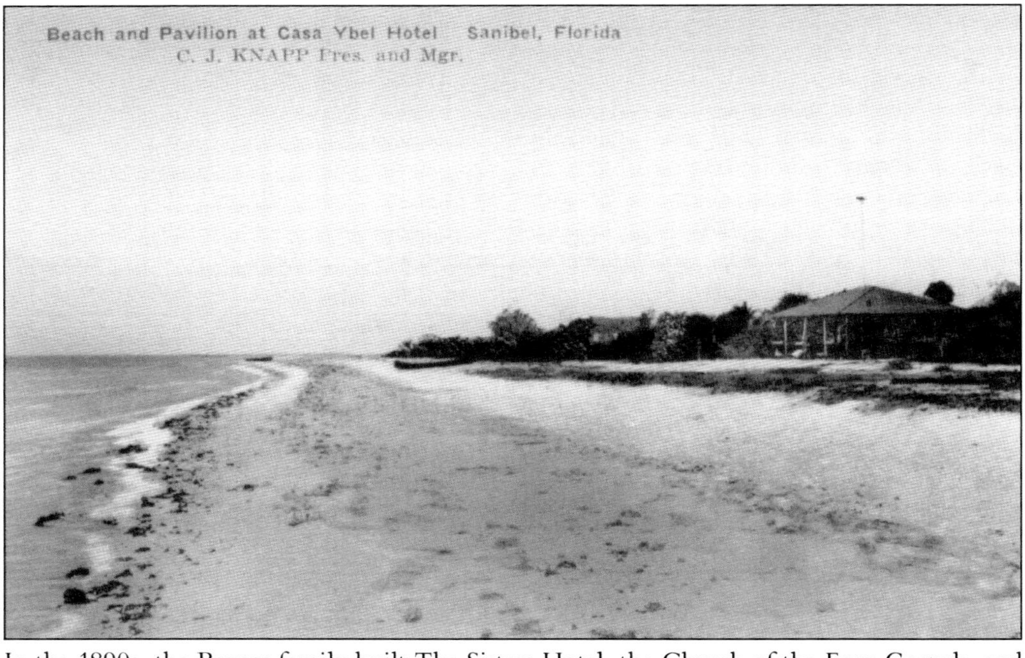

In the 1890s, the Barnes family built The Sisters Hotel, the Church of the Four Gospels, and Thistle Lodge. The Sisters was renamed Casa Ybel Hotel in 1906 and offered hunting, fishing, shelling, and a retreat from northern winters. The Knapp family from Cleveland bought the property in 1923, after building a home and the Green Lawn Lodge on Captiva. In 1945, Casa Ybel was purchased by the Howard Dayton Hotels and by Mariner Properties in 1977. (Courtesy of Charles LeBuff collection.)

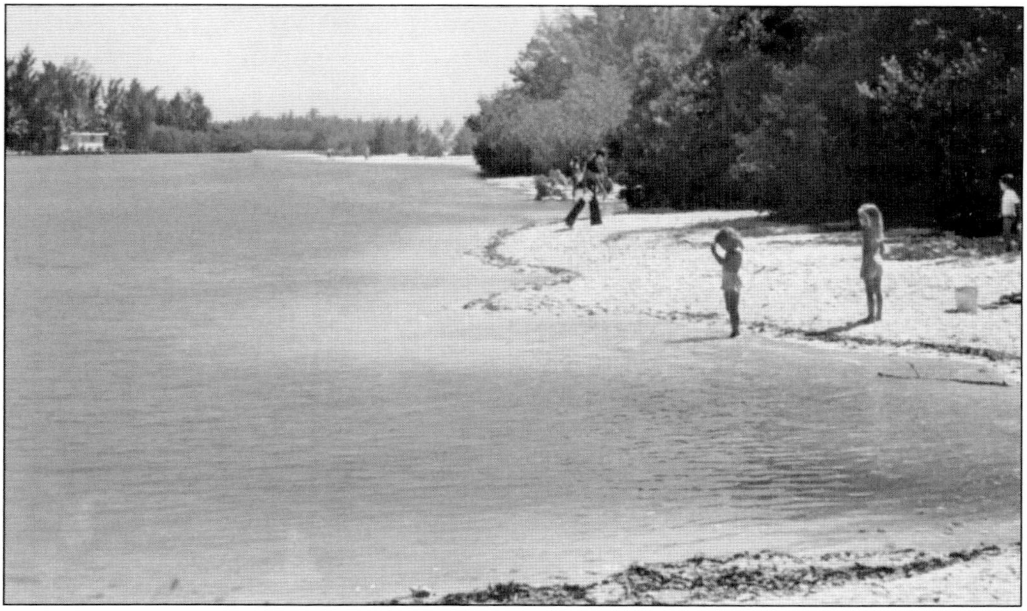

This beach was part of the Blind Pass Inlet. The homes on the east side of Blind Pass were part of Sanibel, and those walking or shelling on the west side had only a short distance to cross over to begin their walk on Captiva's Turner Beach. By the 1980s, much of Turner Beach had eroded away and many of the Blind Pass Sanibel homes were gone or endangered. (Courtesy of Sanibel Historical Museum and Village.)

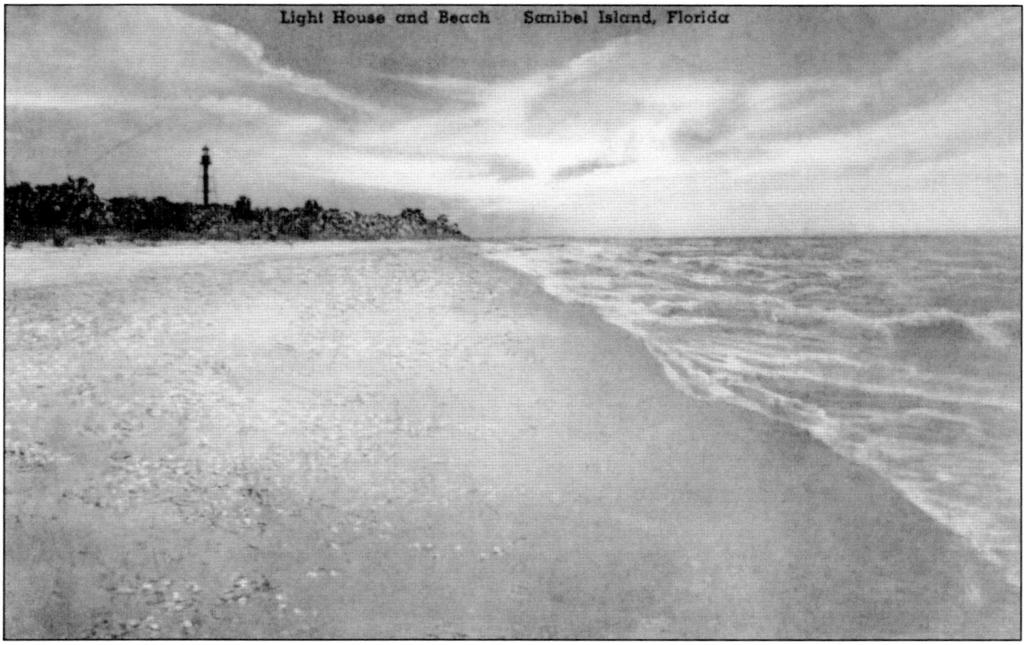

This iconic view of Sanibel was one of the Sanibel Packing Company postcards. Note that no boats, birds, buildings, or people are pictured. Given the scarcity of shells and flotsam on the beach, this photograph was likely taken in calm weather, when a visitor could enjoy the weather and solitude. It would also be perfect conditions for the old island hobby of driving a car down the beach, towing a water skier. (Courtesy of Islander Trading Post.)

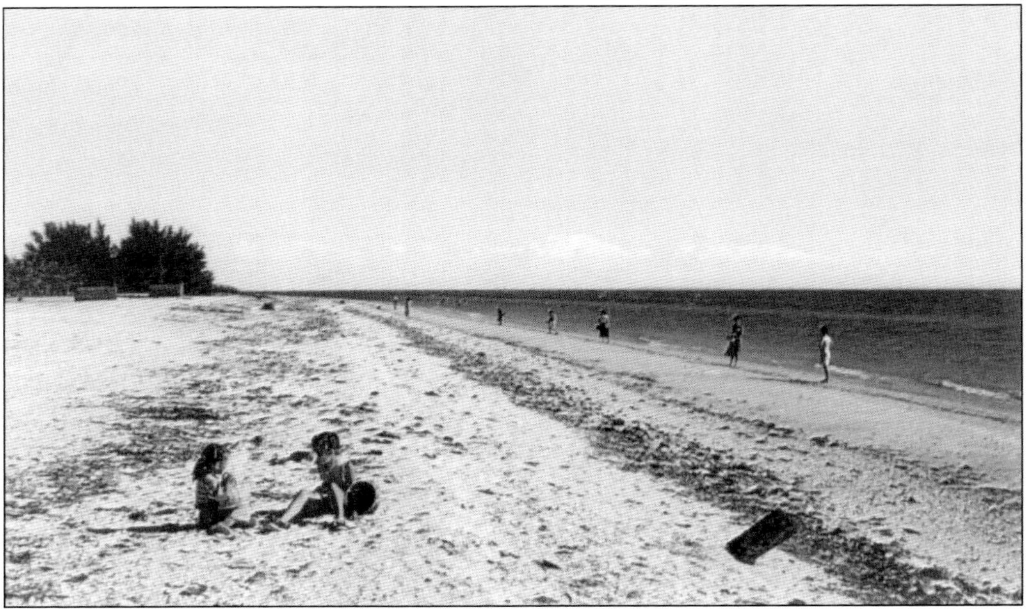

Shelling is often best at low tide. Not only is more of the beach exposed, but also a greater variety of shell species may appear where tides usually cover. The windbreaks or cabanas high on the beach were often constructed of a few boards and an overlay of cabbage palm fronds. Today, permanent cabanas or palm huts are not allowed, as they are a detriment to nesting sea turtles and shorebirds. (Courtesy of Deborah Gleason collection.)

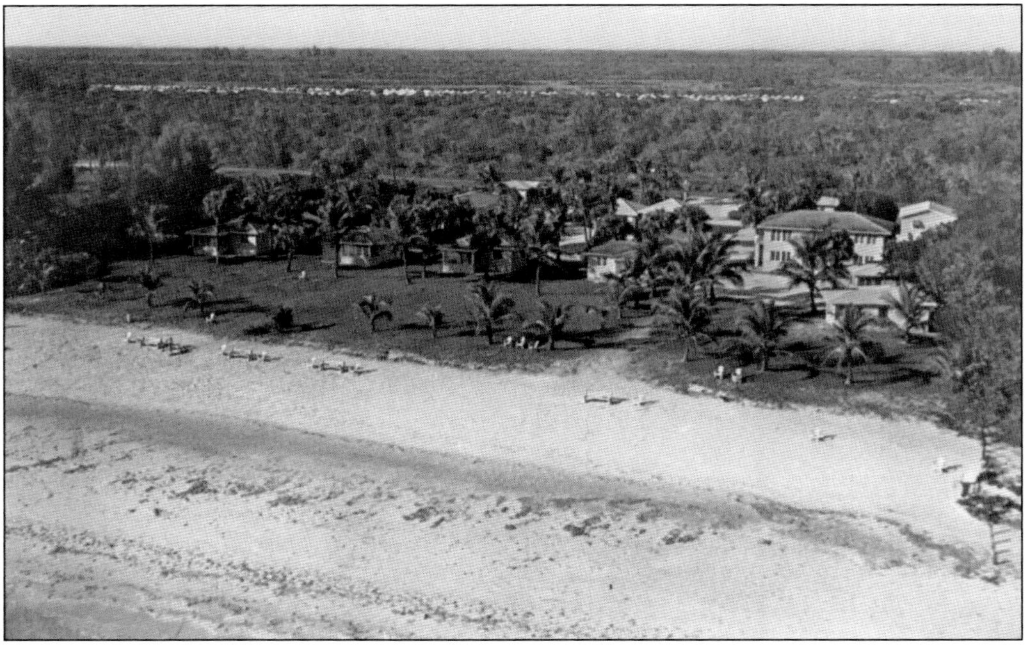

One of the first motels to be built after World War II was Hiers By the Sea. Martin and Sadie Hiers made their own concrete blocks from beach sand. Gulf Drive was once in front of the cottages. The white hills in the background of this photograph are sand mounds from a dragline-dug canal for landing Tommy Wood's seaplane. Wood was the first manager of J.N. "Ding" Darling National Wildlife Refuge. (Courtesy of Islander Trading Post.)

Captiva's currents run deeper than on Sanibel's eastern beaches. An Australian pine is leaning, a victim of erosion. The shells are common ark shells. In World War II, many beaches were patrolled, and Bowman's Beach was used for air-to-ground target practice. At that time, residents of both islands were required to black out their windows at night. (Courtesy of Gerri Much.)

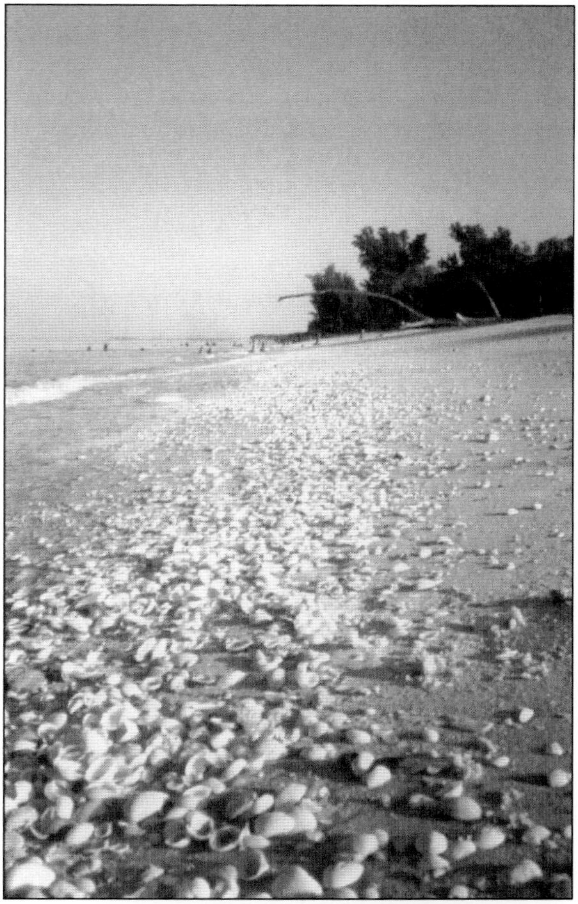

The original Gulf Drive is part of this beach scene, possibly at the Island Inn. Often resort beaches were raked and cleaned, and shuffleboard remains a traditional Florida pastime. Beaches are now encouraged to return to their natural state; sea oats and other native grasses fight erosion and provide natural habitat for shorebirds and animals. (Courtesy of Islander Trading Post.)

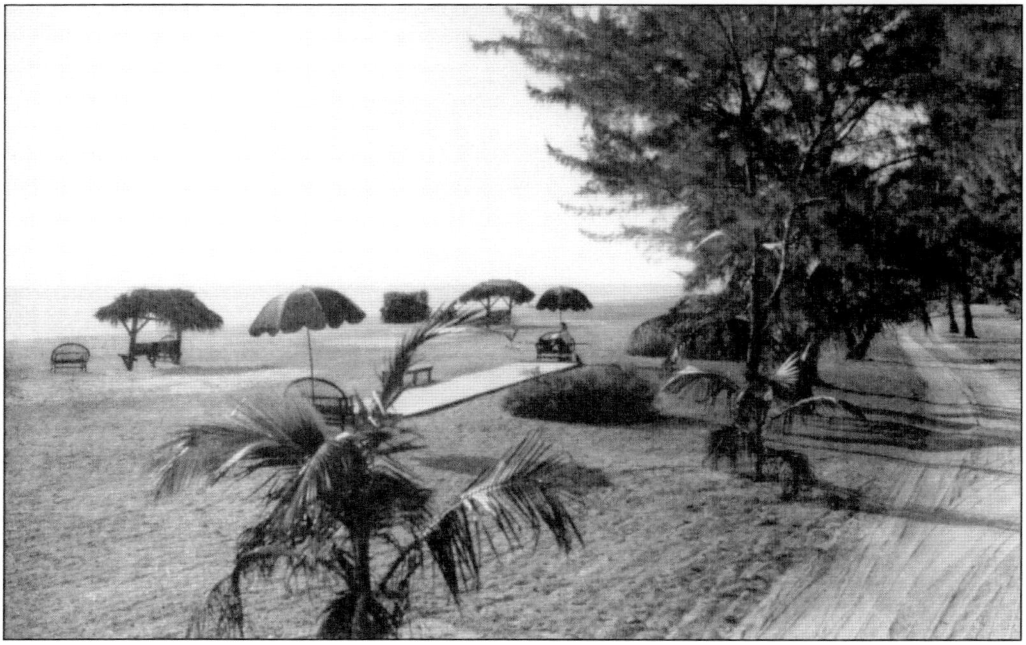

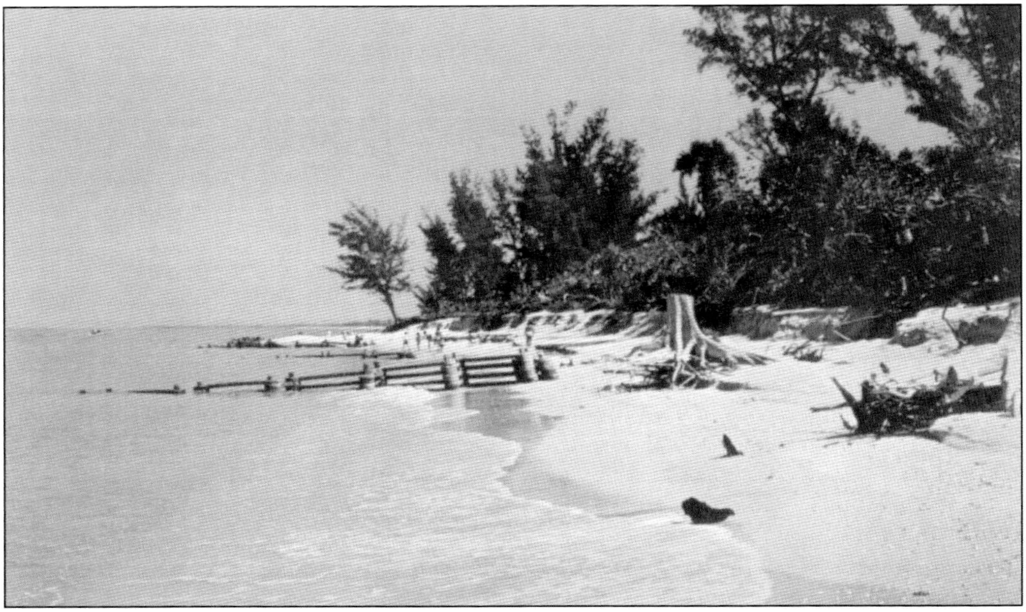

Captiva Island has long fought a war with erosion. One of the earliest weapons was the dog bone groin, thought to be the savior of the beaches. Unfortunately, they were not highly successful in erosion control, and most were lost to wave action or simply covered up by later beach renourishment. They were, however, known to attract sought-after fish and became the go-to fishing spots for local fisherman. (Courtesy of Sanibel Historical Museum and Village.)

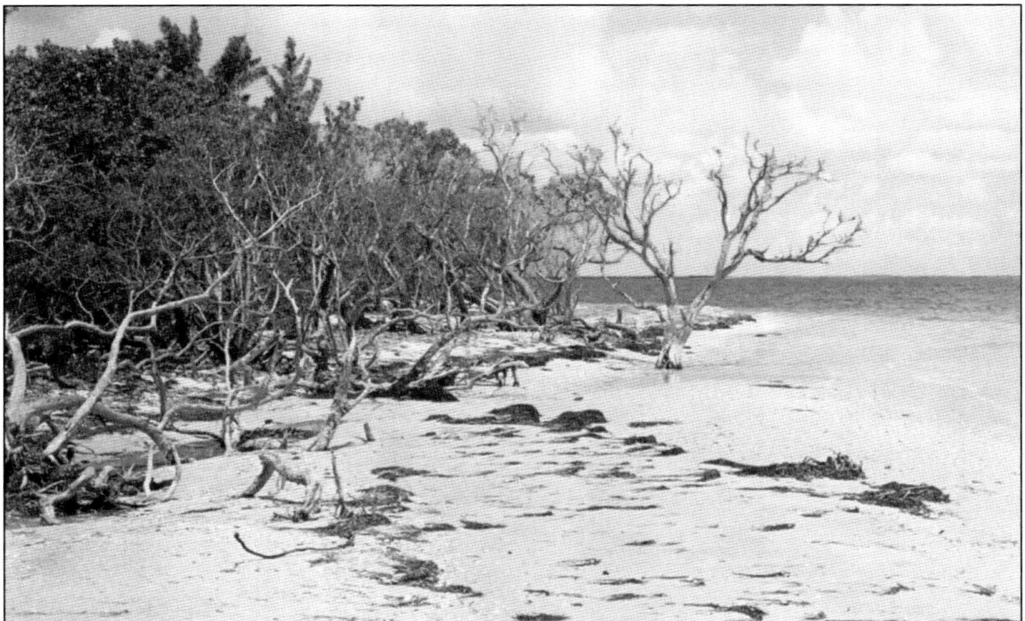

The effects of erosion are not only felt on Gulf-front beaches but bay front as well. Barrier islands can erode from any shore, whether it is from natural causes or manmade ones. The best natural defense is planting and maintaining the native plants, including mangrove, buttonwood, seagrape, and sea oats. The lighthouse beach has seen years of extreme erosion and then, inexplicably, the sand begins to accrue. (Courtesy of Charles LeBuff collection.)

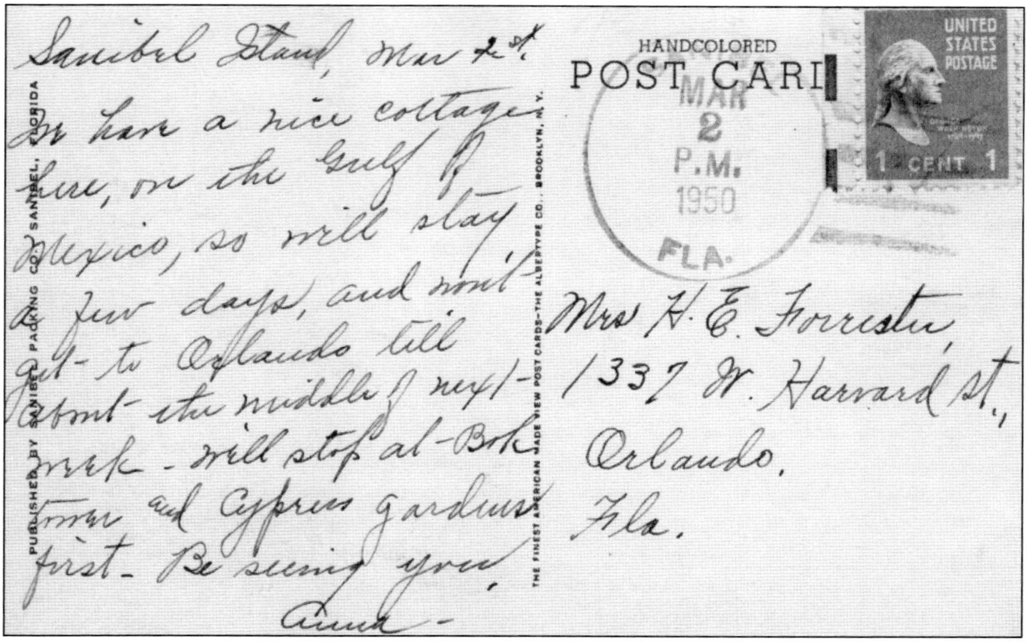

PUBLISHED BY SANIBEL PACKING CO., SANIBEL, FLORIDA

Sanibel Island, Mar 2nd.
We have a nice cottage here, on the Gulf of Mexico, so will stay a few days, and won't get to Orlando till about the middle of next week - will stop at Bok tower and Cypress gardens first. Be seeing you,
Anna -

THE FINEST AMERICAN MADE VIEW POST CARDS—THE ALBERTYPE CO., BROOKLYN, N.Y.

HANDCOLORED
POST CARI

UNITED STATES POSTAGE
1 CENT 1

MAR
2
P.M.
1950
FLA.

Mrs H. E. Forrester,
1337 W. Harvard St.,
Orlando,
Fla.

In 1950, a postcard message cost only 1¢. This visitor delayed her trip to Orlando for a "nice cottage on the Gulf of Mexico." She was referring to a cottage at Island Inn, and now, after 60 years, that cottage is still available for vacationers. Chances are, according to the postmark, this traveler also attended the Sanibel Shell Fair, held the first weekend of March for the last 75 years. (Courtesy of Islander Trading Post.)

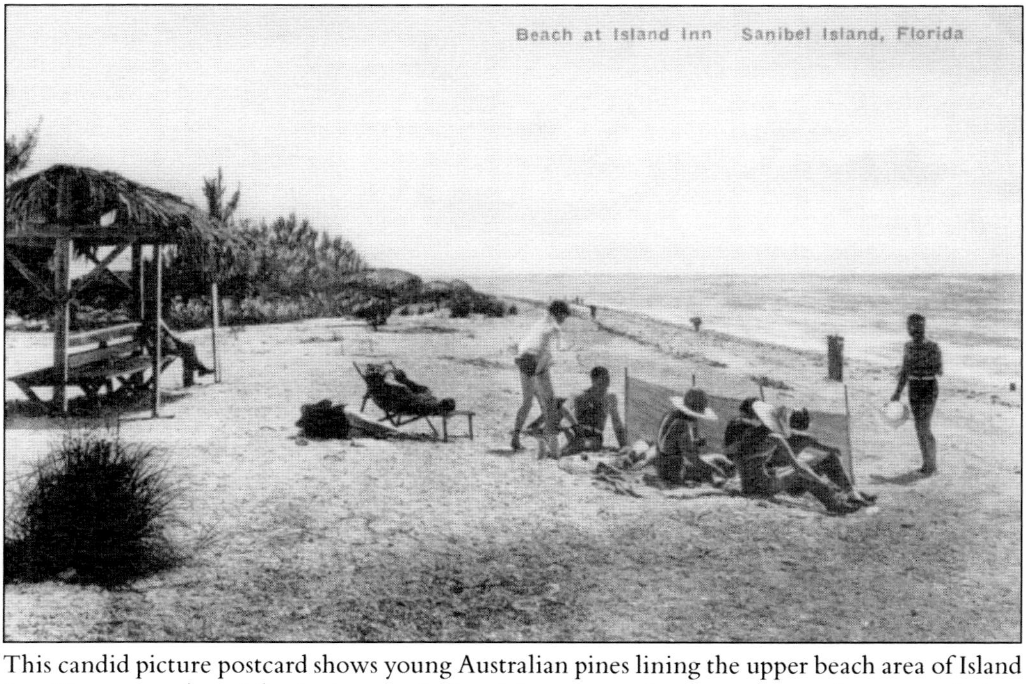

This candid picture postcard shows young Australian pines lining the upper beach area of Island Inn. Pines were planted for shade and windbreak but are now known to uproot in strong winds as well as discourage native plant growth. During the 1960s and 1970s, the Island Inn was managed by Jack and Milbrey Rushworth. (Courtesy of Islander Trading Post.)

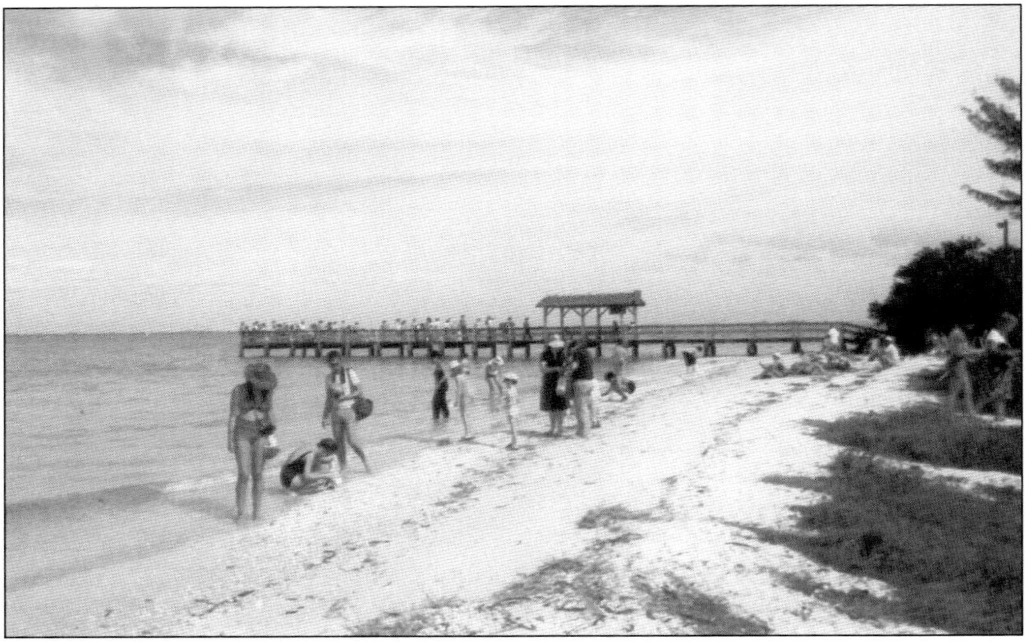

The first lighthouse wharf, at 162 feet long, was built in 1884 to facilitate construction of the lighthouse and keepers quarters. The fishing pier was built and later rebuilt after damage by a tropical storm. The strategic bay-to-Gulf location of the pier makes it a popular fishing location both day and night. The beach there is known for fishing and shelling, but swimming is not recommended because of strong currents. (Courtesy of Islander Trading Post.)

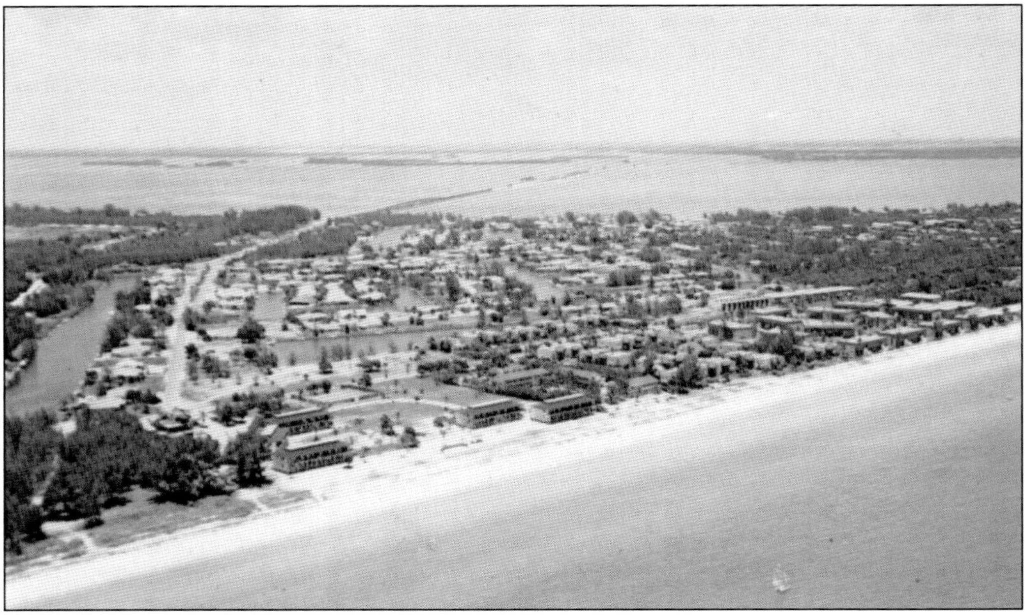

Once the Sanibel Causeway was in place, larger hotels, condominium complexes, commercial tracts, and dozens of homes were built within a decade. In 1974, residents voted to incorporate and control the rampant growth. A well-conceived land use plan was soon put in place, and the threat of high rises and the paving of paradise was averted. The beaches have remained in near-pristine condition and continue to attract visitors annually. (Courtesy of Islander Trading Post.)

Five

Gifts from the Sea

No one appreciated seashells more than Sanibel and Captiva's first inhabitants—the Calusa Indians. Their culture depended on shells, whether for food, tools, or the shell mounds that kept their villages high above the tides, away from bugs and foraging animals.

When Sanibel and Captiva Islands were discovered by modern man, seashells were an instant curiosity. The pioneers, intent upon agriculture, spent much of what little leisure time they had exploring the beaches for the endless varieties of shells.

Since many vacationers are interested in shelling, Sanibel and Captiva have had scores of shell shops and gift shops featuring things directly or indirectly related to seashells. The early shell shops were some of the only retail establishments on the remote islands. Restaurants had paper tablemats with shell illustrations and identification, Bailey's General Store had buckets and shell postcards, but only in the intimate shops like Mary Cunningham's, Glory of the Sea, Ken Havourd's Sanibel Seashell Industries, and Jim's Shell Shop was the rare junonia, or lion's paw. Often, folks were willing to buy the shells that had eluded them on their vacation. At those shops, many were drawn into shell craft once they saw the artistic floral pictures, shell-framed mirrors, or comical shell animals. That was before the days of television or computer distractions, and folks enjoyed the simple pastime of using shells to adorn everyday items.

Collectors picked up any shell they wanted, inhabited or not. Most motels had a shell-cleaning station that included a hot plate and pot to boil out the shell's animal. Of course, today's laws prohibit the taking of live shells, protecting each species so they might reproduce and ensure that the beaches will always be a treasure trove of shells.

In 1927, the tradition of the Sanibel Shell Fair began, where residents and visitors could display their collections of local shells. During World War II, the fair was postponed but continues today as an international event featuring worldwide shells. In 1995, the Bailey-Matthews Shell Museum opened, giving island visitors the ultimate education in shells.

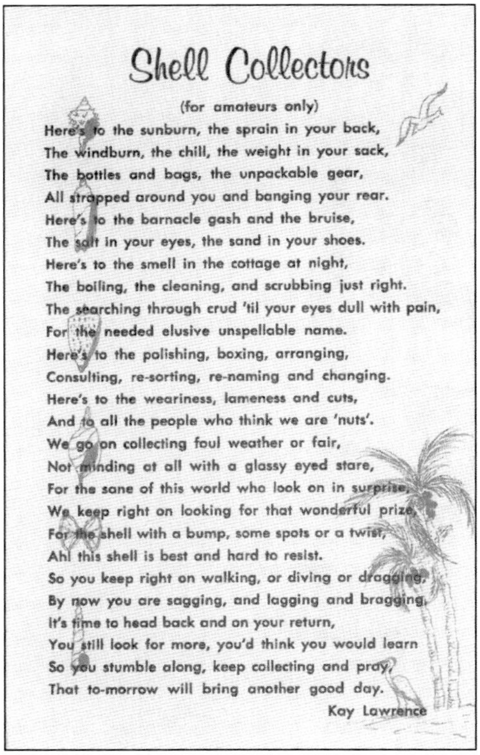

Shell Collectors

(for amateurs only)

Here's to the sunburn, the sprain in your back,
The windburn, the chill, the weight in your sack,
The bottles and bags, the unpackable gear,
All strapped around you and banging your rear.
Here's to the barnacle gash and the bruise,
The salt in your eyes, the sand in your shoes.
Here's to the smell in the cottage at night,
The boiling, the cleaning, and scrubbing just right.
The searching through crud 'til your eyes dull with pain,
For the needed elusive unspellable name.
Here's to the polishing, boxing, arranging,
Consulting, re-sorting, re-naming and changing.
Here's to the weariness, lameness and cuts,
And to all the people who think we are 'nuts'.
We go on collecting foul weather or fair,
Not minding at all with a glassy eyed stare,
For the sane of this world who look on in surprise,
We keep right on looking for that wonderful prize,
For the shell with a bump, some spots or a twist,
Ah! this shell is best and hard to resist.
So you keep right on walking, or diving or dragging,
By now you are sagging, and lagging and bragging,
It's time to head back and on your return,
You still look for more, you'd think you would learn
So you stumble along, keep collecting and pray,
That to-morrow will bring another good day.

Kay Lawrence

Kay Lawrence seldom missed a day on the beach. She continually searched for rare seashells that were delivered to the beach by wind and tide. Well-known for her shelling knowledge and fine collection, she was involved in all aspects of the activities associated with the annual Sanibel Shell Fair. She accurately describes her take on the art of seashell collecting from a serious collector's mind-set on this postcard from the 1960s. (Courtesy of Deborah Gleason collection.)

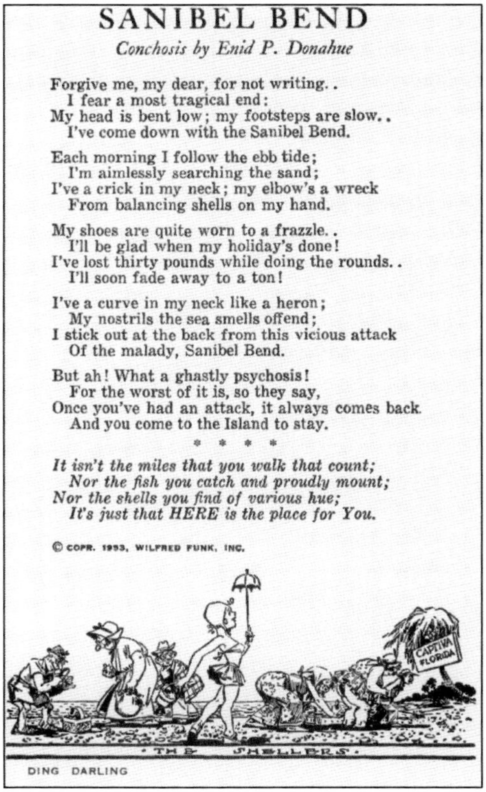

SANIBEL BEND

Conchosis by Enid P. Donahue

Forgive me, my dear, for not writing. .
I fear a most tragical end:
My head is bent low; my footsteps are slow. .
I've come down with the Sanibel Bend.

Each morning I follow the ebb tide;
I'm aimlessly searching the sand;
I've a crick in my neck; my elbow's a wreck
From balancing shells on my hand.

My shoes are quite worn to a frazzle. .
I'll be glad when my holiday's done!
I've lost thirty pounds while doing the rounds. .
I'll soon fade away to a ton!

I've a curve in my neck like a heron;
My nostrils the sea smells offend;
I stick out at the back from this vicious attack
Of the malady, Sanibel Bend.

But ah! What a ghastly psychosis!
For the worst of it is, so they say,
Once you've had an attack, it always comes back
And you come to the Island to stay.

* * * *

It isn't the miles that you walk that count;
Nor the fish you catch and proudly mount;
Nor the shells you find of various hue;
It's just that HERE is the place for You.

© COPR. 1953, WILFRED FUNK, INC.

Enid Donahue's poem about the Sanibel Bend appeared on this postcard in the late 1950s. It includes a cartoon by Captiva winter resident J.N. "Ding' Darling, which depicts busy, stooped-over shellers scrutinizing the surface of the Captiva beach, looking for that special shell. In those days, islanders referred to their islands as "the place where shellers go to bed at 7 and the hellers go to bed at 9." (Courtesy of Deborah Gleason collection.)

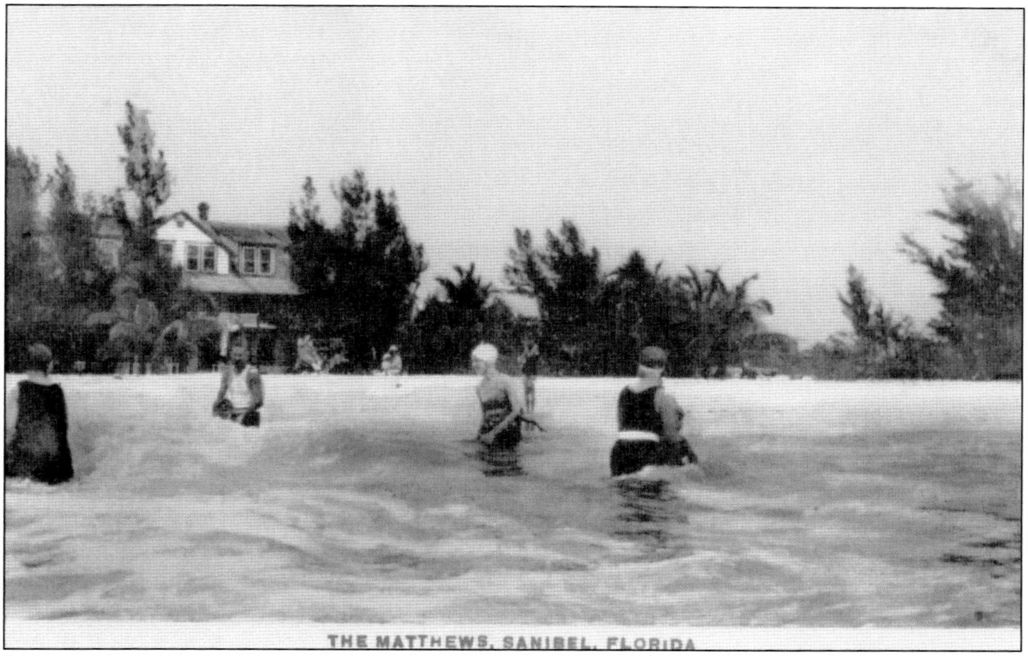

Many rely on their feet to find shells. At the wrong time, this is a dangerous practice. Stingrays congregate in shallows and can inflict painful wounds to shellers who may step on a hidden ray. Not only is the "Sanibel Bend" a common posture, so too is the "Stingray Shuffle." When walking in shallows, it is wise to shuffle one's feet. (Courtesy of Islander Trading Post.)

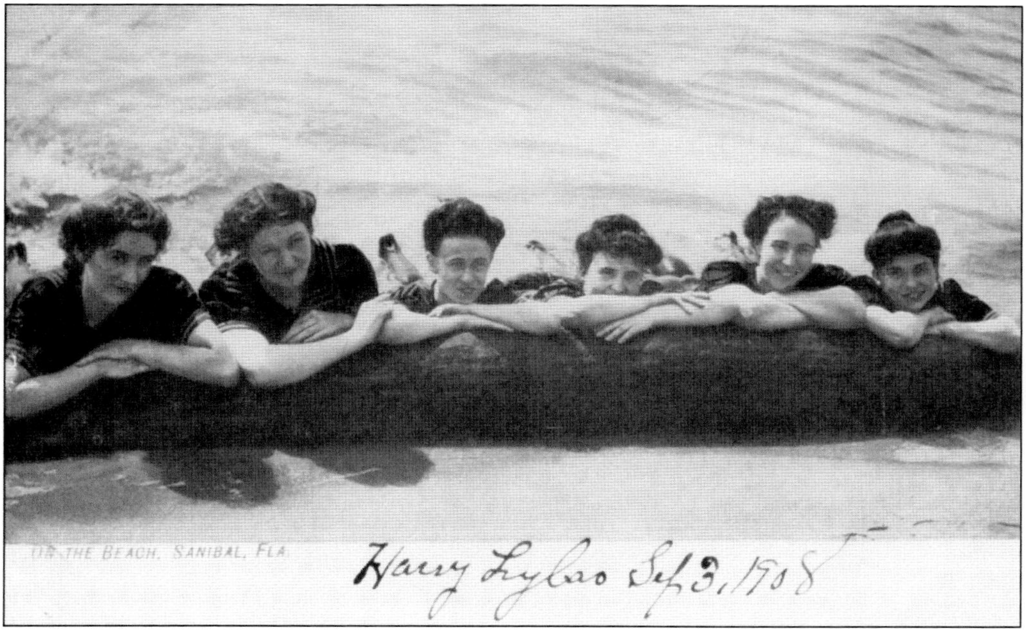

Seashell collecting is always best in the winter. After the passage of cold fronts with strong northwest winds, shells are heaped on the beach. The winds break shells loose from the bottom, and if the wind is strong enough, marine organisms of all kinds get to the beach in a hurry. Summer weather patterns tend to clean the beach. The ladies on this postcard are taking a cooling break from summer shelling. (Courtesy of Islander Trading Post.)

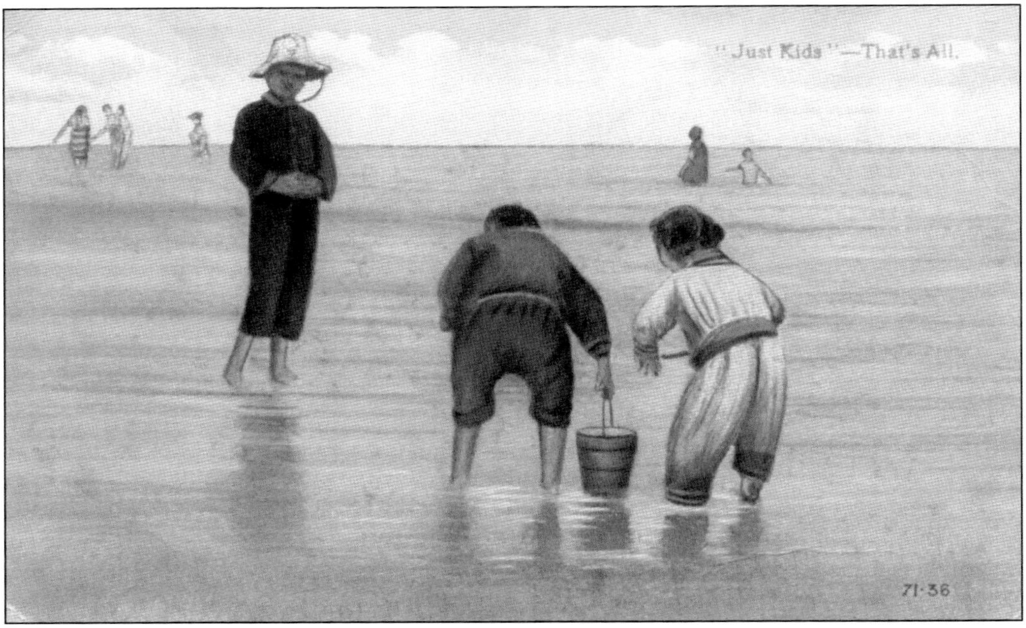

Two wading shellers are pictured doing the Sanibel Bend. Those shellers farther out are wading along a sandbar that parallels much of Sanibel. In that habitat, sand dollars and live mollusk species can be found. Collecting live shells and even living sand dollars is prohibited on Sanibel. Visitors should acquaint themselves with local regulations and learn about seashells by visiting the Bailey-Matthews Shell Museum. (Courtesy of Sanibel Historical Village and Museum.)

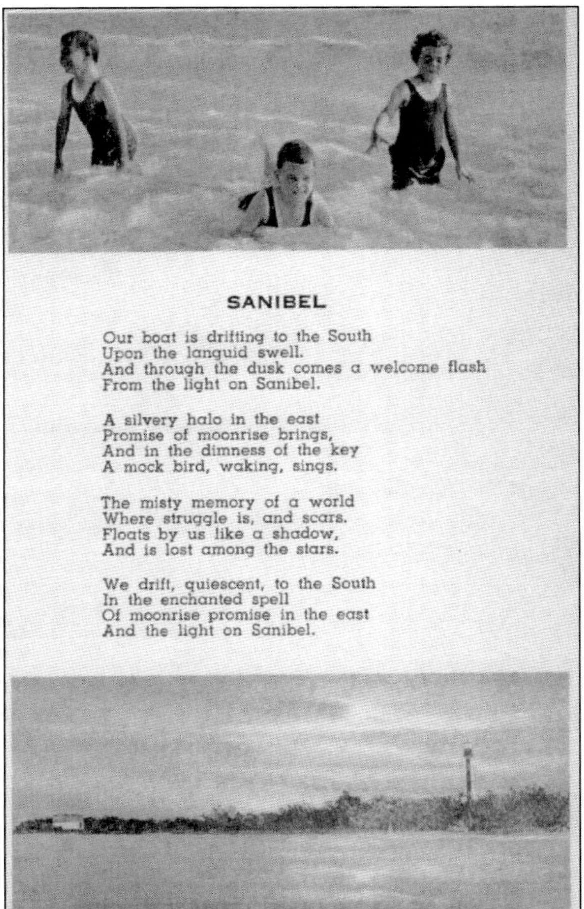

The top of this postcard shows the young Bailey boys. From left to right are John, Francis, and Sam. Francis, the eldest, spent a lifetime managing Bailey's General Store. John left the islands as a young man, as did Sam, the youngest, who became a university athletic director. He returned to the store after retirement. The poem features the Sanibel Lighthouse, as does the bay-front view at the bottom. (Courtesy of Charles LeBuff collection.)

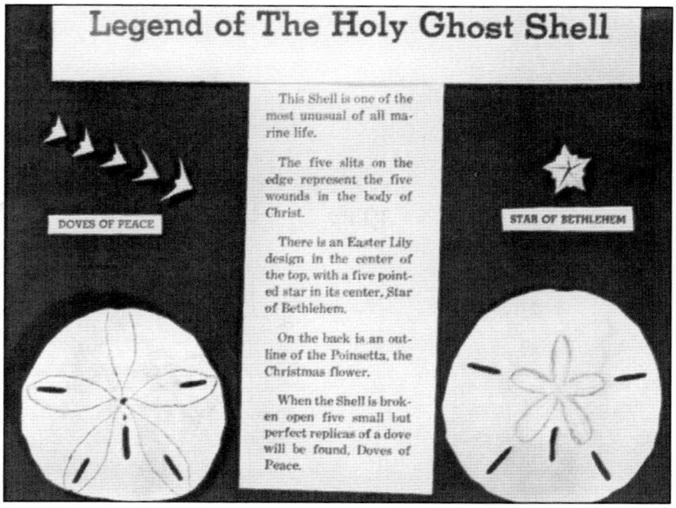

This postcard was popular in the 1950s and 1960s. It conveyed a religious theme based on an interpretation of a sand dollar's skeletal remains. Living sand dollars have a velvet-like covering. They move across the bottom using small projections that are known as tube feet. They eat plankton and algae that are swept to their mouth by hair-like, mucous-coated cilia. Food is moved to the centrally located mouth on their underside. (Courtesy of Deborah Gleason collection.)

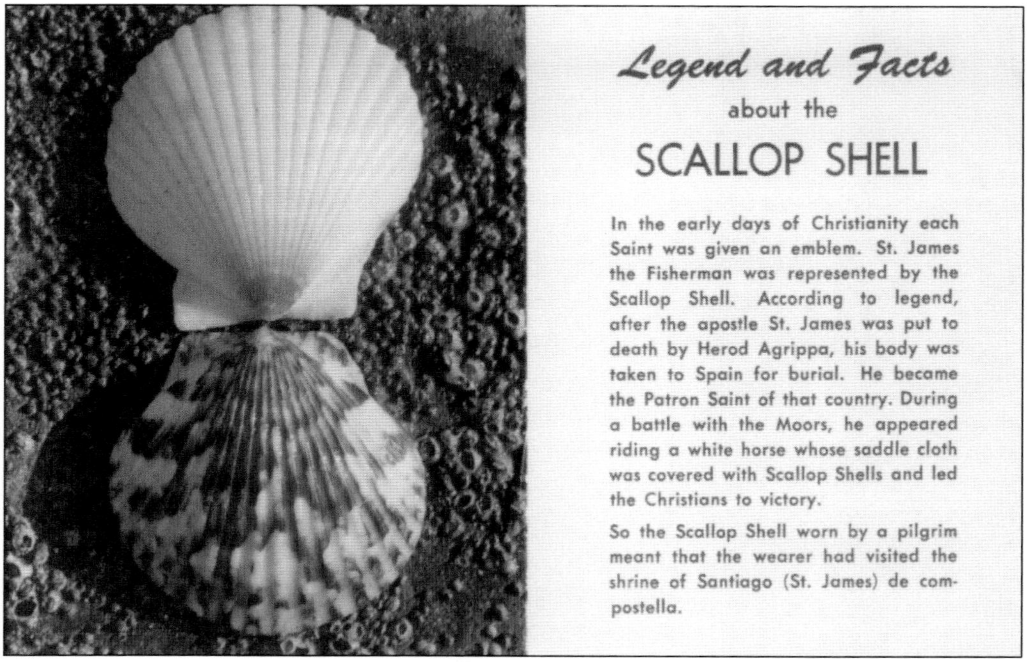

Another postcard with a religious connotation conveyed a legend about the pecten or scallop shell. These edible bivalves were common locally and were harvested throughout Pine Island Sound. Scallops were seasonally abundant in the sound up until the Sanibel Causeway was built. Its dredged spoil islands altered salinity and tidal flow to the degree that bay scallops, which are intolerant to water quality changes, have nearly disappeared from local inshore waters. (Courtesy of Deborah Gleason collection.)

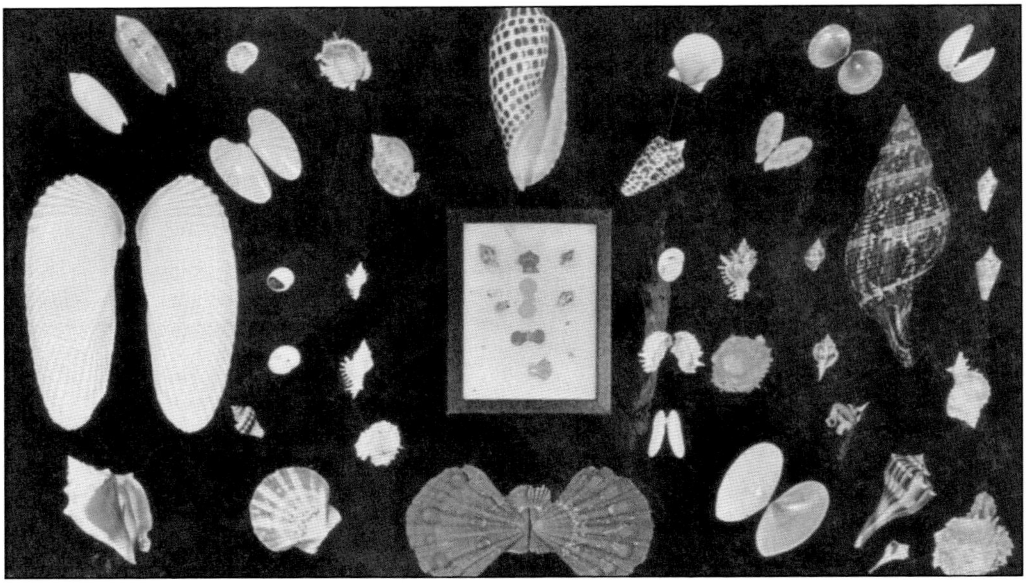

This postcard features a collection of specimen (high-quality individuals) shells from Sanibel and Captiva Islands. This representative collection of the most sought-after island seashells won first prize at the 1962 Sanibel Shell Fair. Inset at the center is another framed collection of miniature seashells. Some serious shell collectors no longer do the Sanibel Bend, they sit on the beach and sort through shell deposits looking for rare miniatures. (Courtesy of Deborah Gleason collection.)

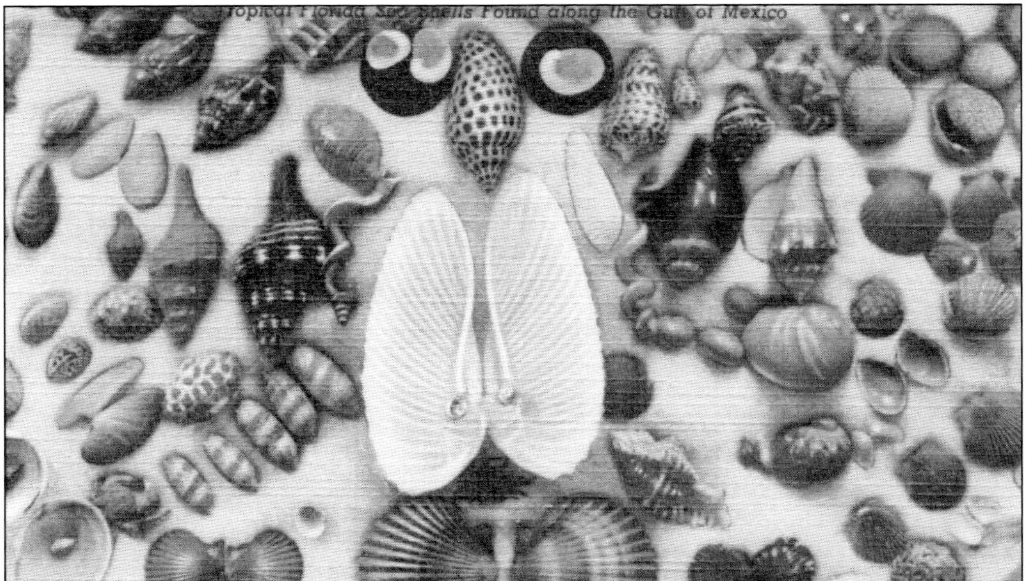

This shell-filled postcard from the 1940s includes a variety of local seashells. Sanibel and Captiva have long-standing reputations as being the shell-collecting capital of the western hemisphere. Everyone who has ever walked these beaches has picked up and admired a beautiful seashell. Just about every visitor to the islands, back in the day, when postcards were at their greatest popularity, sent a postcard adorned with seashells back home to family and friends. (Courtesy of Ralph Curtis.)

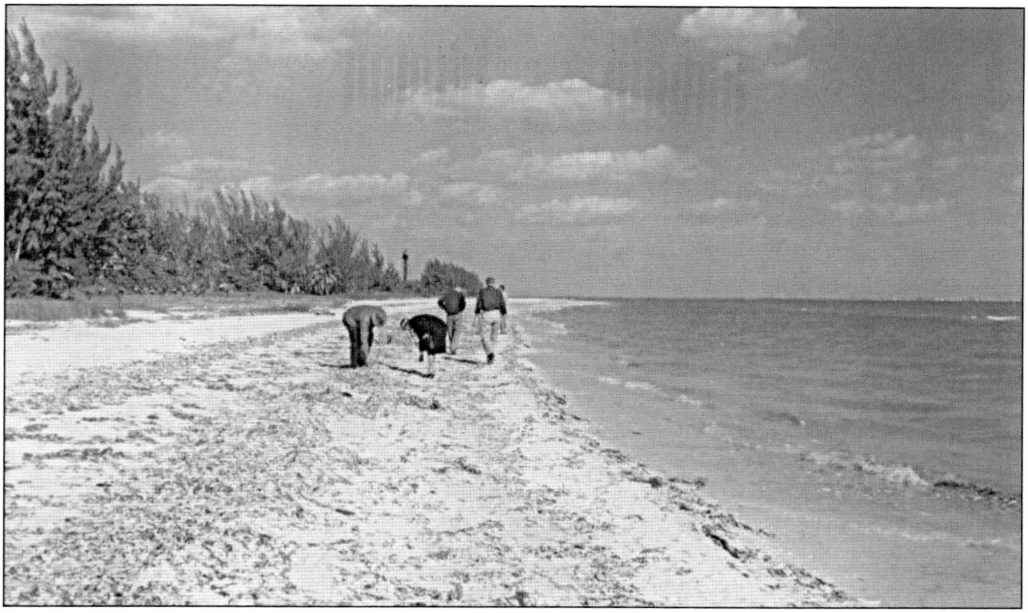

People search for shells on Point Ybel in the winter. The lighthouse is in the background, and this section of the waterfront is blanketed with a mix of marine organisms. The clutter on the beach is parchment worm cases intermixed with seashell treasures. Sanibel does not permit raking or cleaning of its beaches, fully recognizing the biological importance of such natural deposits. (Courtesy of Alvin Lederer.)

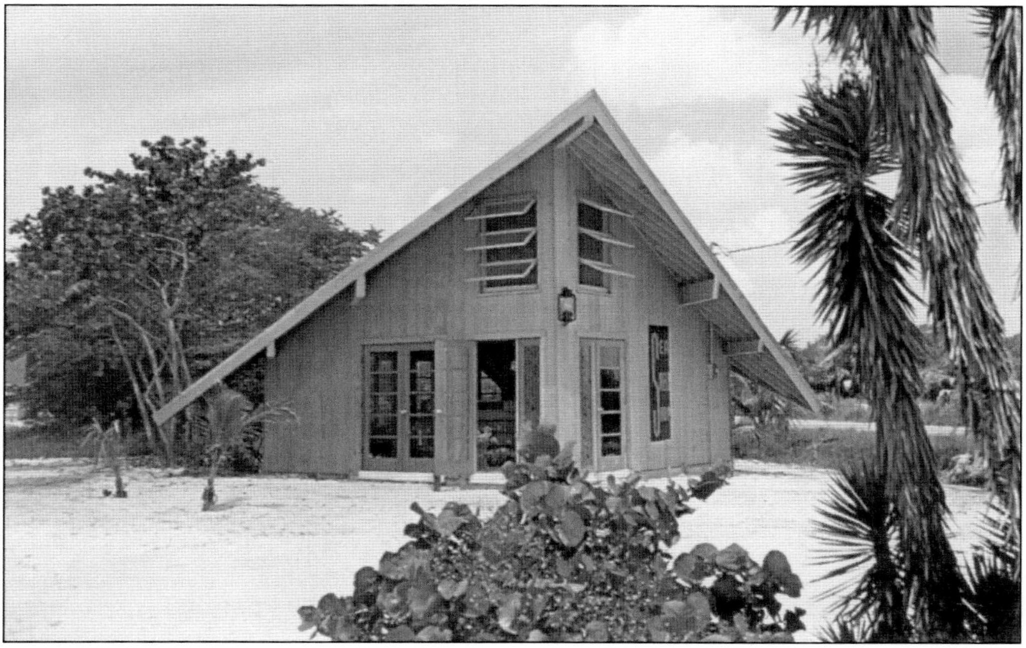

The first shell shop on Sanibel is said to have been Ken Havourd's Sea Shell Industries on Fitzhugh Street. Opened in about 1945, the business continues under the ownership of the Strange family and very close to the original site. As tourism flourished, shell shops expanded. This building, located on what is now West Gulf Drive, housed the shell shop of Hayes Hudson back in the 1950s. It is currently a realtor's office. (Courtesy of Deborah Gleason collection.)

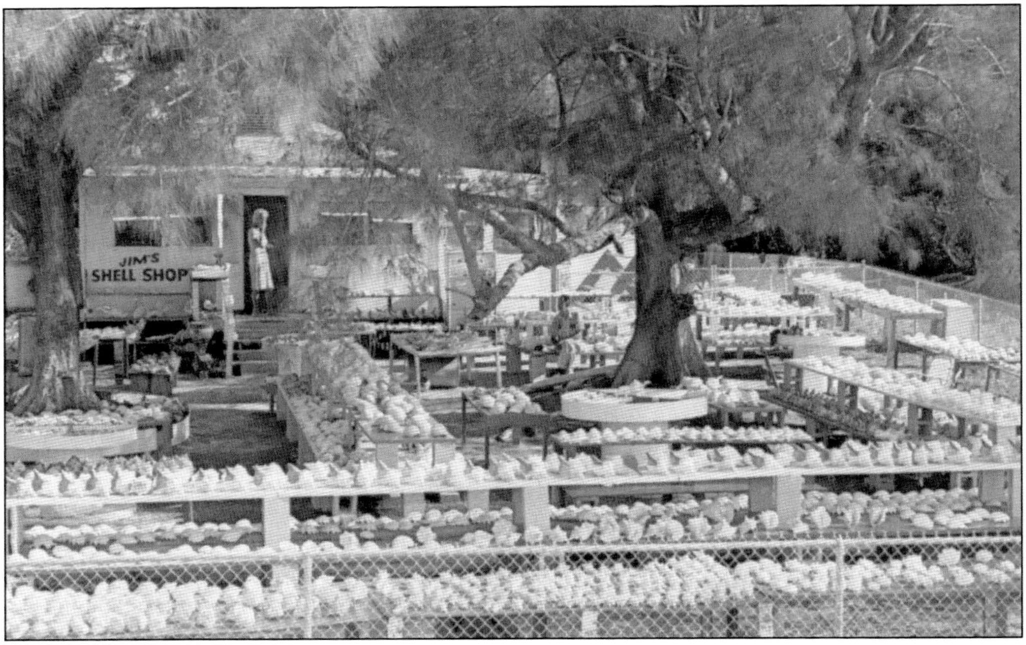

Jim's Shell Shop was mostly an open-air operation on the beach next to the lighthouse at the site of The Palms Hotel. Pictured in the doorway is Katherine "Snooky" Shanahan Williams, granddaughter of former lighthouse keeper Henry Shanahan. Her husband, James Williams, sits beneath the Australian pine. A victim of polio, James stayed at Warm Springs in Georgia along with Pres. Franklin D. Roosevelt and helped write some the president's speeches. (Courtesy of Islander Trading Post.)

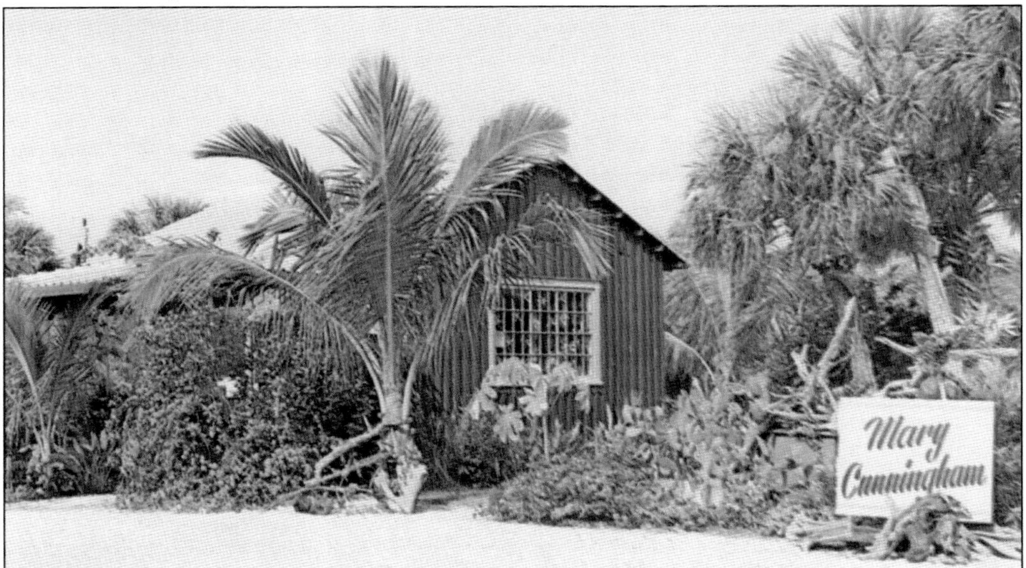

Mary Cunningham's shell shop on Captiva Island featured some of the best collectable seashells available anywhere. She was a guru in the local shell-collecting field, and both experts and high-level amateur collectors from all over the country made it a point when visiting the islands to frequent her shop to share information on shells, including recent rare shell finds, their identification, cleaning, and shell-craft creations. (Courtesy of Islander Trading Post.)

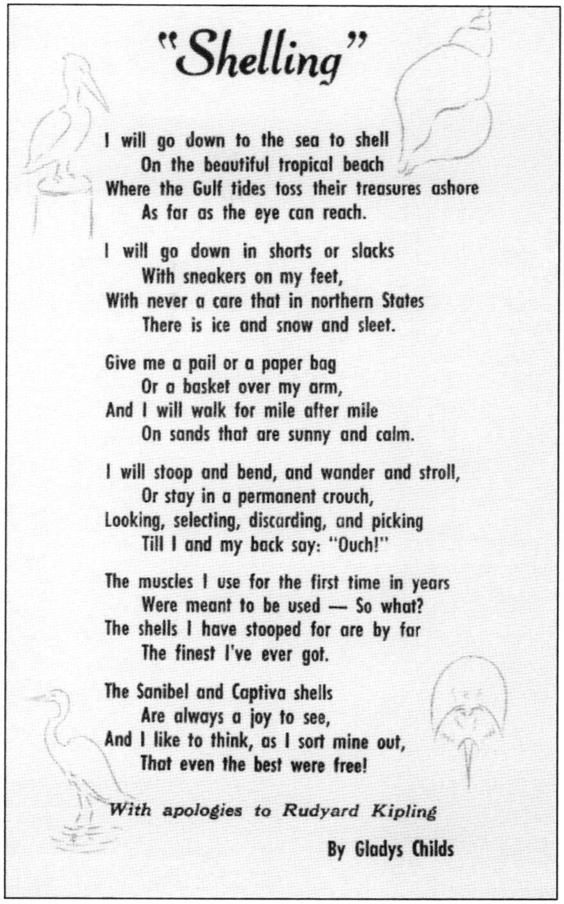

"Shelling"

I will go down to the sea to shell
On the beautiful tropical beach
Where the Gulf tides toss their treasures ashore
As far as the eye can reach.

I will go down in shorts or slacks
With sneakers on my feet,
With never a care that in northern States
There is ice and snow and sleet.

Give me a pail or a paper bag
Or a basket over my arm,
And I will walk for mile after mile
On sands that are sunny and calm.

I will stoop and bend, and wander and stroll,
Or stay in a permanent crouch,
Looking, selecting, discarding, and picking
Till I and my back say: "Ouch!"

The muscles I use for the first time in years
Were meant to be used — So what?
The shells I have stooped for are by far
The finest I've ever got.

The Sanibel and Captiva shells
Are always a joy to see,
And I like to think, as I sort mine out,
That even the best were free!

With apologies to Rudyard Kipling

By Gladys Childs

Gladys Childs was not only an artist who preserved elements of the barrier island lifestyle, she was also a poet who accurately portrayed shelling during her time. This Sanibel-Captiva postcard captured her sentiments on the skill and hardships faced by shellers on the island winter beaches. Her prose conveys a time when shelling was exceptional and describes the fortitude mustered by a serious seashell collector visiting in the wintertime. (Courtesy of Charles LeBuff collection.)

Outdoor advertising was in its infancy in the 1950s, but island businesses used it to their advantage wherever possible. After all, the majority of enterprises on the islands, other than overnight sleeping accommodations and a few eateries, were seashell-related. This portable signboard was parked to the right of the Punta Rassa ferry landing. The ladies on this postcard are potential shell collectors carefully perusing the seashell display. The building is the office of the Kinzie Brothers Steamer Line. (Courtesy of Sanibel Public Library.)

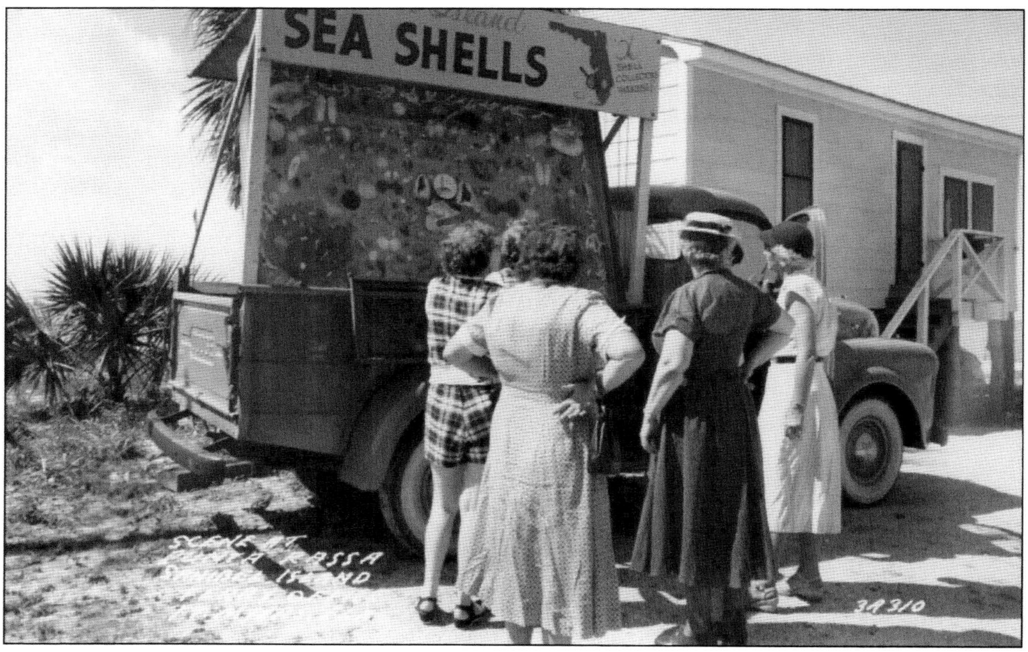

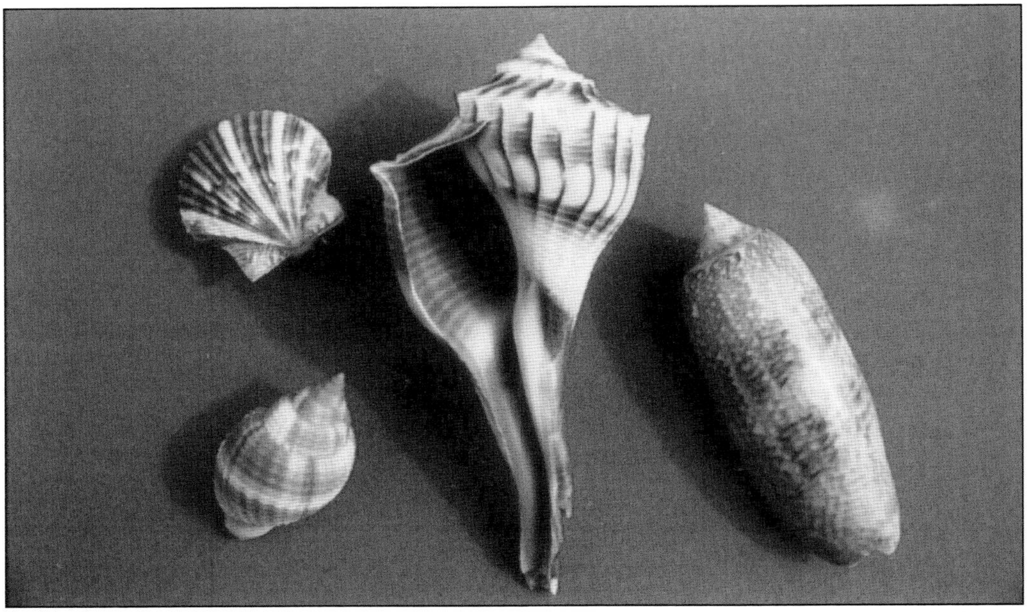

This postcard features four common shells that could trigger a lifelong hobby. Pictured clockwise are, from the bottom left, the common nutmeg, a bay scallop or pecten, a lightning or left-handed whelk, and a lettered olive shell. All are univalves, except the scallop, which is a bivalve. It has two parts that open along a hinge, and the oversized muscle of the connection is edible. (Courtesy of Sanibel Public Library.)

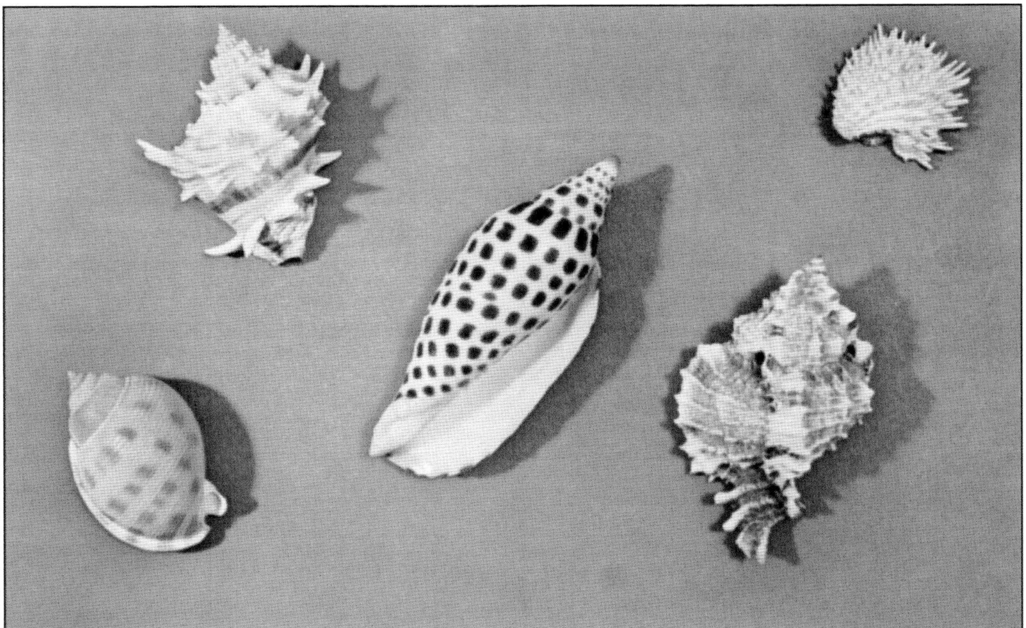

This shell postcard contains some collectable seashells that are sought by serious shellers. The center shell is the deep-water junonia, which every sheller seeks. Some island beachfront residents seed their beach with expensive junonias when a holiday visit from their grandchildren is imminent. At the top are the king's crown conch (left) and the spiny jewel box. On the bottom are the Scotch bonnet (left) and the apple murex. (Courtesy of Sanibel Public Library.)

Six

Bridges through Time

By the time the authors arrived on the islands in 1958, the bridge that connected Captiva to Sanibel had long been taken for granted by residents. Through time, the islands were sometimes also connected by land in the form of an unbroken barrier beach. This depended on the effects of the Gulf of Mexico on the seaward opening of Blind Pass. This section of island coast is dynamic and constantly changes due to the random but natural opening or closing of the Gulf entrance of the pass.

The first bridge that connected the islands was storm-damaged and replaced by another wooden span a little farther north near the location of the present bridge. The first concrete bridge, the Alvin Gorton Bridge, was completed in 1954. Gorton was a two-time Lee County commissioner (1929–1934, 1937–1958). The Gorton Bridge was replaced in 1990 by another concrete structure (the present Blind Pass Bridge) at a cost of $2.8 million.

Talk of a bridge that would connect the barrier islands of Sanibel and Captiva to the mainland often came up. This idea was never taken seriously until the late 1950s, after work started on a privately owned causeway and bridges that were to connect more northerly positioned Gasparilla Island (Boca Grande) to the Charlotte County mainland. In 1960, the Lee County commissioners were straining to see the offshore islands developed to increase the tax base. The commission announced that it was planning a bridge system to connect eastern Sanibel to Punta Rassa. This resulted in a public uproar, and the majority of Sanibel and Captiva residents opposed the idea of a bridge. Objections ranged from fear of high-density development to damage to the estuary because of the causeway's design. Lee County won the legal battle, and the Sanibel Causeway opened for traffic on May 26, 1963. The cost of all components of the causeway was $2.73 million, paid for by bonds and to be repaid by a $3 toll. Construction of three new bridges started in 2004, and the new spans opened in 2007, at a cost of $137 million with a toll increase to $6.

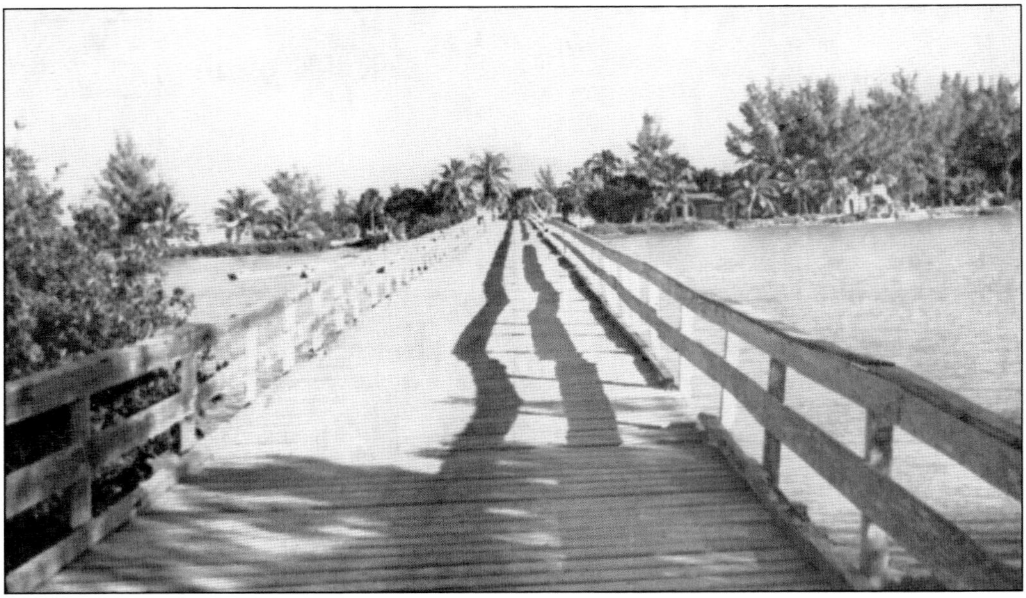

A one-lane wooden bridge first spanned Blind Pass in 1918. Automobiles were almost nonexistent on the islands in those days, so if two horse- or mule-drawn wagons approached opposite ends of the structure at the same time, one had to yield. If a Captiva-bound car approached the bridge, it backed up if a car was already on the bridge. Sanibel-bound traffic had the right of way. (Courtesy of Deborah Gleason collection.)

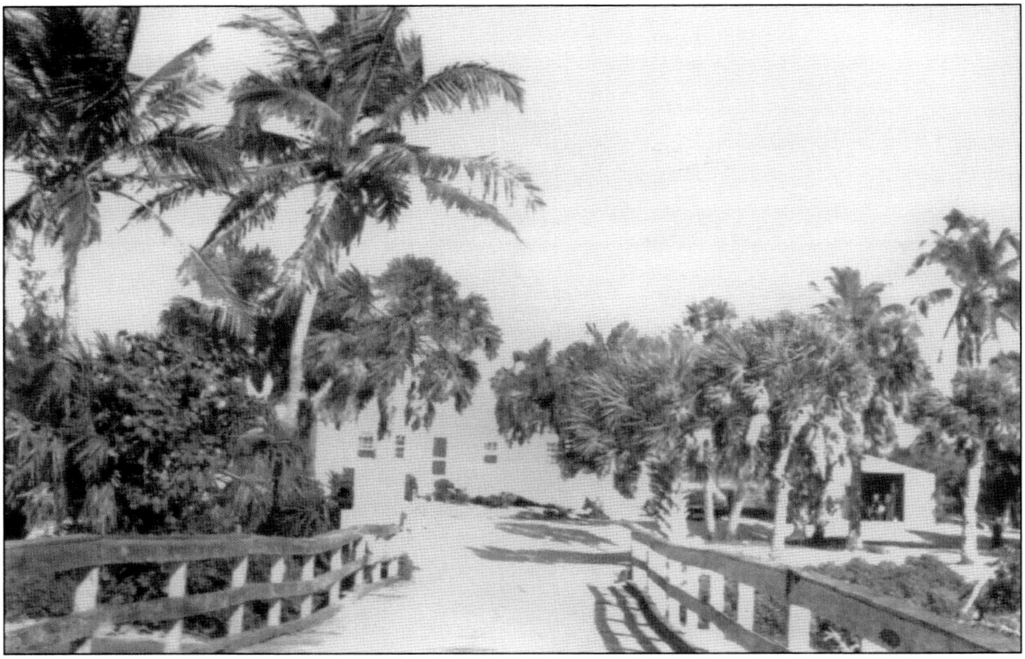

A small neighborhood, Santiva, is pictured here. Houses, cottages, and marinas developed near the Sanibel Island end of the pass bridge early in the 20th century. Land on the Captiva side was narrow and never really saw much development. In the early days, there were some stilt houses in Blind Pass south of the original bridge, but when a hurricane took out the first bridge, they went too. (Courtesy of Captiva Island Historical Society.)

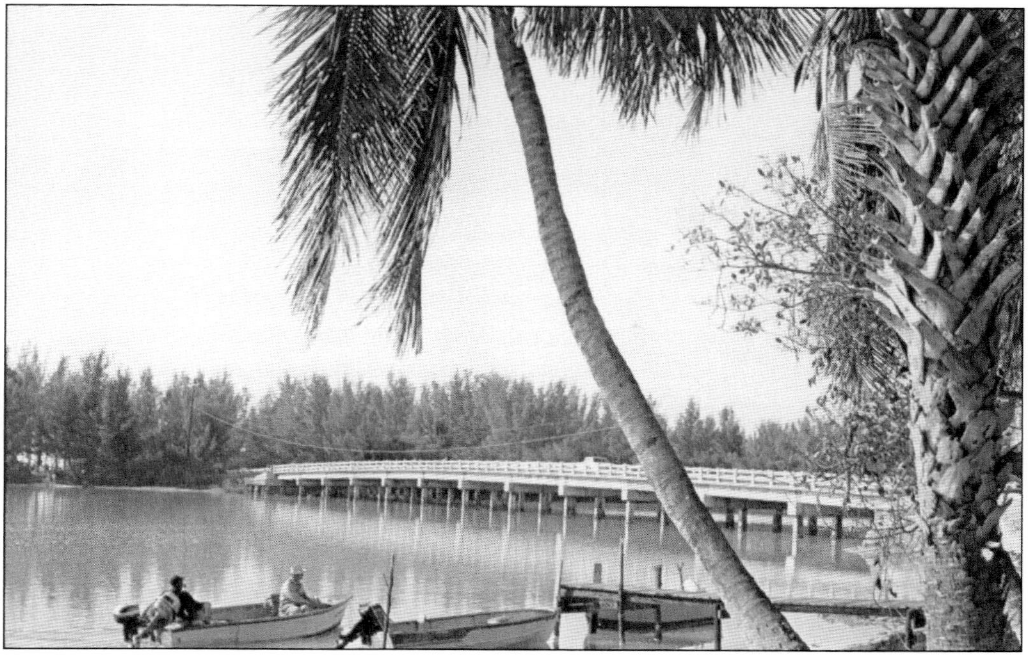

Skiffs in the foreground of this postcard are at the former Castaways Marina when its docks were directly on the Blind Pass waterfront. When Blind Pass closed in the late 1960s, accreted sand eliminated the waterway between the two islands at the bridge. The concrete, two-lane Alvin Gorton Bridge is in the background, as are young Australian pine trees that have become established on the Captiva Gulf beach. (Courtesy of Sanibel Historical Museum and Village.)

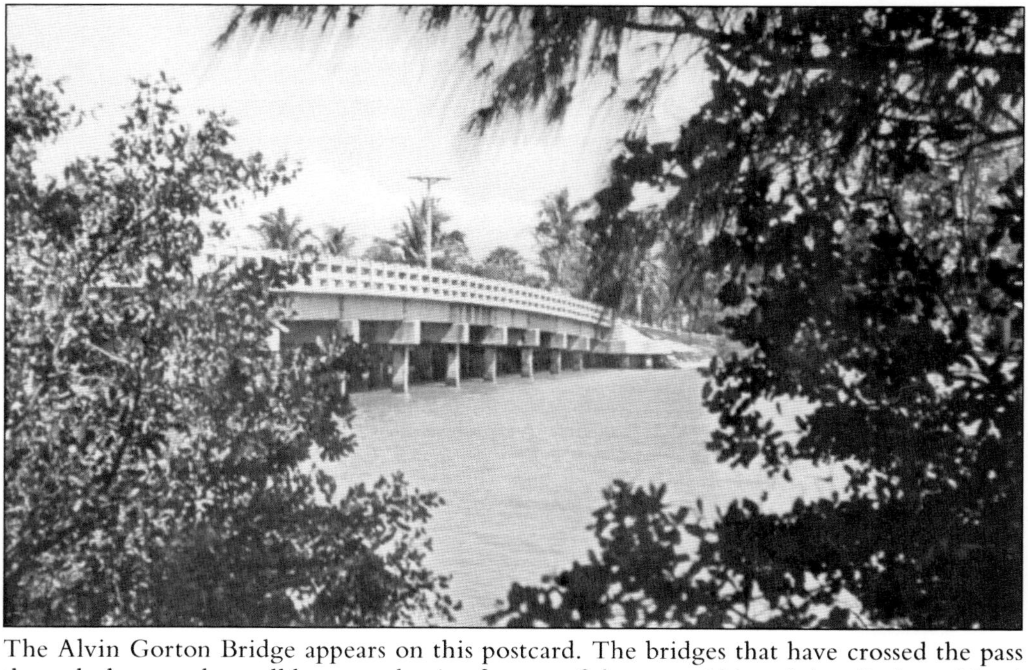

The Alvin Gorton Bridge appears on this postcard. The bridges that have crossed the pass through the years have all been productive for sport fishermen. Although bag limits and legal sizes and seasons have changed, the Blind Pass Bridge is still popular among snook-seeking anglers. (Courtesy of Sanibel Historical Museum and Village.)

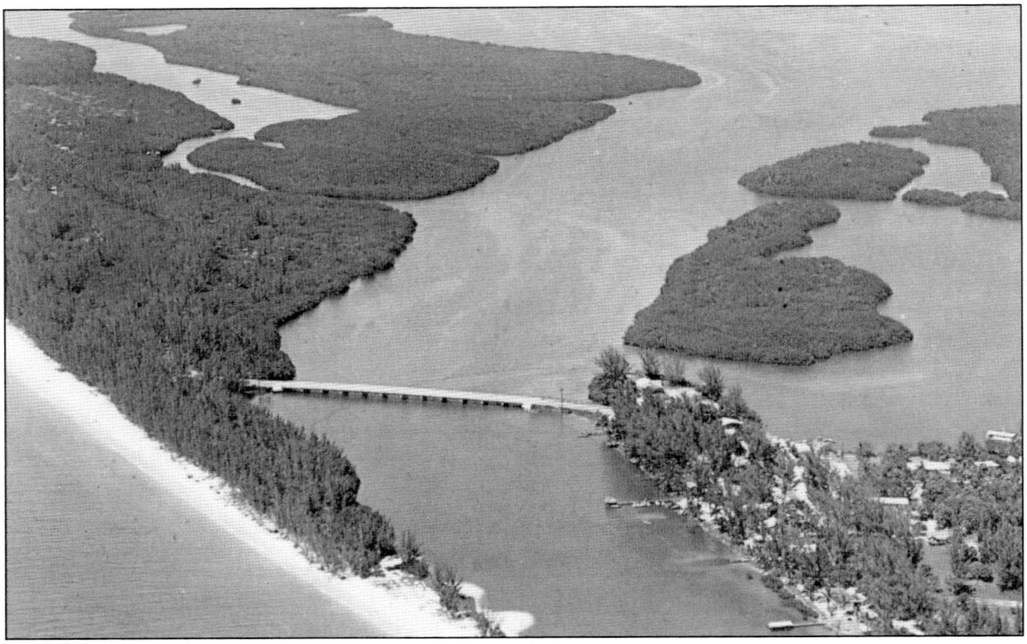

This aerial postcard of Blind Pass clearly shows the small Santiva community of western Sanibel, when Castaways Marina was a functioning headquarters for fishermen and live shell-seekers. The southward extension of Captiva (left) later migrated and joined the islands together. Buck Key and Roosevelt Channel, which separates it from Captiva, are visible in the upper left. (Courtesy of Deborah Gleason collection.)

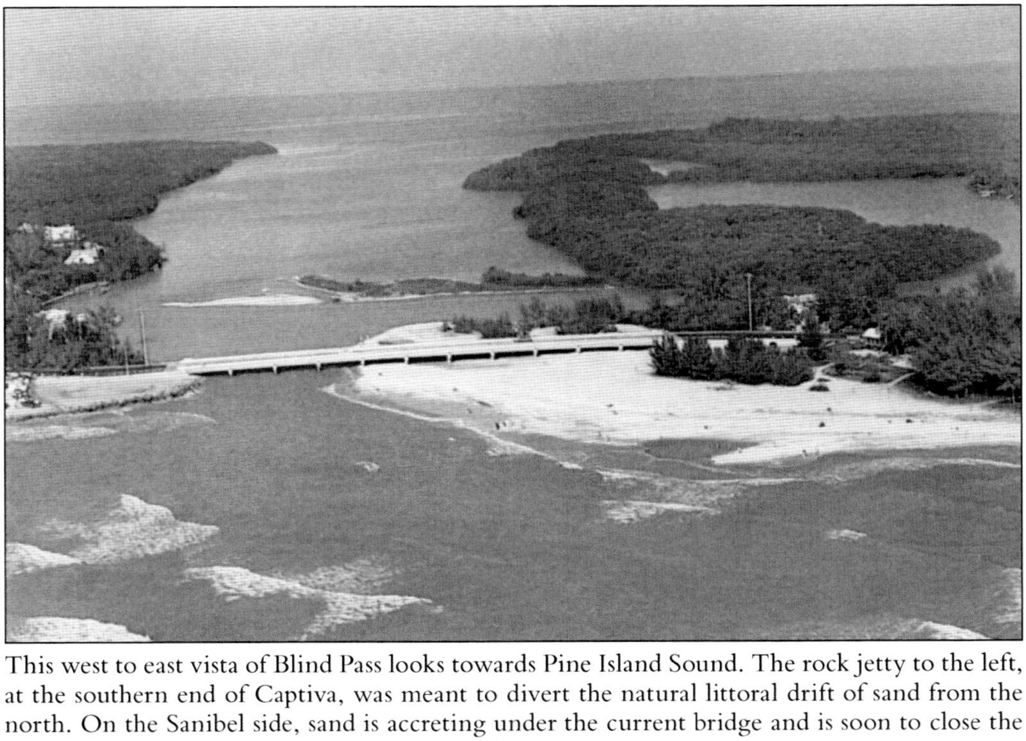

This west to east vista of Blind Pass looks towards Pine Island Sound. The rock jetty to the left, at the southern end of Captiva, was meant to divert the natural littoral drift of sand from the north. On the Sanibel side, sand is accreting under the current bridge and is soon to close the pass again. (Courtesy of Deborah Gleason collection.)

This postcard provides a glimpse of an early wooden bridge that crossed the Sanibel River. This bridge spanned the waterway at today's Donax Street. At the time of the photograph, this street was known as Tulipa Way. (Courtesy of Sanibel Historical Museum and Village.)

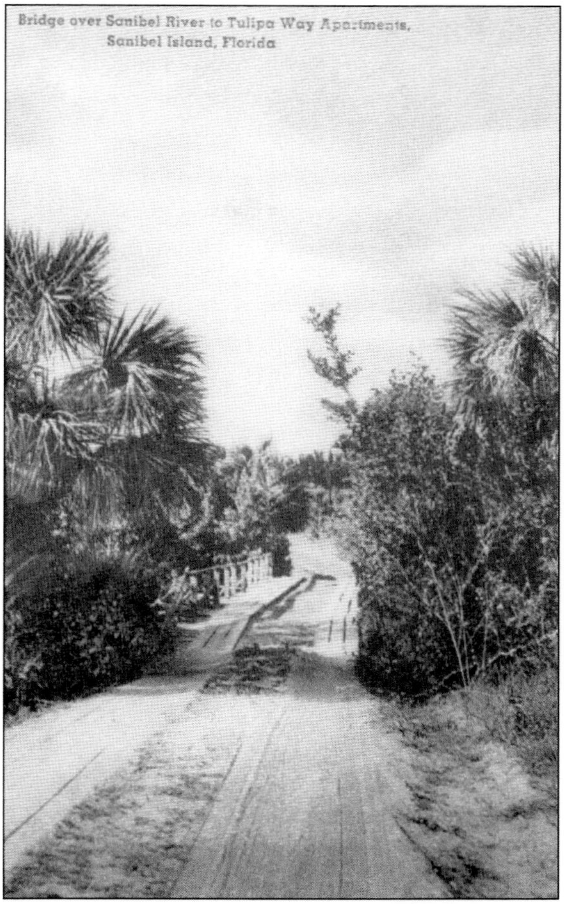

Blind Pass is pictured at a time when the island beaches were connected and a barrier beach has closed the pass. With extra-high tides coincidental with storms, loads of sand over-washed this narrow beach, and soon there was dry beach under the bridge. Expensive hydraulic dredging followed to open the pass, but within a couple of years, it was closed again. With fiscal abandon of public funds, Blind Pass was dredged again. (Courtesy of Deborah Gleason collection.)

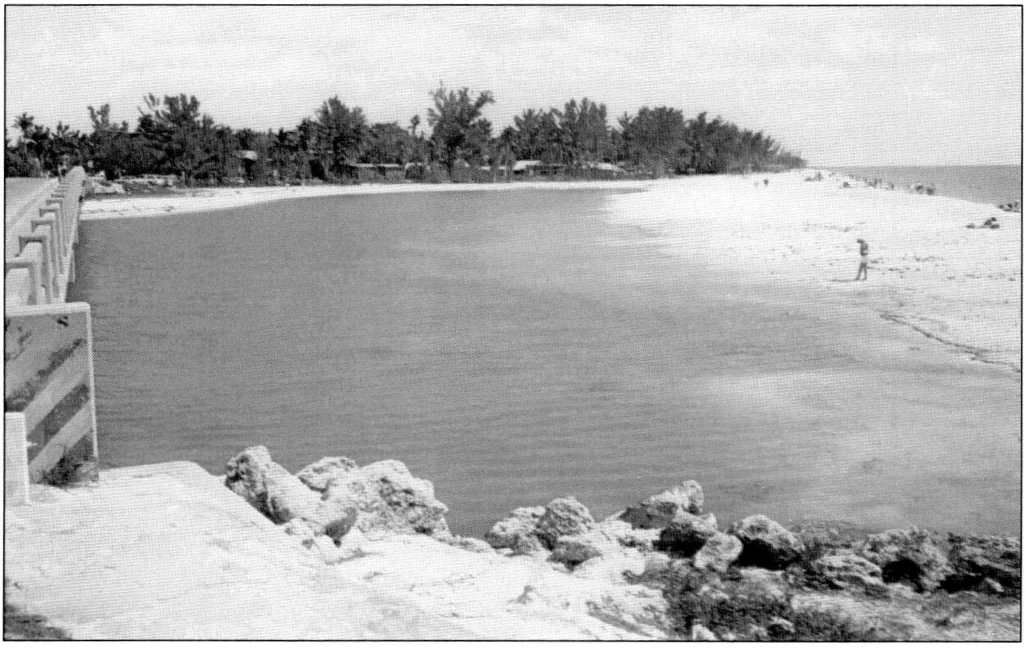

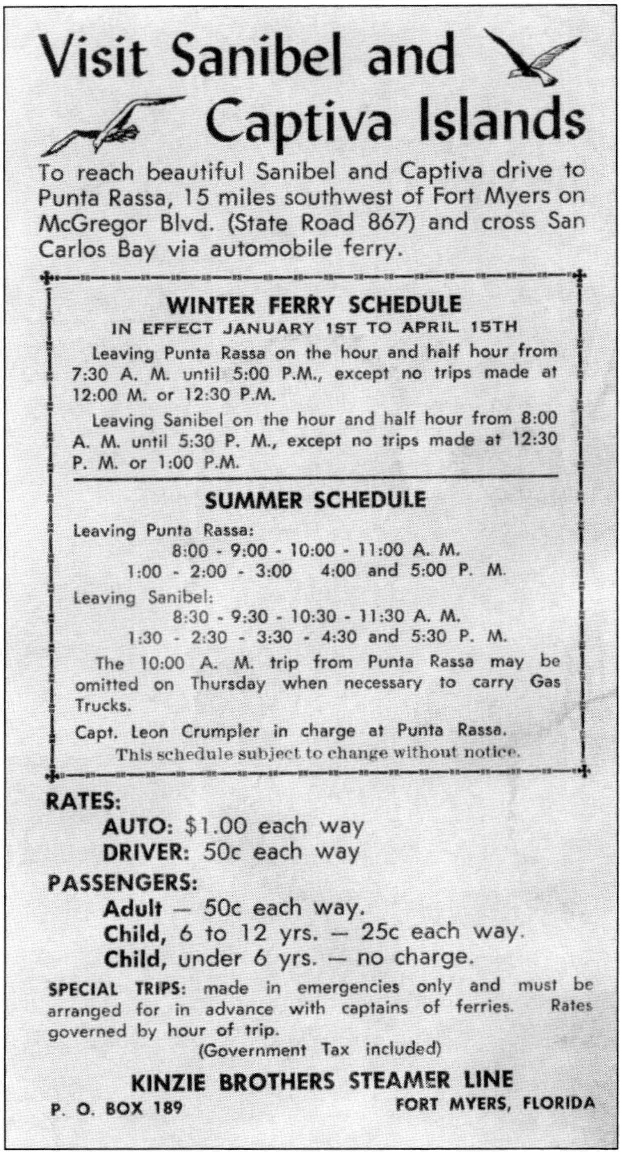

Visit Sanibel and Captiva Islands

To reach beautiful Sanibel and Captiva drive to Punta Rassa, 15 miles southwest of Fort Myers on McGregor Blvd. (State Road 867) and cross San Carlos Bay via automobile ferry.

WINTER FERRY SCHEDULE
IN EFFECT JANUARY 1ST TO APRIL 15TH

Leaving Punta Rassa on the hour and half hour from 7:30 A. M. until 5:00 P.M., except no trips made at 12:00 M. or 12:30 P.M.

Leaving Sanibel on the hour and half hour from 8:00 A. M. until 5:30 P. M., except no trips made at 12:30 P. M. or 1:00 P.M.

SUMMER SCHEDULE

Leaving Punta Rassa:
8:00 - 9:00 - 10:00 - 11:00 A. M.
1:00 - 2:00 - 3:00 4:00 and 5:00 P. M.

Leaving Sanibel:
8:30 - 9:30 - 10:30 - 11:30 A. M.
1:30 - 2:30 - 3:30 - 4:30 and 5:30 P. M.

The 10:00 A. M. trip from Punta Rassa may be omitted on Thursday when necessary to carry Gas Trucks.

Capt. Leon Crumpler in charge at Punta Rassa.
This schedule subject to change without notice.

RATES:
AUTO: $1.00 each way
DRIVER: 50c each way

PASSENGERS:
Adult — 50c each way.
Child, 6 to 12 yrs. — 25c each way.
Child, under 6 yrs. — no charge.

SPECIAL TRIPS: made in emergencies only and must be arranged for in advance with captains of ferries. Rates governed by hour of trip.
(Government Tax included)

KINZIE BROTHERS STEAMER LINE
P. O. BOX 189 FORT MYERS, FLORIDA

The ferry schedule and pricing from 1955 is pictured here. For a family with two adults and two children with their car, round-trip cost for a ferry crossing was $5; there were no discounts. After ferry service ended, the boats were sold. The *Best* went to Puerto Rico; the *Islander* went to Omaha, Georgia; the *Rebel* went to Portland, Maine; and the *Yankee Clipper* went to Put In Bay, Ohio, on the Great Lakes. (Courtesy of Islander Trading Post.)

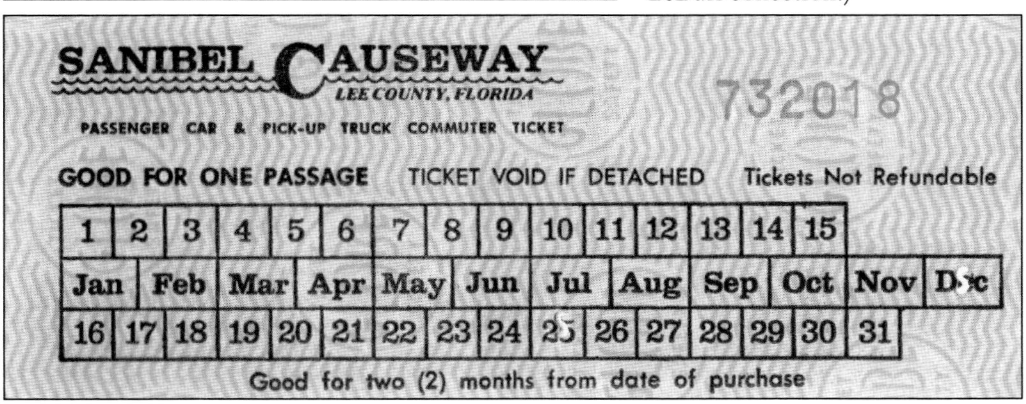

SANIBEL CAUSEWAY
LEE COUNTY, FLORIDA
732018
PASSENGER CAR & PICK-UP TRUCK COMMUTER TICKET
GOOD FOR ONE PASSAGE TICKET VOID IF DETACHED Tickets Not Refundable

1	2	3	4	5	6	7	8	9	10	11	12	13	14	15

Jan	Feb	Mar	Apr	May	Jun	Jul	Aug	Sep	Oct	Nov	Dec

16	17	18	19	20	21	22	23	24	25	26	27	28	29	30	31

Good for two (2) months from date of purchase

At first, round-trip on the causeway was $3. Years later, a commuter program reduced the toll to 50¢, and anyone could buy a book of 20 tickets for $10, but they were supposed to be void if removed from the book. This was ignored by toll officials, and mainland businesses passed out tickets to their patrons. This, and the increase in day-trippers, became a point of contention between island residents and Lee County officials, factors that led to Sanibel's incorporation. (Courtesy of Charles LeBuff collection.)

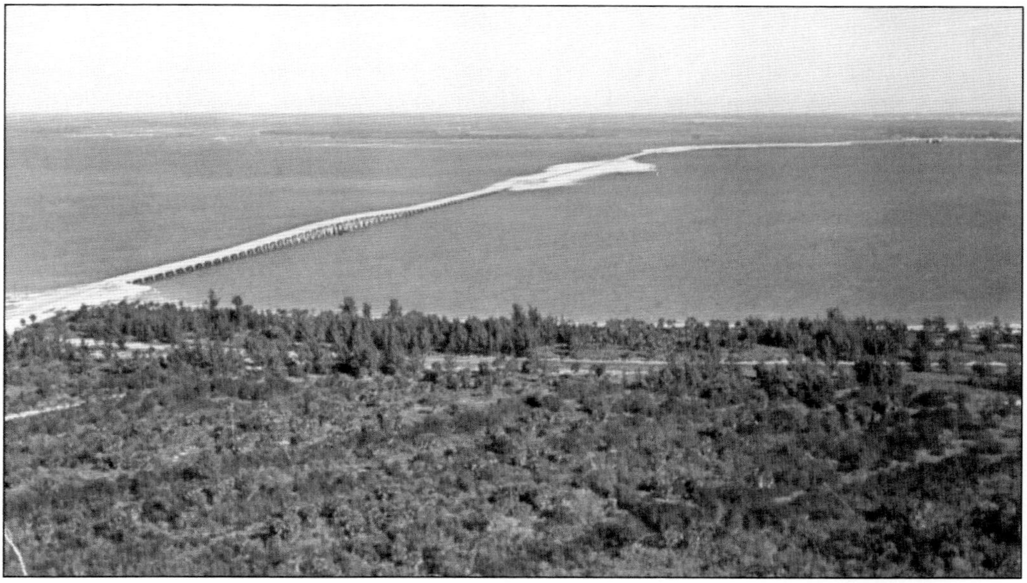

The brand-new causeway is pictured in 1963. The viewpoint looks north from the wild lands of the Sanibel bridgehead. The bare sand on the spoil islands attracted colonies of ground-nesting birds like least terns and black skimmers. Bird mortality on the road overwhelmed islanders, and another conflict arose with Lee County. The county refused to lower the speed limit (then 45 miles per hour) but did allow the Sanibel-Captiva Audubon Society to install "Slow—Bird Crossing" signs. (Courtesy of Charles LeBuff collection.)

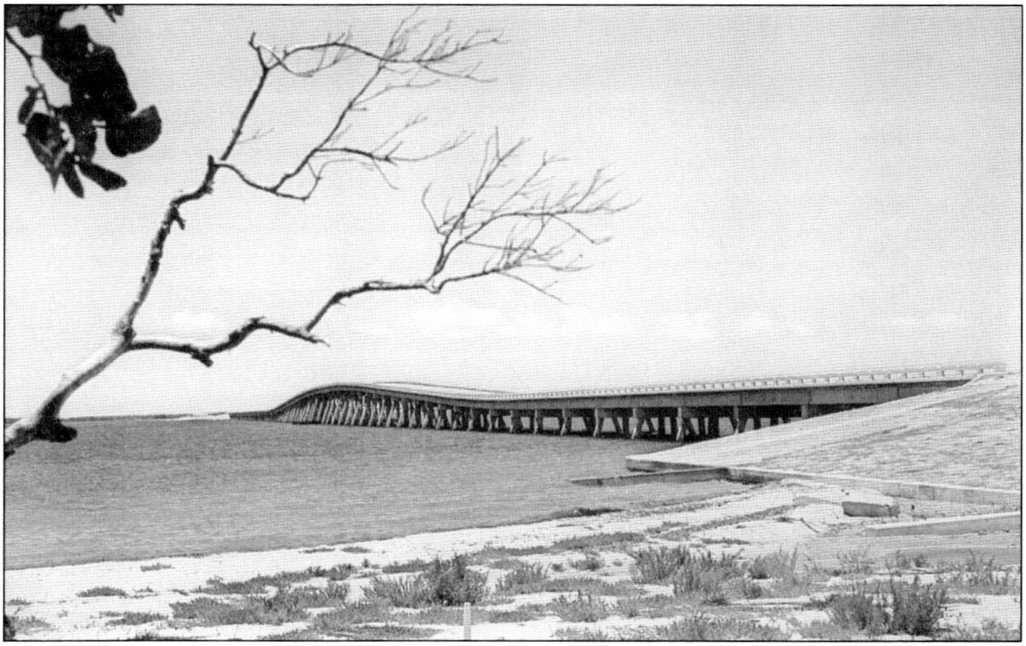

This postcard features the Sanibel bridgehead of the new causeway in 1963. Originally, Lee County planned to bring the bridge in to Sanibel at a point near the tree to the left. Francis Bailey, who owned the land and was anti-bridge, refused to give them a right-of-way, and the bridge was realigned to connect to the land of pro-bridge property owner Hugo Lindgren. (Courtesy of Charles LeBuff collection.)

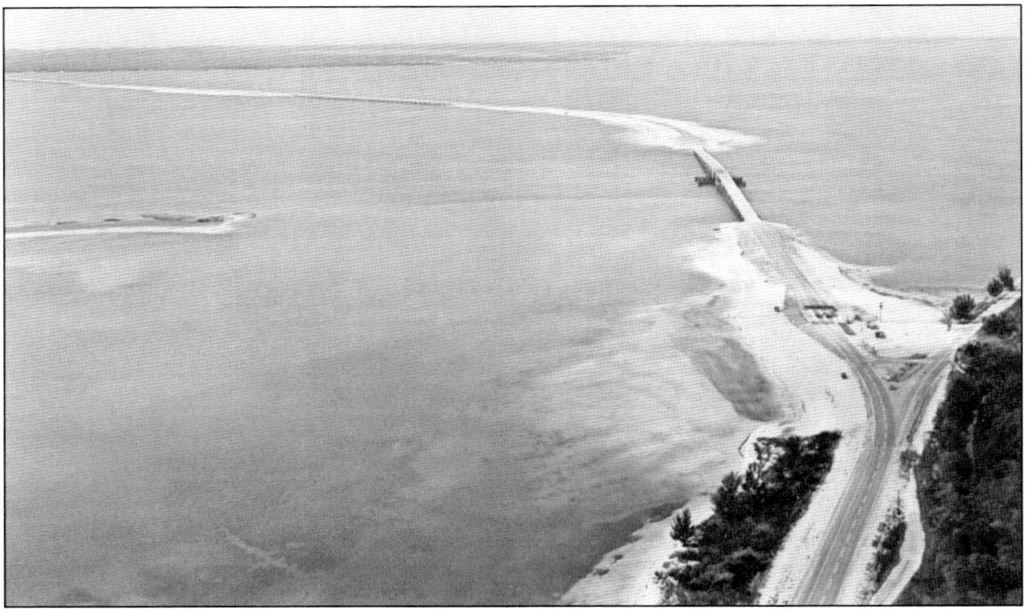

The causeway is pictured to the west with the toll plaza in the center right. The small spoil island on the left was from channel dredging, and over the years, it slowly disappeared. Today, the remnants of this little island, which formerly supported Australian pines and sea oats and remarkably resembled a miniature Sanibel in shape and alignment, is still visible on neap tides. None of it remains above water at high tide. (Courtesy of Charles LeBuff collection.)

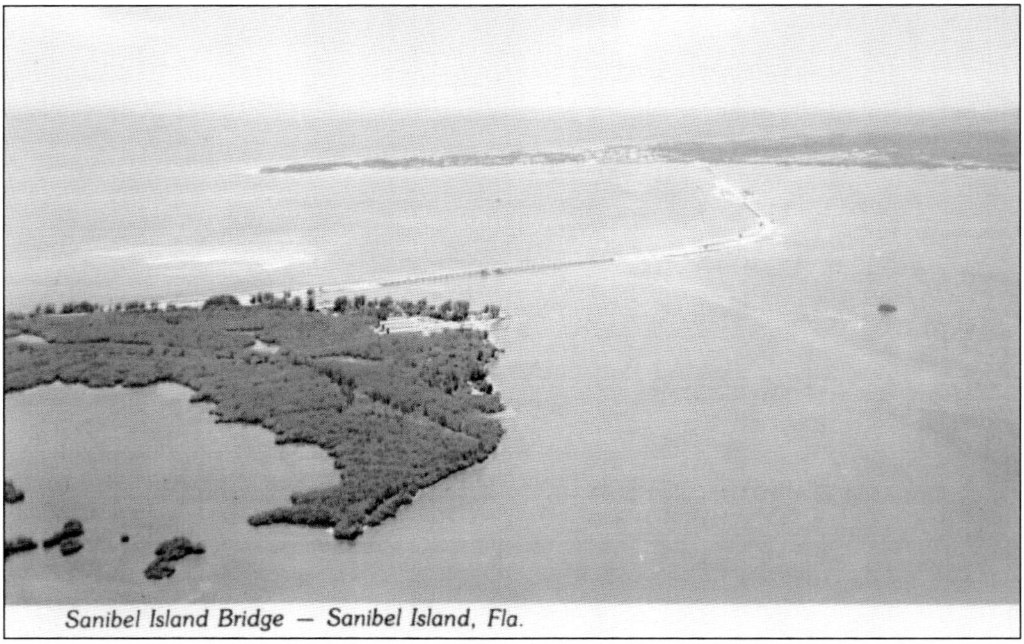

San Carlos Bay and the Gulf of Mexico beyond are shown on this c. 1965 aerial view postcard. Punta Rassa, once a bustling cattle-shipping port, an early haven for tarpon fishers, and the mainland hub of the Kinzie Brothers Steamer Line is in the left foreground. The first Sanibel Causeway and bridges span the bay and Point Ybel where the historical Sanibel Lighthouse is located at the upper left. (Courtesy of Charles LeBuff collection.)

Seven

Churches, Businesses, and Early Eateries

Thanks in part to being a vacation destination, Sanibel and Captiva Islands have a plethora of postcards detailing community buildings, early businesses, and restaurants. Each card is a snapshot in time, and without these cards, much of the early island history would fade. In 1984, the Sanibel Historical Museum and Village was founded, and the preservation of island history, including postcards, was started in earnest.

Most of the images in this book are pre-causeway, so one has to consider that many of these buildings were constructed with supplies that were ferried, barged, or shipped by steamer. Islanders often gathered together to build their homes, schools, and businesses. With remarkable ingenuity, they wielded heavy wood support beams and made concrete blocks of beach sand. Heavy machinery was next to impossible to transport, so mules and men accomplished the physical labor.

Not all island churches are represented in this book as not all churches produced postcards. Sanibel and Captiva have no less than six places of worship, and only three have been represented in this publication. Both islands have community or civic centers that have been, and continue to be, central to the social life and concerns of islanders.

Restaurants on Sanibel and Captiva often started in conjunction with an inn, such as with the Island Inn, Casa Ybel, Castaways, and 'Tween Waters. When the ferryboats started their service, Miss Charlotta's Tea Room and Casa Marina opened to serve those passengers. Later, restaurants like Isabel's Tavern (Scotty's), Jack's Place, Golden Sands, Coconut Grove, and Sunshine Café opened on the main Sanibel-Captiva road.

Island businesses were often born of necessity, as were Sanibel Packing Company (Bailey's), Nave Plumbing, and J.P. Carter Trucking. Once the link to the mainland was in place, businesses changed as they catered to the hundreds of visitors arriving daily. As the islands were "discovered," new islanders came to live and enjoy the weather, wildlife, and seclusion, but they did not realize their very presence would change the ambiance forever. As previously mentioned, the population of Sanibel and Captiva in 1956 was approximately 200. In 2010, it was approximately 7,000.

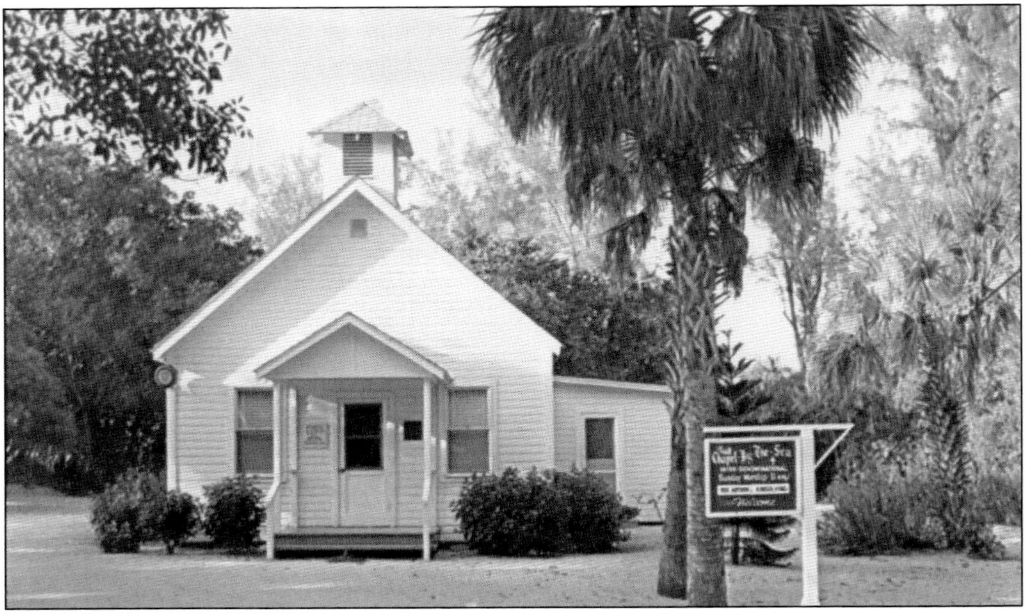

Chapel By The Sea, built in 1901, was first a schoolhouse used as a church monthly when a circuit preacher visited. Another schoolhouse was constructed, and the building was fully converted into a church. In 1921, the Methodist Conference bought the building from the county, and in 1954, Captiva residents purchased it. Graves in the adjoining cemetery are dated as early as 1897 and bear the names of many pioneer families. (Courtesy of Islander Trading Post.)

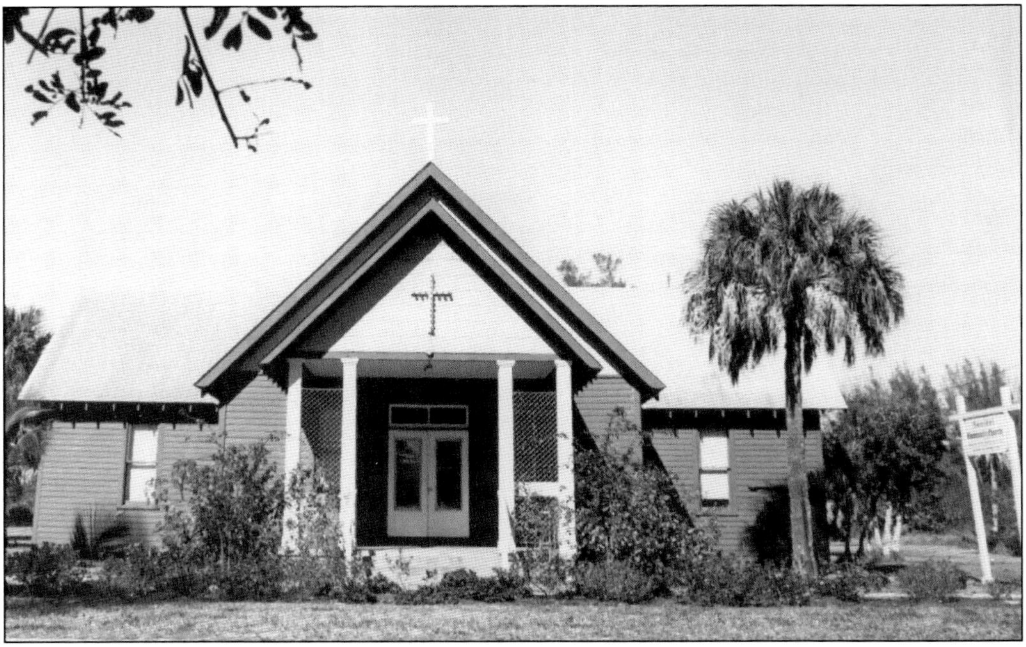

The construction of Sanibel Community Church was started in 1914 and completed in 1917. This nondenominational church was built on land donated by the Mitchell family. Those in the community paid for the building materials and provided the labor to construct it. Built with lumber preserved and stained brown with creosote and linseed oil, it was named The Little Brown Church. It stands today with extensive additions. (Courtesy of Sanibel Public Library.)

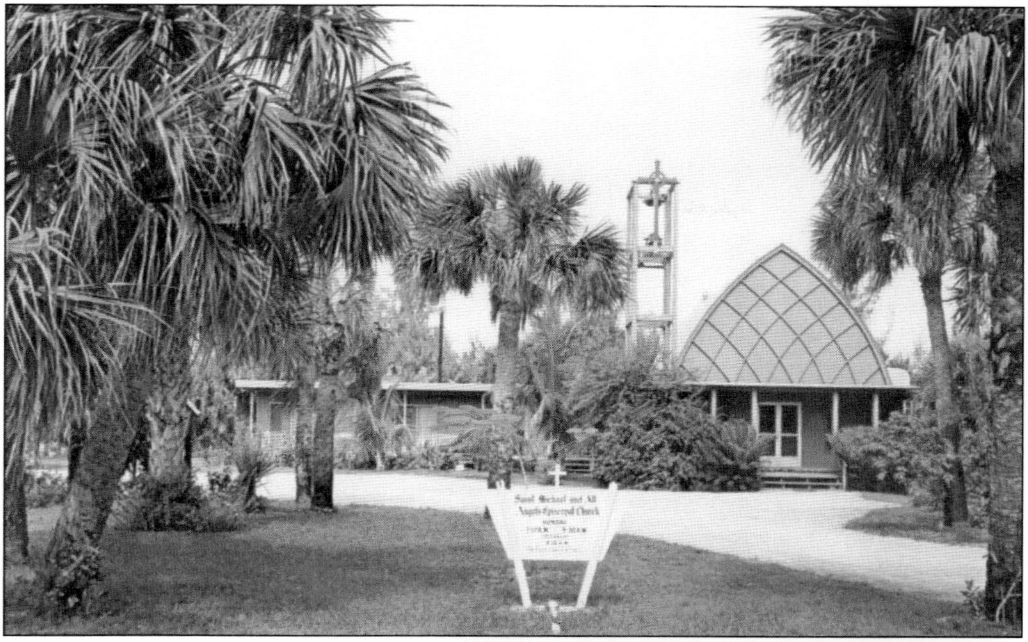

The Sanibel Episcopal Church held its first services on Wednesday mornings at the Sanibel Community Church but soon moved to Casa Marina restaurant, located at the ferry landing. In 1961, the new church, St. Michaels and All Angels, was completed, and in 1963, Fr. Thomas Madden and his congregation made it Sanibel's first racially integrated church. There have been several additions to the building, including the popular Noah's Ark Thrift Shop. (Courtesy of Deborah Gleason collection.)

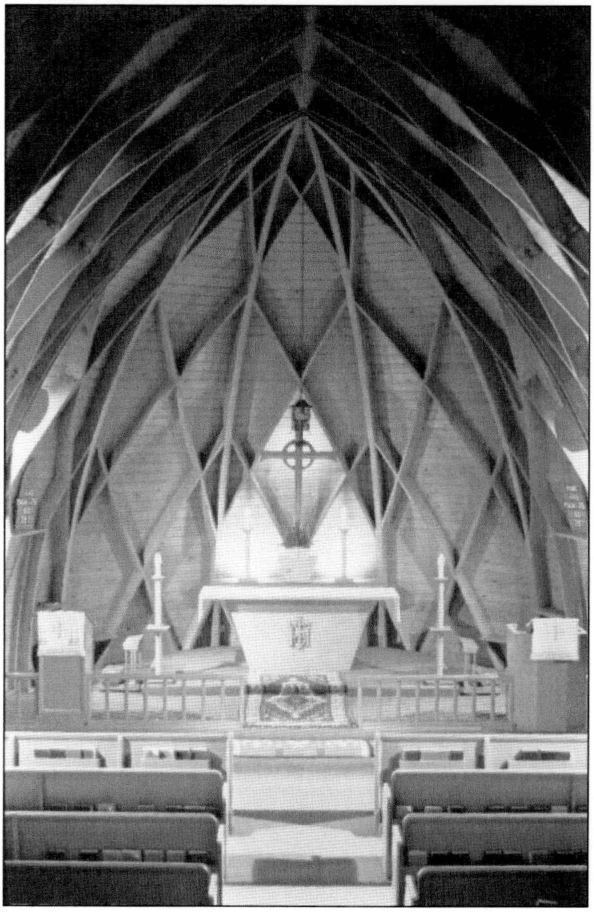

Winter visitor and architect Gustel Kiewitt donated his time and design for St. Michaels and All Angels Episcopal Church. The Gothic design, with interior walls and ceiling arches carrying the weight of the structure without central pillar support, was unique for island building. Fr. Thomas Madden realized the need to care for all of God's creatures on Sanibel by helping to start PAWS, an organization dedicated to caring for homeless cats. (Courtesy of Islander Trading Post.)

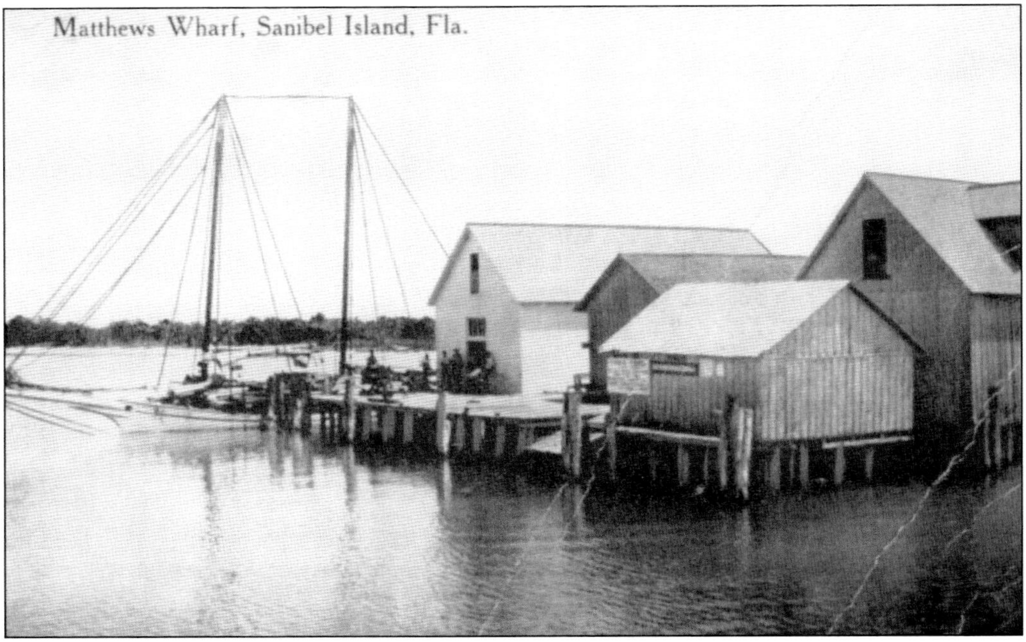

Matthew's Wharf was built in 1896 by Jane Matthews for the use of all islanders. Will Geraty and Steele Doyle ran the wharf plantation store until the Bailey brothers bought them out in 1899. The Bailey groves, gardens, and store became Sanibel Packing Company. It was a popular landing for steamers and schooners, bringing passengers and freight to and from the islands until it was destroyed by the hurricane of 1926. (Courtesy of Islander Trading Post.)

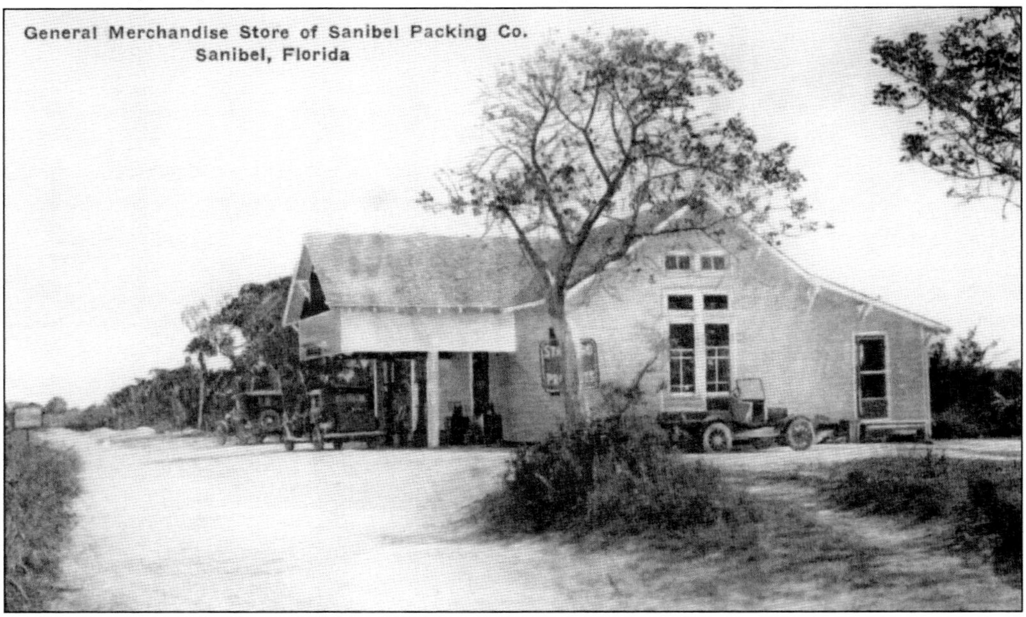

The 1927 Bailey's General Store was built solidly on a sand ridge after the demise of Bailey's store on Matthew's Wharf. Only the safe was recovered and remains in the 1927 store today in the Sanibel Historical Museum and Village. While this store was being constructed, a makeshift store was opened in a small building (later Miss Charlotta's Tea Room) that had been planned as a gas station. (Courtesy of Islander Trading Post.)

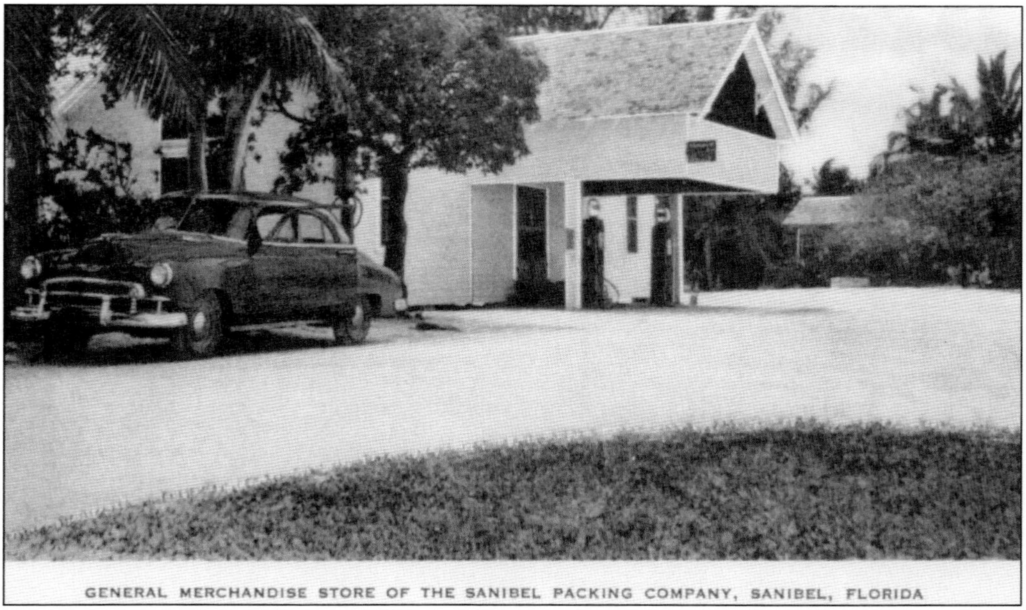

During the 1930s and 1940s, gasoline and just about anything else could be purchased at Bailey's General Store. A true general store, it carried food, clothing, seed, tools, hardware, medicine, and fishing supplies. Frank Bailey coined the phrase, "If we don't have it you don't need it." When the ferry dock was moved east, the gas pumps were removed and a new gas station was built at the corner of Periwinkle Way and Bailey Road. (Courtesy of Islander Trading Post.)

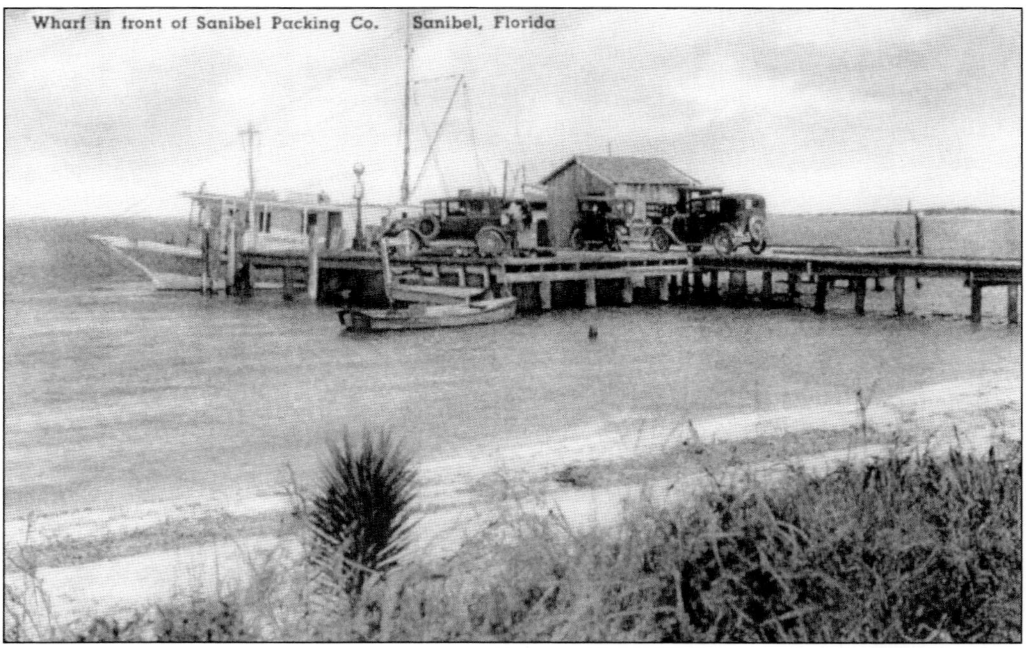

After the 1926 hurricane, a new wharf was built for the arrival of steamers, schooners, and mail boat. Citrus and vegetables were still being shipped out, although in much smaller amounts after the 1926 storm surge left salt in the fields. Large blocks of ice came by ship to be cut into manageable sizes for home iceboxes. The three Bailey kids enjoyed using the ice shavings to have "snowball" fights. (Courtesy of Islander Trading Post.)

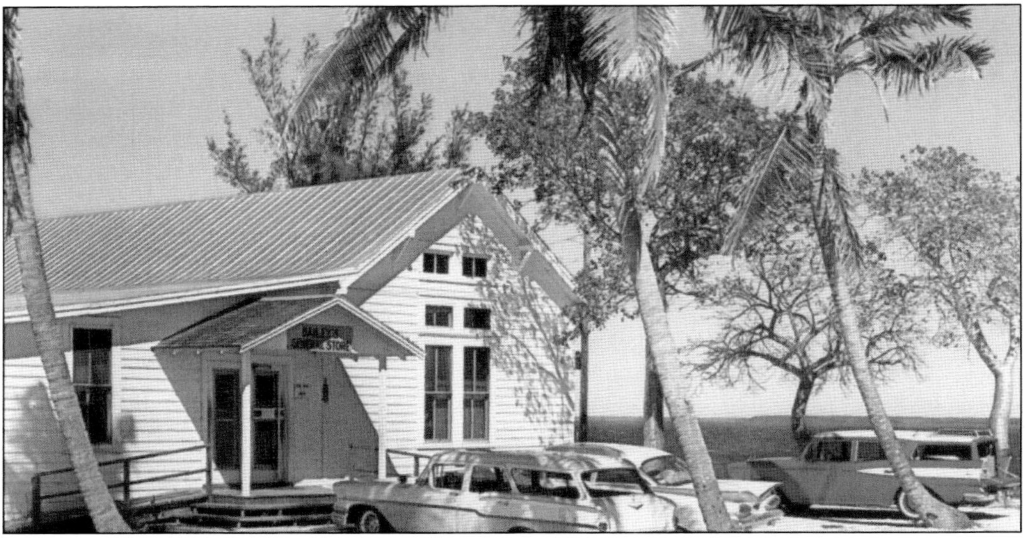

Bailey's General Store was reconfigured in the 1950s, with the entrance facing the parking lot. The store remained the island hub with Western Union, the mail boat stop, and cold Coca-Cola. In 1963, the new bridge meant a new Bailey's, and this old building became the Red Pelican import shop, a dance studio, and later The Children's Center Pre-school. Donated by the Bailey family, this vintage store can be seen today at the Sanibel Historical Village. (Courtesy of Charles LeBuff collection.)

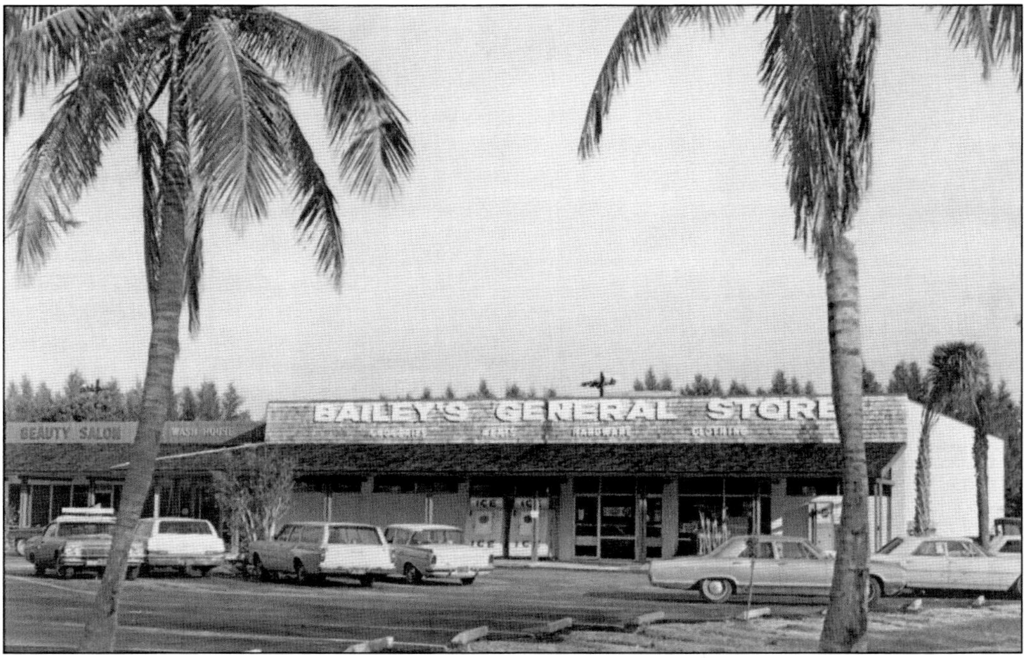

The third Bailey's General Store was built inland about 1966 at a central location at the intersection of Tarpon Bay Road and Periwinkle Way. This new location placed it with a laundromat, beauty salon, and Coconut Grove Restaurant. The post office was across the street and a small movie theater soon joined the complex, making it the closest thing to a downtown that Sanibel had ever seen. (Courtesy of Deborah Gleason collection.)

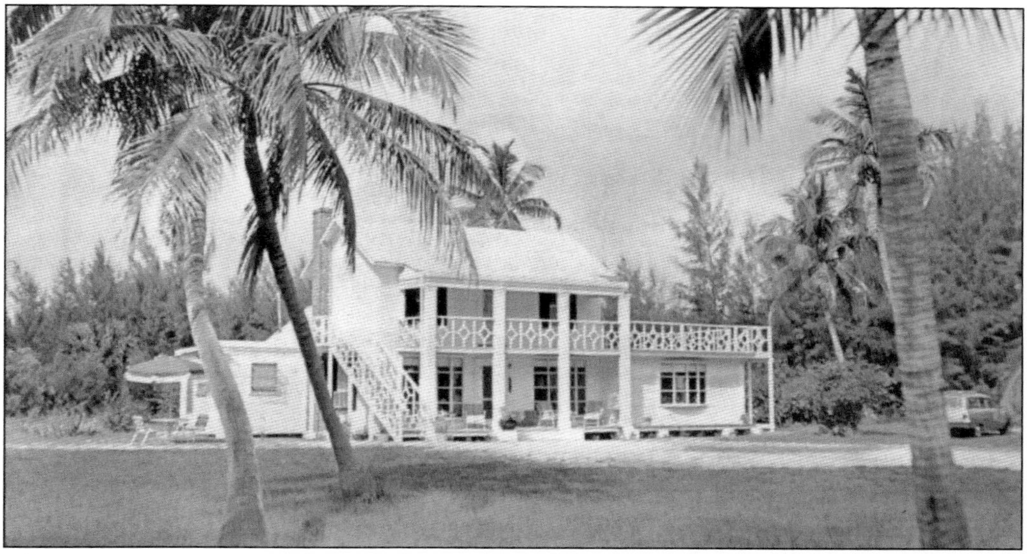

This large home was built in 1891 by the homesteading Cooper family. They grew tomatoes, peppers, eggplant, and watermelon. The Coopers owned a packinghouse and several boats to deliver crops and goods. George Cooper was probably Sanibel's first postman; twice weekly he picked up the mail at Pine Island, and residents came to his home to get their mail. This 1960s postcard pictures the building when it was the site of Dotti's Dress Shop. (Courtesy of Deborah Gleason collection.)

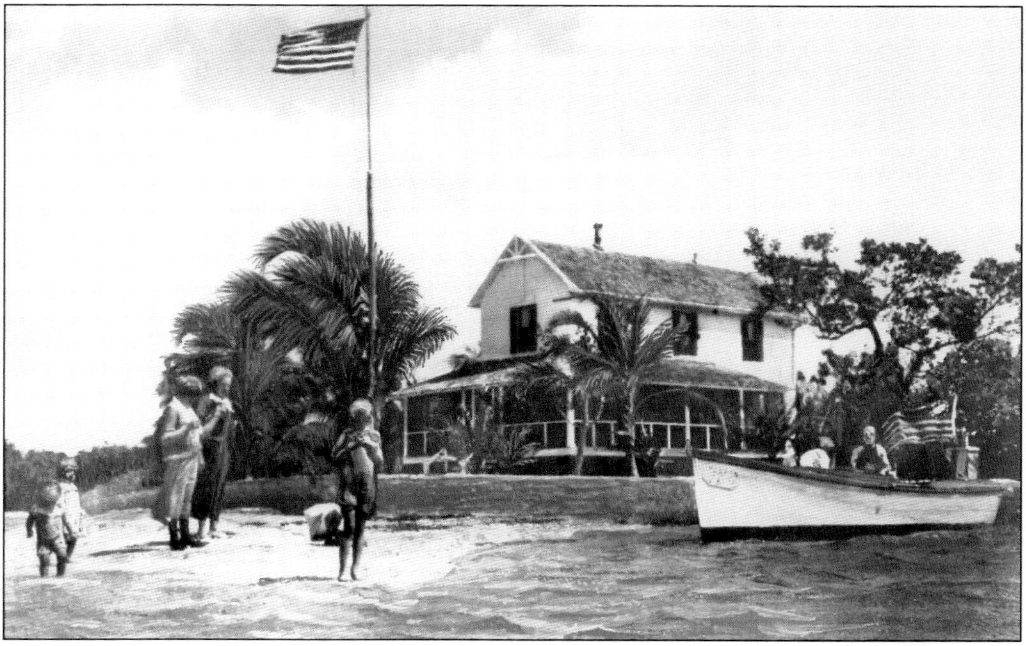

This 1930s family photograph shows one of Sanibel's most lovely outposts, Woodring Point. The home looked out over San Carlos and Tarpon Bays, and the first owners may have been wealthy winter residents. Its last owner was the legendary Tommy Wood, seaplane pilot and manager of the J.N. "Ding" Darling National Wildlife Refuge. To his misfortune, his home burned down in 1974 not long after the Gene Hackman movie *Night Moves* used it as a set. (State Archives of Florida, Florida Memory.)

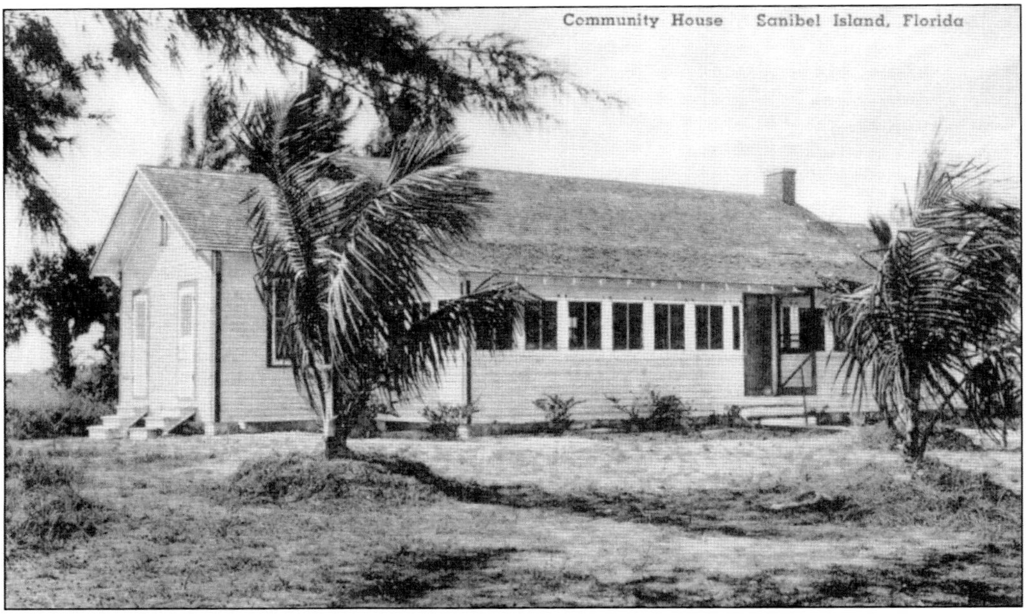

Curtis Perry, a winter visitor from Maine, collected funds to construct the Sanibel Community House in 1927, on land donated by Cordie Nutt. Dances, dinners, holiday events, lectures, plays, and the annual Sanibel Shell Fairs were, and still are, held there. Every Christmas Eve, Santa arrived with a present for each island child. Both the Sanibel Library and chamber of commerce got their start there. (Courtesy of Jim Pickens.)

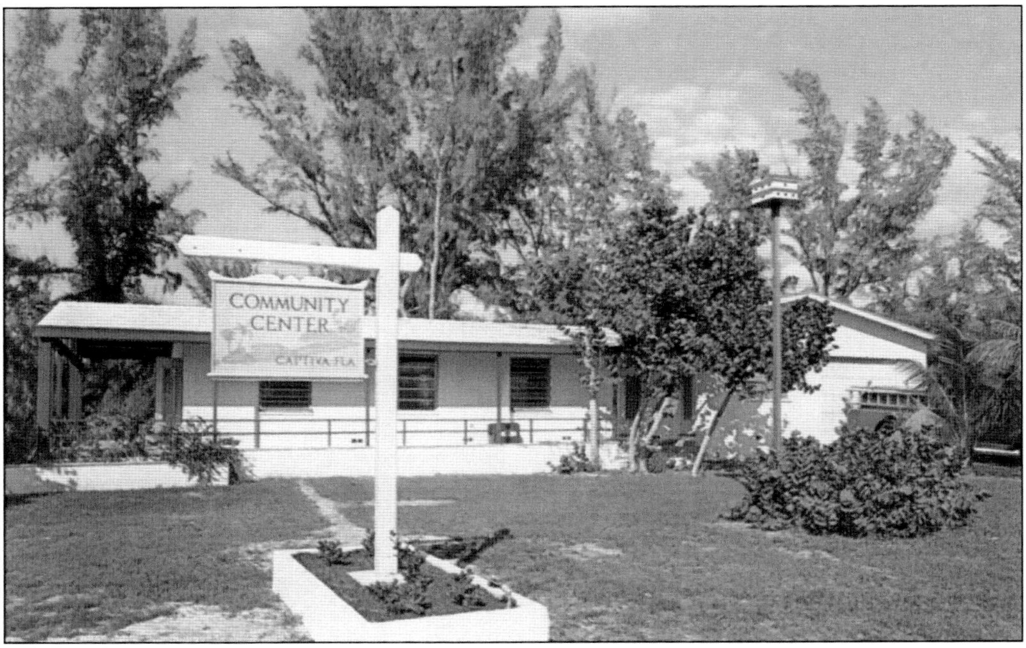

The Captiva Civic Association was founded in 1936, but it was not until 1960 that the Community Center was built at 11560 Chapin Lane. It housed the early Captiva Library and the Captiva Fire Department. In 1970, the Captiva Memorial Library addition was built onto the center, and in 1980, the Captiva Fire Department Station was moved to 14981 Captiva Drive. (Courtesy of Islander Trading Post.)

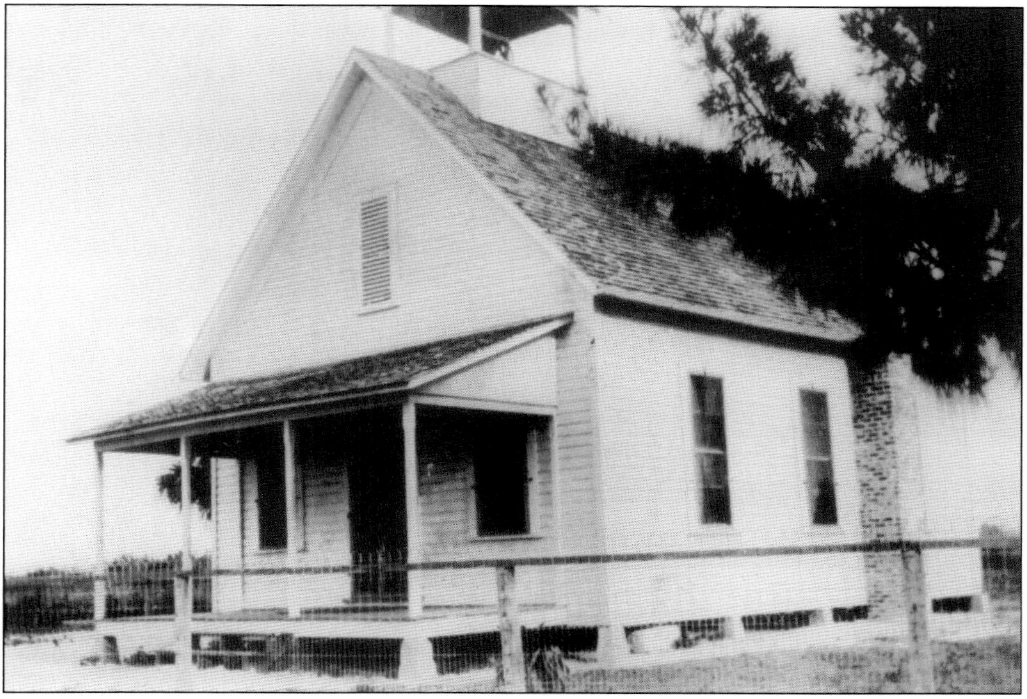

Schools came and went on the islands. This Sanibel Schoolhouse was constructed on the corner of Bailey Road in 1894 and moved to a central location on Periwinkle Way in 1903. Around 1930, Captiva children were bused via touring car to attend classes there. In 1937, a second room was added for the younger children. When a new school was built in 1963, the abandoned building became Phillip and Ruth Hunter's Pirate Playhouse. This building is now part of the Sanibel Historical Village. (Courtesy of Sanibel Public Library.)

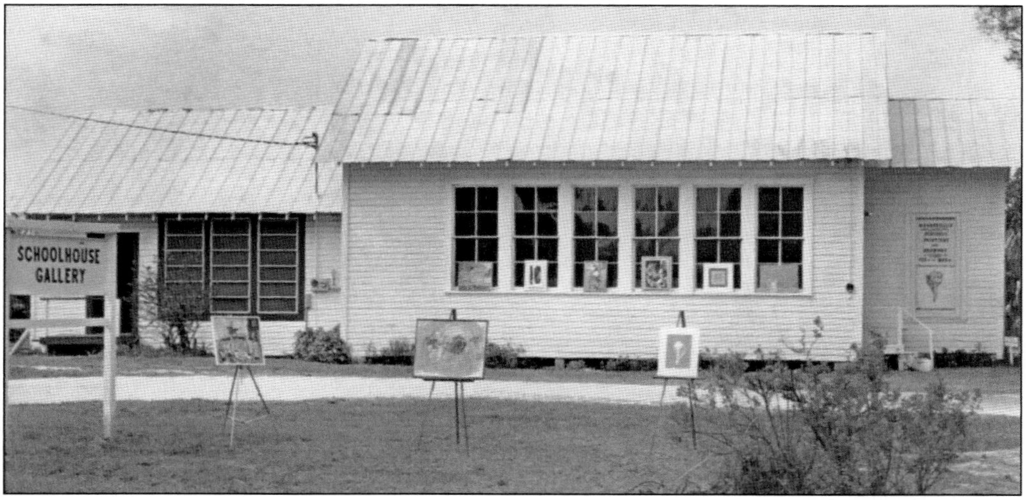

Constructed in 1914 as a Baptist church, this building became the schoolhouse for black children around 1927. Children from the Gavin, Jordan, Preston, and Walker families attended. Closed in the early 1950s, black children were bused via ferryboat to schools in Fort Myers until 1964, when the new Sanibel School became the first in Lee County to be racially integrated. In the National Register of Historic Places, it is also part of the Florida Black Heritage Trail. (Courtesy of Islander Trading Post.)

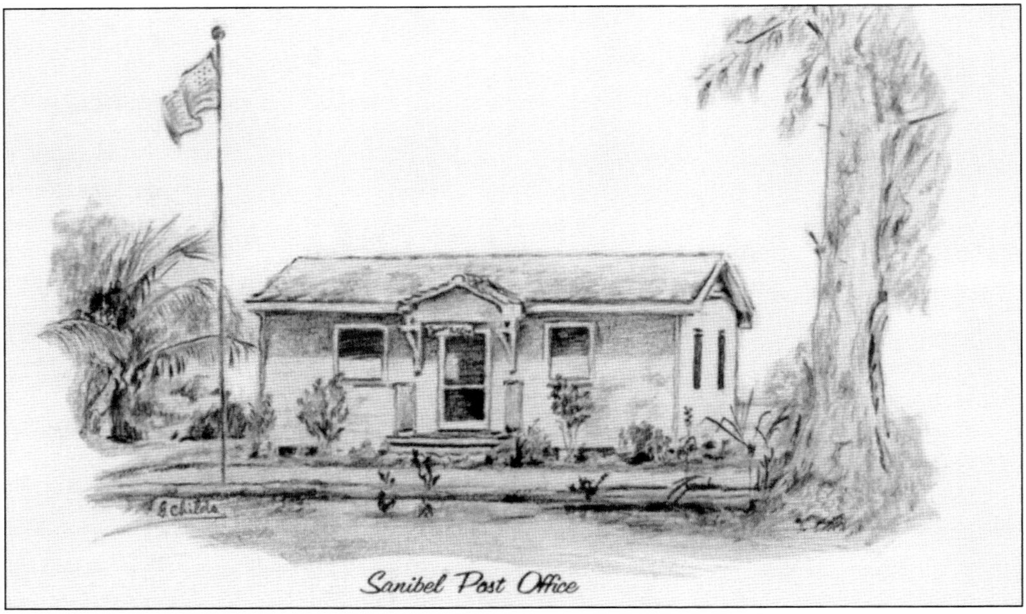

Located on Ferry Road, this 1954 building replaced an earlier, smaller structure. Scotia Bryant of the Captiva pioneer family was Sanibel's postmistress from 1943 to 1967. Before 1943, the post office was at Reed's Landing (1894), where Will Reed served as postmaster for 44 years. The postal service was vital to homesteaders, as what was not available at the general store had to be mail ordered. (Courtesy of Islander Trading Post.)

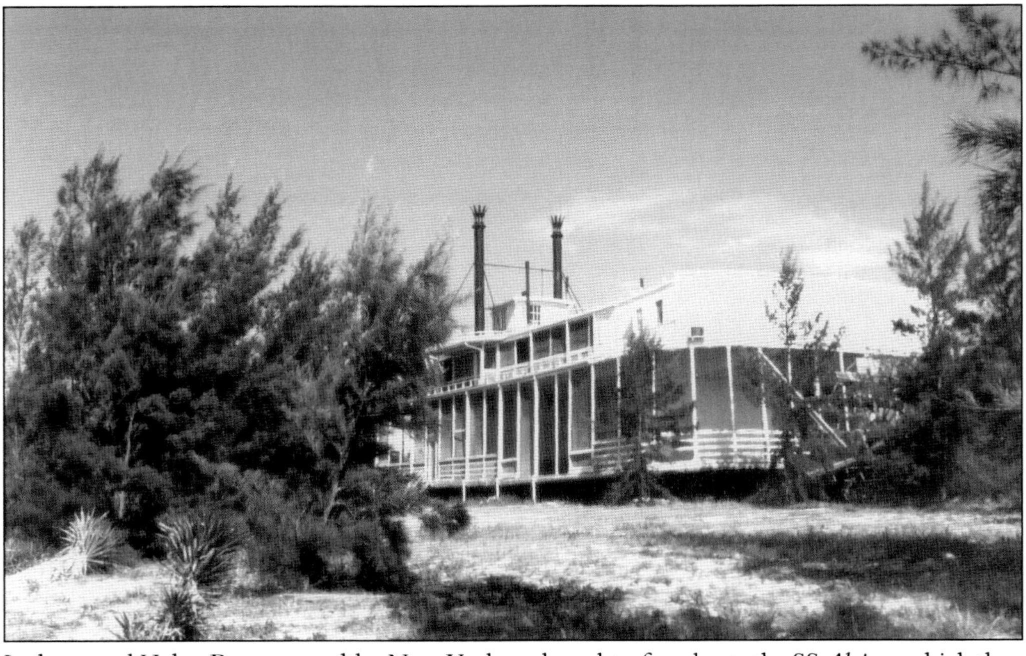

Lathrop and Helen Brown, wealthy New Yorkers, bought a ferryboat, the SS *Algiers*, which they renovated into an elegant home in the style of a Mississippi riverboat. In 1960, the 150-foot boat was towed from Fort Myers to a Gulf-front site that was dredged, then filled. Unfortunately, Lathrop Brown did not live long enough to truly enjoy the ornate home. It stood empty and dilapidated until the City of Sanibel bought the land for a park. (Courtesy of Jean and Tom Quinby.)

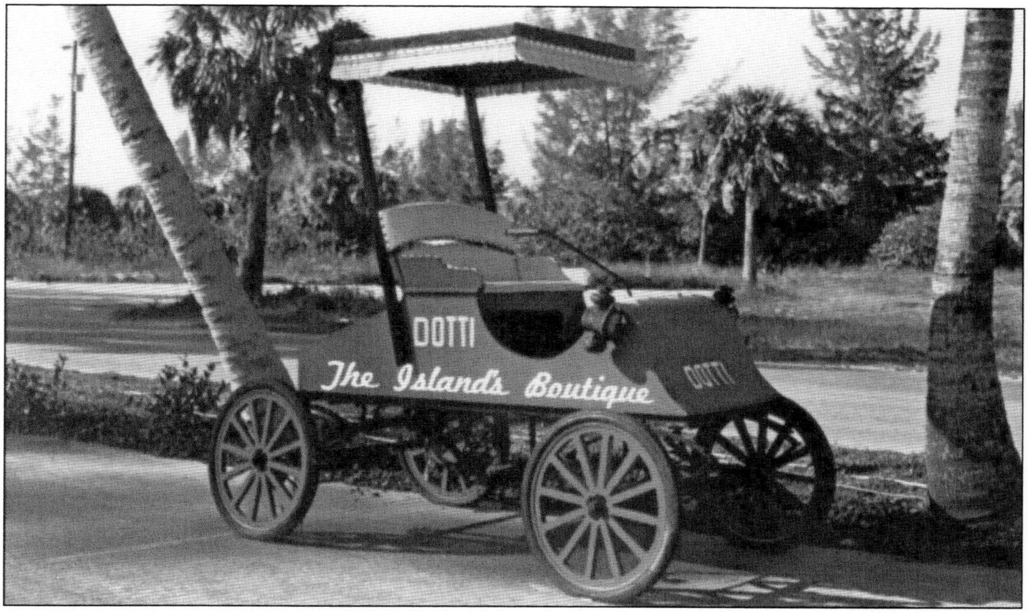

Islander and coauthor Charles LeBuff built this "horseless carriage" in the mid-1960s and drove it around the islands for several years. He then sold it to Dotti Booker to advertise her dress shop, Dotti's, which was then located on Periwinkle Way. The empty parking lot in the background was the site where a 1972 tornado tore down three commercial units, just missing the Sanibel Community Church. (Courtesy of Charles LeBuff collection.)

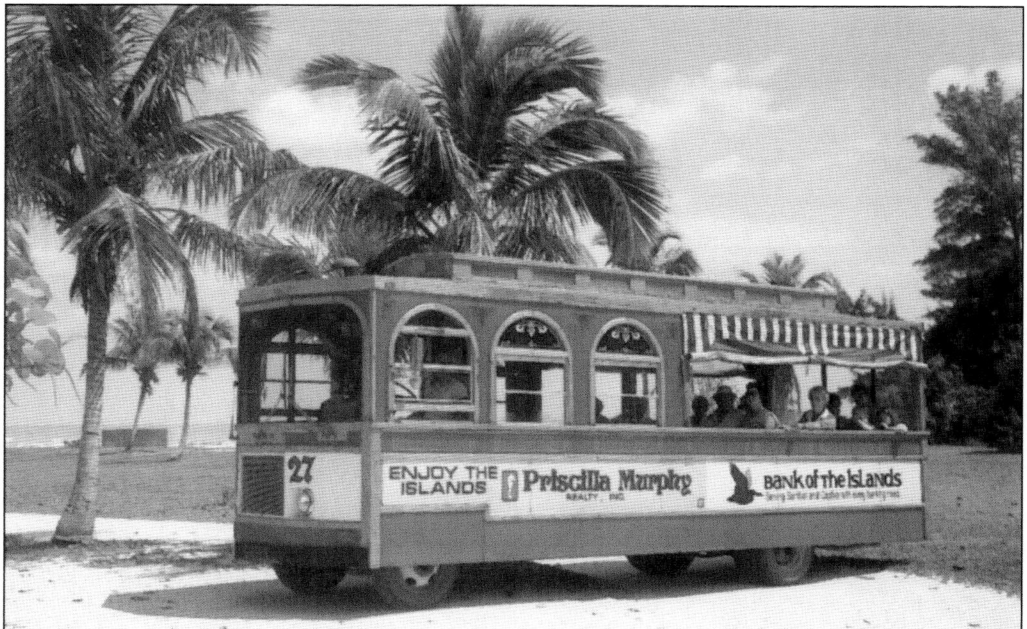

This unique vehicle was part of the island landscape in the 1980s. Jim and Betty Anholt, who owned the Standard Station (1969), felt the islands could support public transportation. The Sanibel Trolley was not only public transportation, but also a guided tour, deftly combining the past with the present. They continued the trolley service into the 1990s. (Courtesy of Jim and Betty Anholt.)

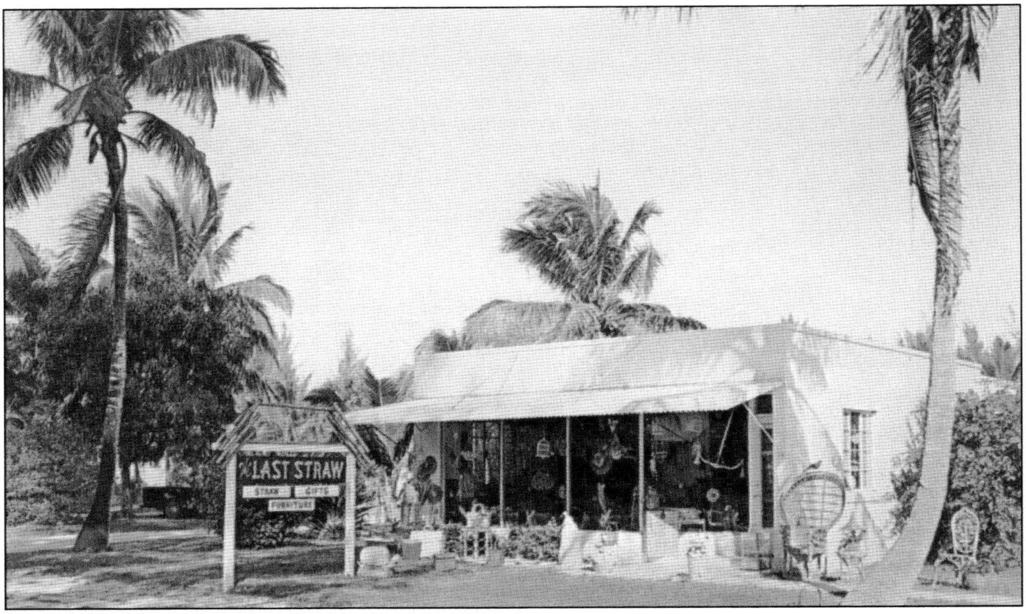

One could find anything made of straw in Charlie Holland's 1960s–1970s shop, The Last Straw. The building showcased Nave Plumbing until it moved to a larger shop in the back of Sanibel Square Center. Alan and Goldie Nave owned the complex and lived in the gray house next door. This building, once expanded, was also home to Caloosa Canvas Co., The Nimble Thimble, and Dunham's of Maine. (Courtesy of Islander Trading Post.)

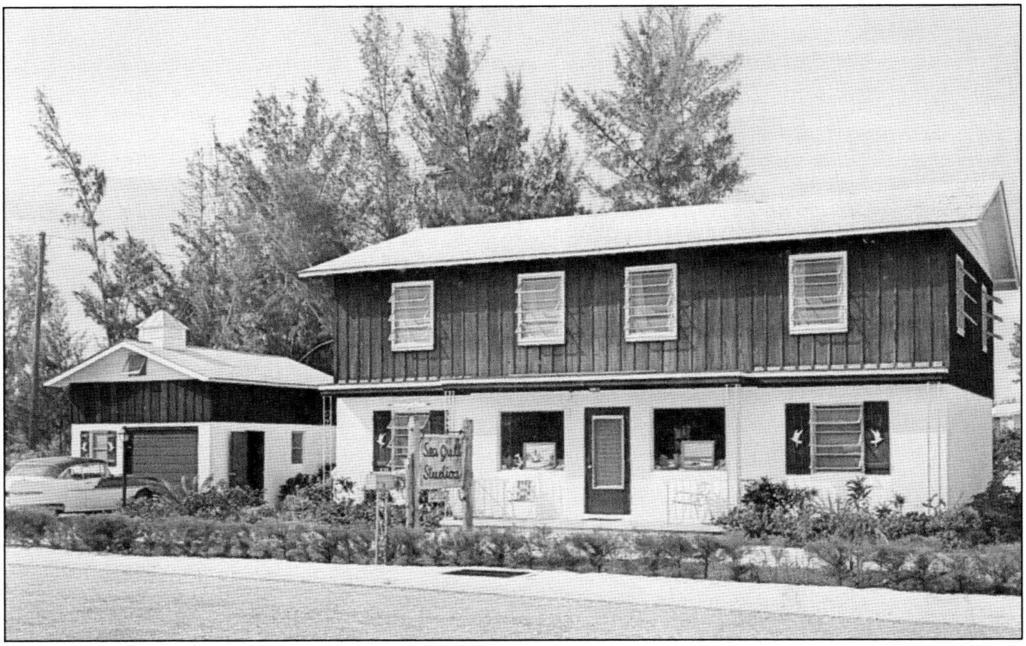

This West Gulf Drive gallery, Sea Gull Studios, was owned by the artistic Klotz family in the 1960s. There, one could find international and local art of many genres, with an island touch. The building later became a well-known Italian restaurant, Letizias, owned by Lou Letizia, and later, Bob Janes, before he became a Lee County commissioner. It is now the site of the Lantana Condominium. (Courtesy of Deborah Gleason collection.)

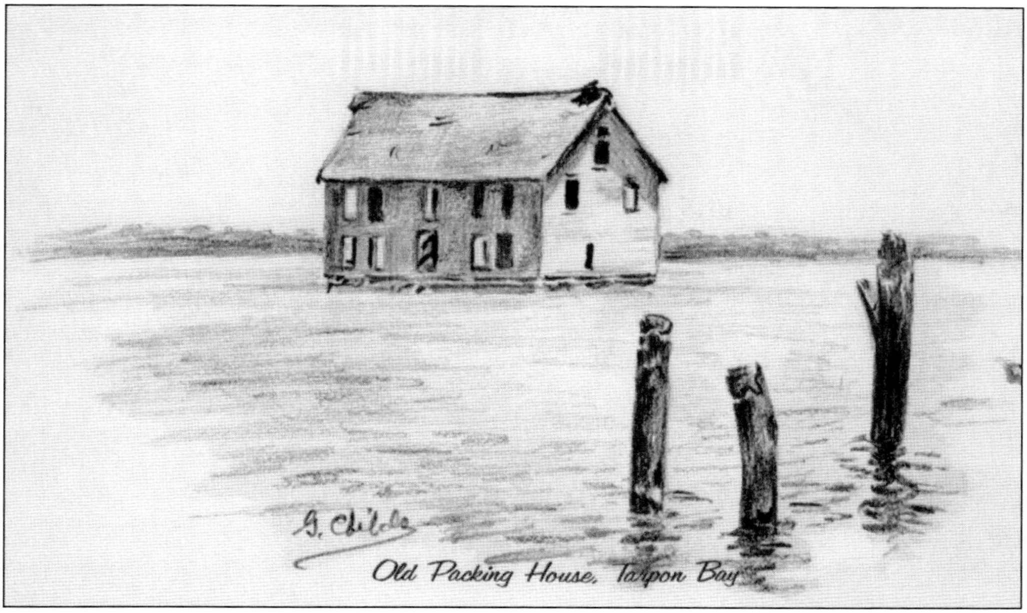

This drawing by Gladys Childs is of a deserted packinghouse on Tarpon Bay. Once a thriving link for the transport of island-grown produce, this building is said to have been owned by the partners John Bruaw, Elmer Fentrow, and James Johnson. Their packinghouse was at the end of a long pier, possibly an effort to set it closer to a channel in the shallow bay. It later became a store. (Courtesy of Charles LeBuff collection.)

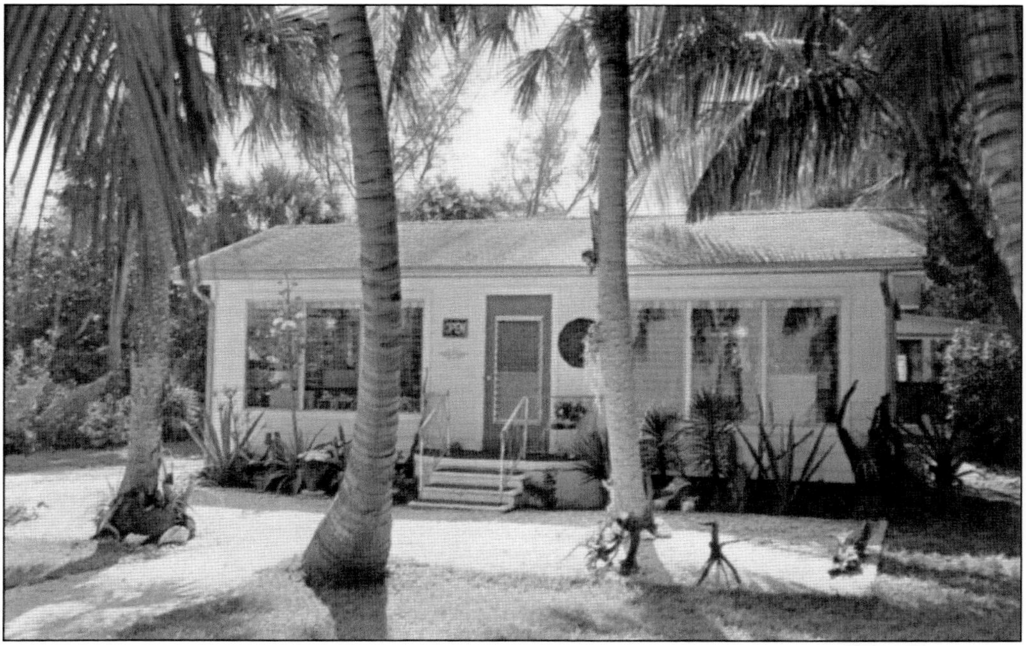

This Captiva building, McCall's Gift Shop, was located on the road to South Seas Plantation. Sometime in the 1970s or 1980s, the building was raised several feet to protect it from storm surge. It was last named the Tree House Shop. The late artist Bob Rauschenberg bought the property to preserve the land from further commercialization, and it is still part of the Rauschenberg estate. (Courtesy of Deborah Gleason collection.)

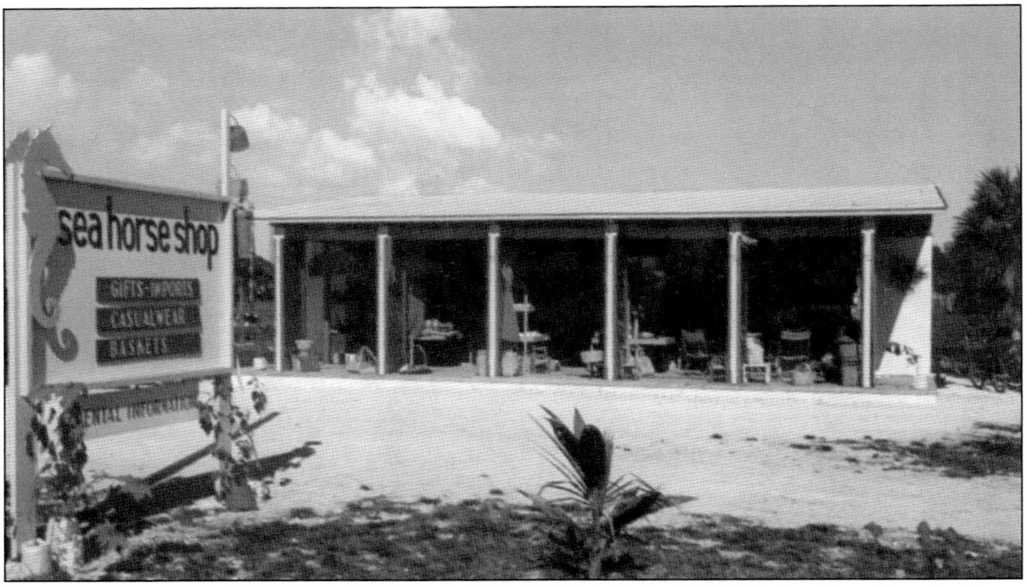

Mary and Joe Gault came to Sanibel in 1953 with their three children, Mary Jo, Christine, and Tim. A former auto designer for General Motors, Joe was an artist and craftsman. Their eclectic store, Sea Horse Shop, was an instant success that expanded yearly, even adding a Japanese garden with a pond. It was Sanibel's small department store with imports, clothing, accessories, jewelry, decor, and furniture. (Courtesy of Islander Trading Post.)

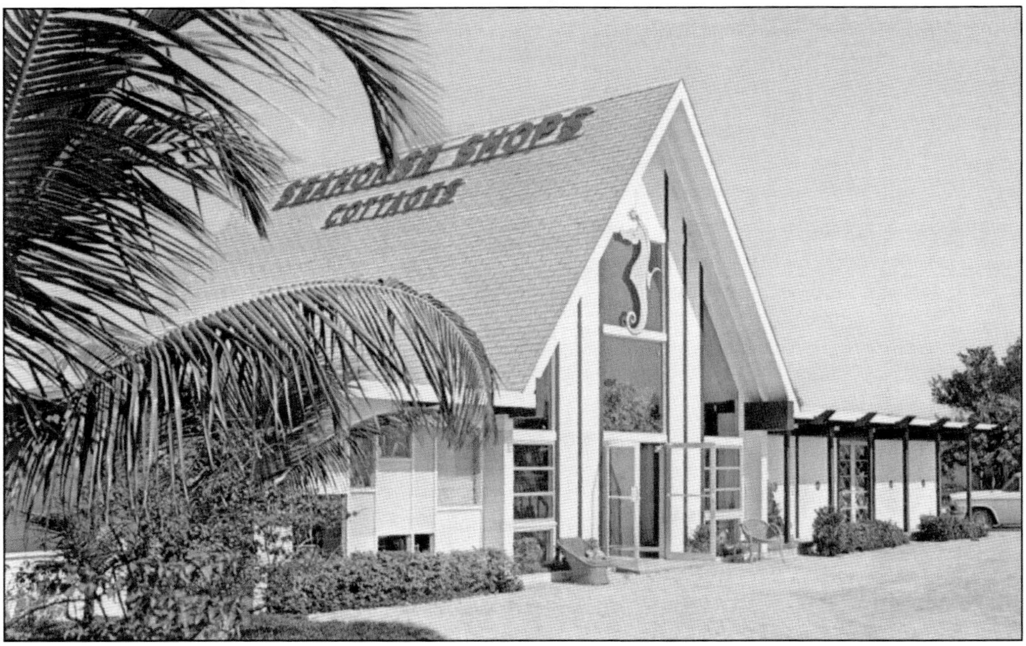

In the 1950s, Sea Horse Shop included a bookshop owned by Bill MacIntosh, which soon moved to a larger location on Periwinkle Way. The Gault family also included grandparents who built and ran rental cottages by the shop and Gulf-front cottages nearby. Later additions to the building included a small restaurant, The Lighthouse Café, and Tuttle's Sea Horse Shell Shop. Now named The Sporty Seahorse, it has retained much of its original ambiance. (Courtesy of Deborah Gleason collection.)

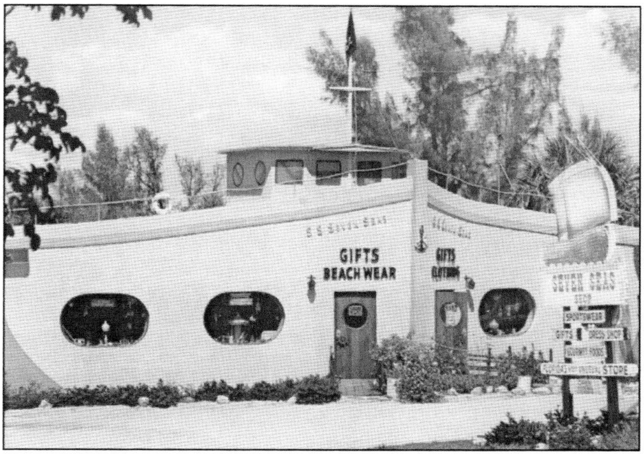

The Seven Seas Shop was a Periwinkle Way wonder when it was built by Paul and Irene Adams in the 1960s. With a moat, wood plank floors, a pilothouse, and portholes for windows, it lived up to its name of the SS *Seven Seas*. It was known for men's and women's clothing, gifts, and souvenirs. It is better known today as the Lazy Flamingo Restaurant, offering seafood, cold beer, and casual fare. (Courtesy of Islander Trading Post.)

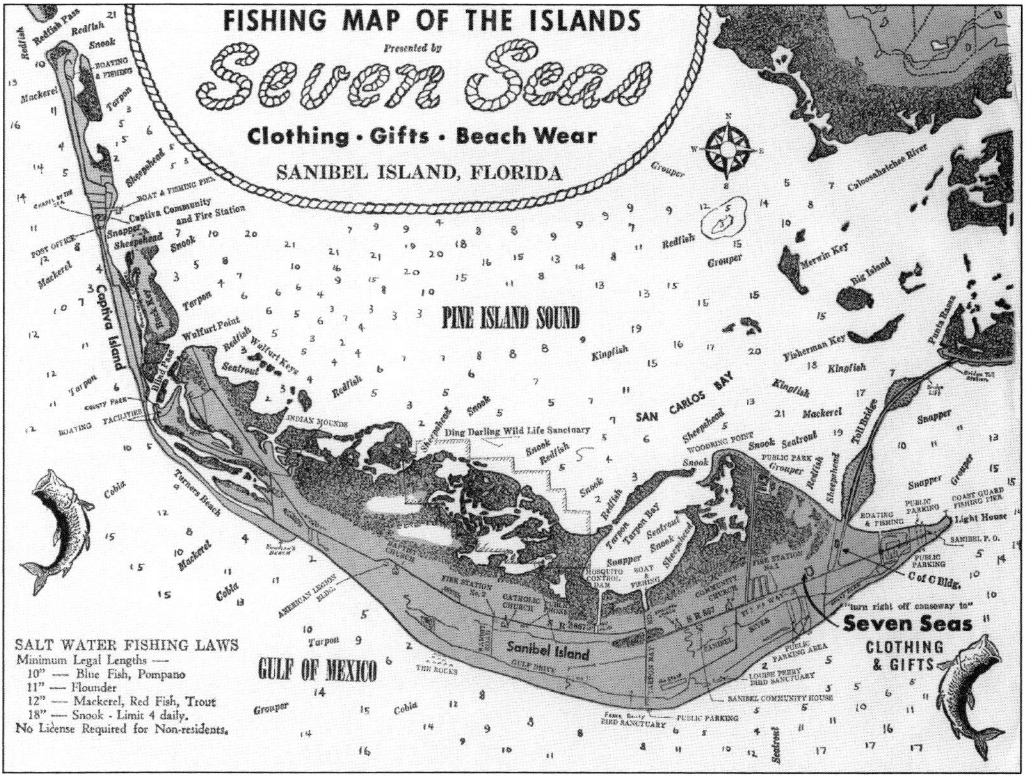

Maps of Sanibel and Captiva were part of commercial island culture. They usually included information on fishing or shelling, and some included the ferryboat and mail boat routes. This Seven Seas fishing map was produced after 1963 and shows the full length of Captiva's Turner Beach, now vanished from erosion. Also of note are the Periwinkle Fire Station, the Ferry Road post office, and the Casa Ybel airstrip. (Courtesy of Islander Trading Post.)

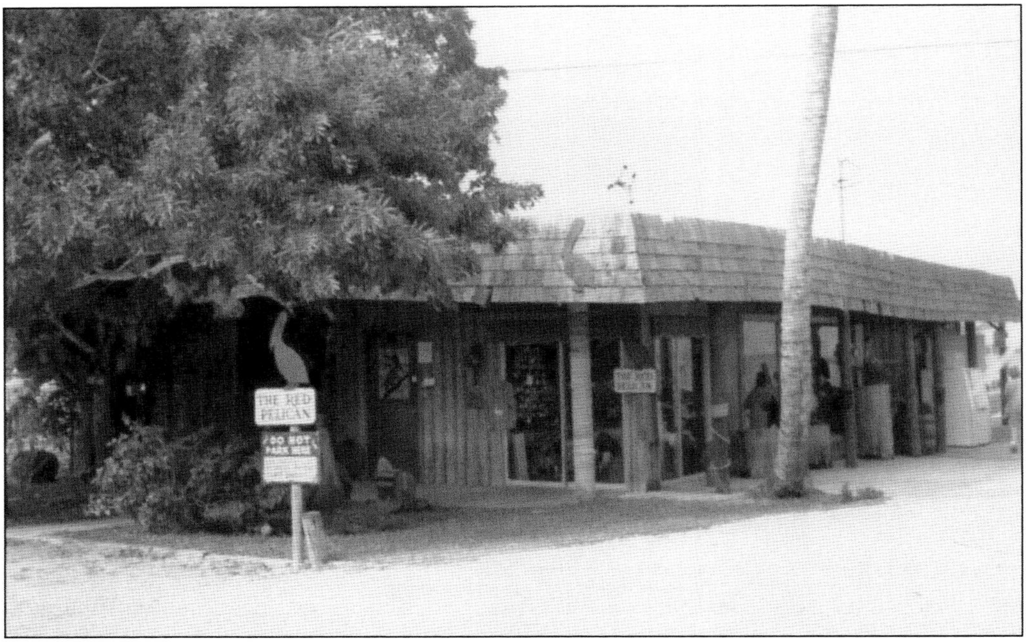

The Red Pelican import shop was created by Adelaide Bailey in the late 1960s, when it was at the old, bay-front location of Bailey's General Store. This postcard shows the next location at Tarpon Bay, where more vacationers likely visited it. The shop featured unique imported women's clothing, sandals, and potpourri. (Courtesy of Deborah Gleason collection.)

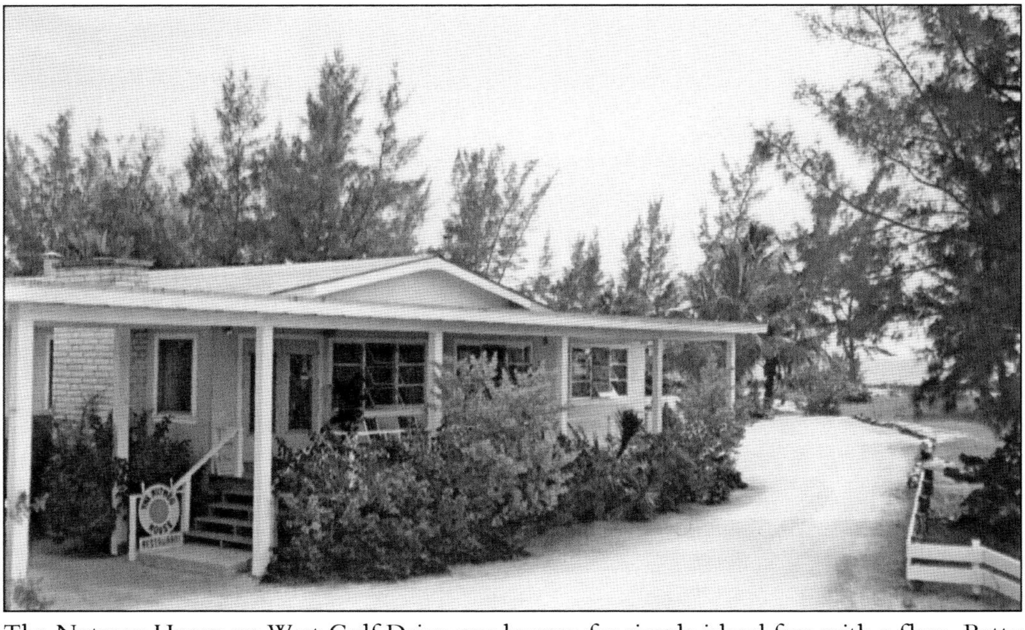

The Nutmeg House on West Gulf Drive was known for simple island fare with a flare. Betty Sears and Evelyn Pearson owned and managed it from the 1960s to the 1980s. No strangers to hard work, they had first run the Casa Marina restaurant (1950s) at the ferry landing. They were both instrumental in establishing the Sanibel Episcopal Church and the Sanibel Historical Museum. The Nutmeg House building is still used as a restaurant today. (Courtesy of Sanibel Historical Museum and Village.)

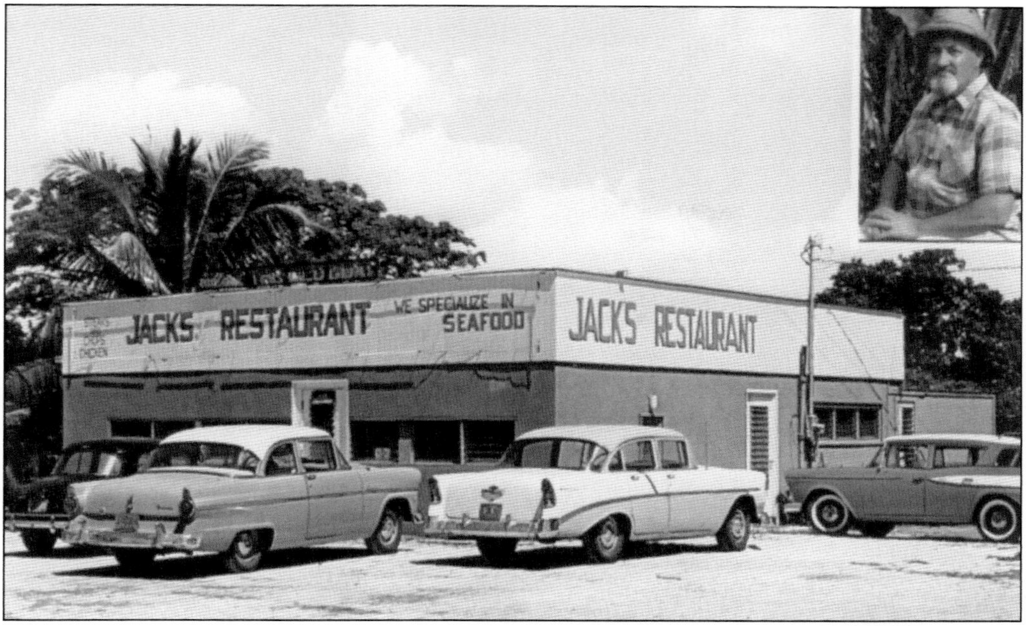

Jack's Place was a Periwinkle Way restaurant owned by Jack and Gertrude Cole. First an open-air tavern, it was soon enclosed, as air-conditioning became available. From the 1970s through the 1990s, the restaurant was known as the Harbor House under two different owners, Don Case and Bill Walters. In the early 2000s, the old structure was torn down; a new building has been home to Dolce Vita and now il Cielo restaurant. (Courtesy of Islander Trading Post.)

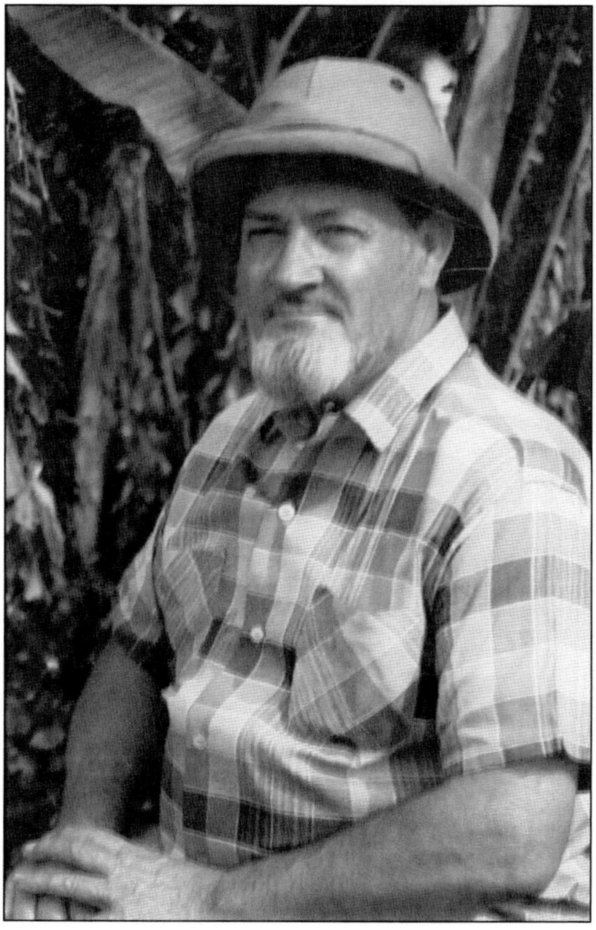

Self-appointed "The Old Goat," this was a popular postcard, as Jack Cole enjoyed giving them out free. When Jack was not flipping burgers, he was in his backyard enjoying pistol practice or working on his atom bomb shelter, not an uncommon practice in the days of the Cold War and the Red Menace (communism). Jack would buy fish from any local fisherman who came to the kitchen door with a large fresh catch. (Courtesy of Deborah Gleason collection.)

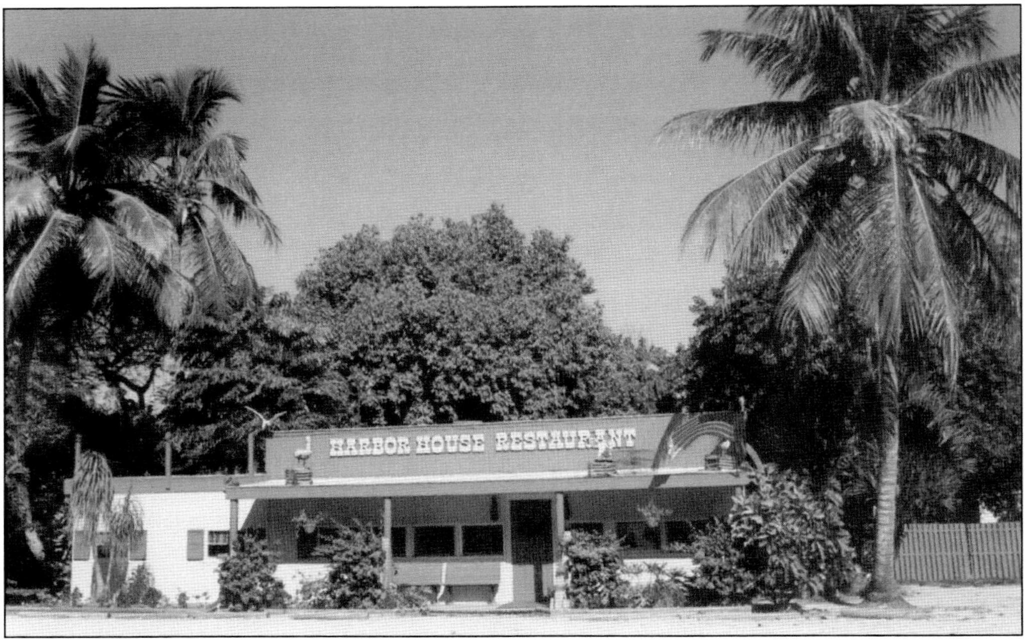

The Harbor House (previously Jack's Place) was a Periwinkle Way seafood restaurant renamed and opened by Bill Walters. Don and Jeanette Case purchased it in the 1970s and raised their family here. Don also served as a full time Sanibel police officer, and his son David is a career professional firefighter on Sanibel. (Courtesy of Islander Trading Post.)

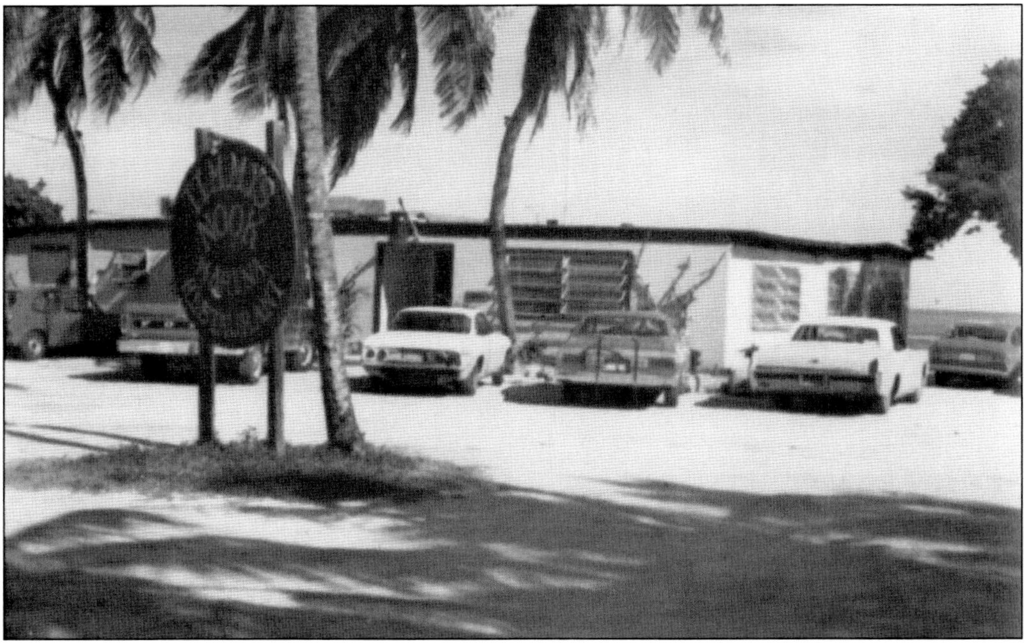

Timmy's Nook restaurant was opened in 1950 by T. "Timmy" M. Wiles and his wife, Beulah, a Captiva native. For decades, it was the Captiva watering hole, where locals and visitors could find fun, fresh fish, and sour cream blueberry pie. Timmy died in 1970, and his daughters ran the restaurant before selling it in the 1990s. The Green Flash restaurant is now in that bay-front location. (Courtesy of Islander Trading Post.)

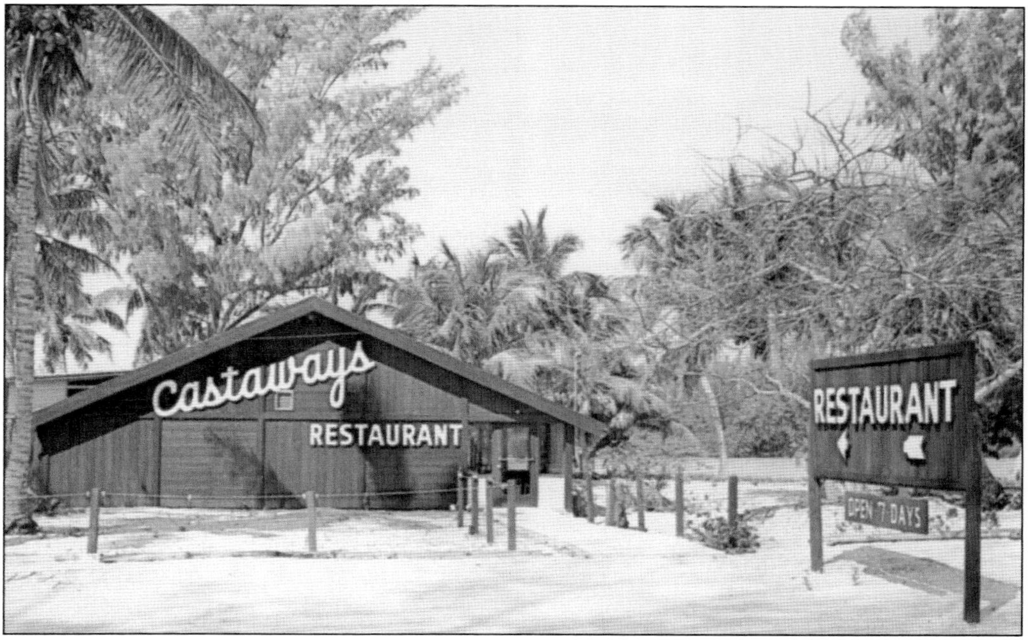

The Castaways Restaurant was an oasis in north Sanibel and claimed a share of Captiva patrons. It had one of the best views on both islands as it sat on Blind Pass and overlooked busy boat docks and Blind Pass Bridge. In the 1960s, when operated by Roy and Gert Webb, it was renowned for its enormous sandwiches. Today, the seasonal restaurant is called the Mad Hatter. (Courtesy of Islander Trading Post.)

Soup du Jour — Cup	.20	Fresh Fruit Cup	.35
Bowl	.40	Fruit Juices	.15 & .25
Small Salad	.40	Full Order Tossed Greek Salad	1.00

HOT ROAST BEEF SANDWICH, Gravy Potato, Vegetable	1.40
HOT TURKEY SANDWICH, Gravy Potato, Vegetable	1.25
HOT HAMBURGER, Gravy Potato, Vegetable	1.00
CHICKEN SALAD ROLL Potato Salad, Sliced Tomato	1.25
TUNA FISH SALAD ROLL Potato Salad, Sliced Tomato	1.25
SHRIMP SALAD ROLL Potato Salad, Sliced Tomato	1.40
LOBSTER SALAD ROLL Potato Salad, Sliced Tomato	1.40

Fresh Fruit Salad Plate
Cottage Cheese
Crackers
1.25

Fried Fish Fillets
French Fries
Salad
Rolls and Butter
1.75

½ Fried Chicken
French Fries
Salad
Rolls and Butter
2.25

Fried Jumbo Shrimp
French Fries
Salad
Rolls and Butter
2.25

GIANT SEAFOOD PLATTER
Fried Lobster Tail, Shrimp, Bay Scallops
Fish Fillets
French Fries
Salad
Rolls and Butter
2.95

The Coconut Grove, at the corner of Tarpon Bay and Periwinkle Way, was a legendary restaurant on Sanibel. It was open for three meals daily and later had a full bar where islanders met and socialized until well past the dinner hour. This menu illustrates the value of a dollar in the 1950s and 1960s; the Greek salad reflects the heritage of owners John and Bella Kontinos. (Courtesy of Islander Trading Post.)

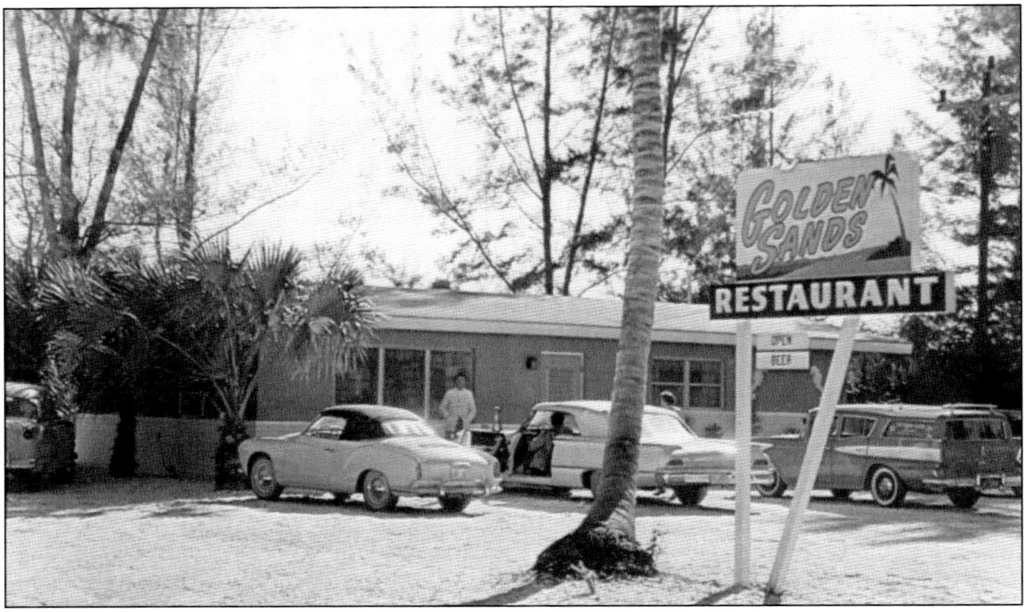

The Golden Sands was a well-respected Periwinkle Way restaurant in the 1960s. It was built by Ted and Allie Defoe, leased by Jake and Pearl Stokes, and taken over by Roy and Gert Webb. The musical Welker twins, Gene and Jim, operated the eatery until it was sold in the 1970s. The restaurant became McT's, a seafood restaurant, sold again in 2011, and is now the Sanibel Fish House. (Courtesy of Deborah Gleason collection.)

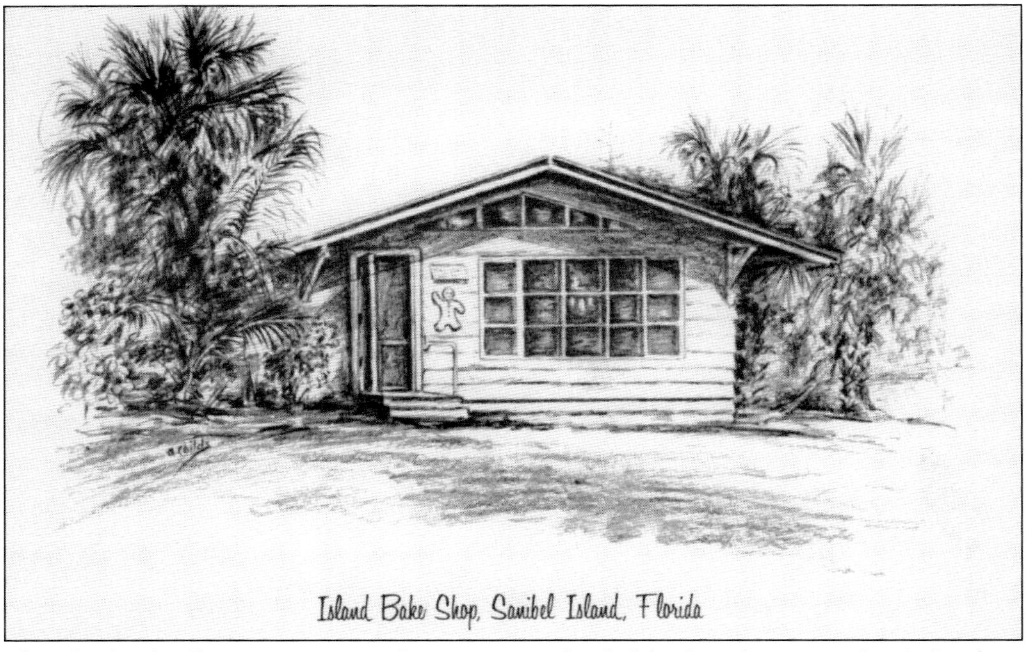

The Island Bake Shop was a treasured sweet spot on Sanibel (and on the way to Captiva), where cakes, pies, cookies, brownies, éclairs, and breads were sold. Jack VanBell was perhaps most famous for his lemon pecten cake, which he baked in a pan shaped like a scallop or pecten shell. Years later, those cake pans were sold at the Unpressured Cooker shop in Periwinkle Place. (Courtesy of Islander Trading Post.)

Eight

Inns . . . and Outs

Sanibel and Captiva Islands have long been home to travelers. Early settlers opened their homes as boardinghouses to others coming to find land to homestead. Dozens of inns, hotels, motels, and cottages have come and gone from the landscape. Some of these were The Sisters, or Casa Ybel, and The Matthews, later named the Island Inn, which began as a home that offered rooms and dining for winter visitors. Reed's Landing had the bay-side Sanibel Hotel, where the Kinzie steamers docked, and those arriving on Captiva may have landed at the Randall dock and stayed at Fisherman's Lodge, 'Tween Waters, or other early inns.

After World War II, new motels evolved. These motels were mom-and-pop establishments of varying sizes but seldom had over 12 rooms or cottages. The summer months were too desolate to sustain larger hotels. Even the ferry service was reduced to one ferry every 1.5 hours.

Winter or summer, the last ferry left the island daily at 5:30 p.m., and it was common for travelers to miscalculate and be forced to find a room for the night.

With the motels came new postcards to be sent from the sunny shores of Sanibel and Captiva. These are perhaps the most prolific of island cards that a collector can attain. Few of the early motels are still in existence, and many have given way to larger condominium projects, as documented by postcards.

In 1963, the advent of the Sanibel Causeway brought new motels, hotels, and condominium complexes. The number of visitors coming to Sanibel and Captiva tripled the first year. In just one decade, many of the quaint mom-and-pop motels were redeveloped into multiunit condominium projects. Suddenly, there was the possibility of high-rise buildings on Sanibel's shoreline, and in 1974, islanders reacted by severing their ties with Lee County and creating a city of their own (with its own growth ordinances). Thus, much of the simple island ambiance and respect for the nature on Sanibel Island has been saved.

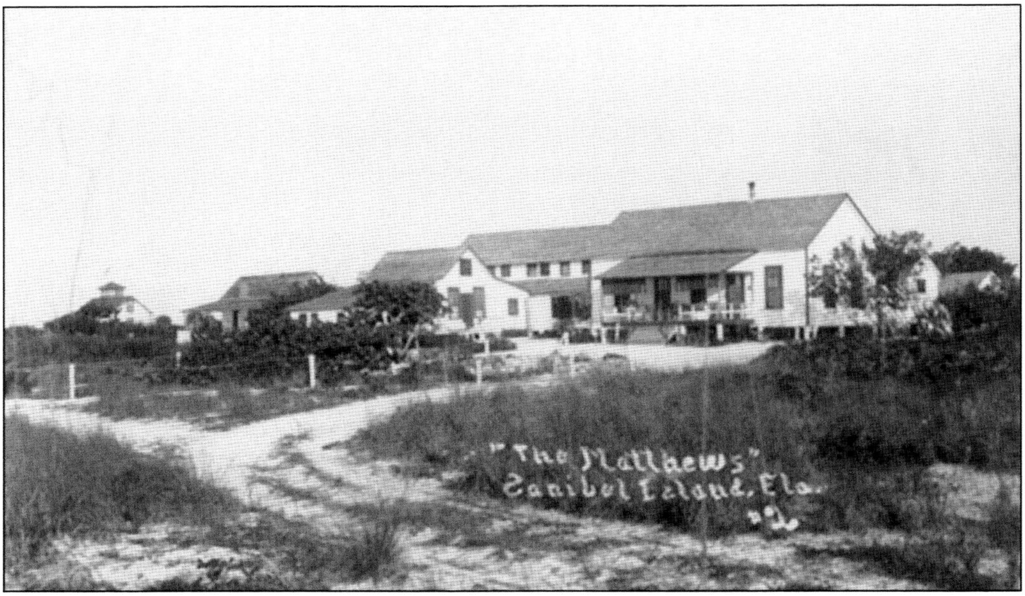

Harriet and Will Matthews of Kentucky arrived on Sanibel in 1895. While trying their hand at farming, they took boarders into their home to make ends meet. Soon, they offered winter visitors land to build a house on if they would take their meals at their inn, The Matthews. This early postcard shows sparse vegetation and the sandy Gulf Drive along the beach. (Courtesy of Charles LeBuff collection.)

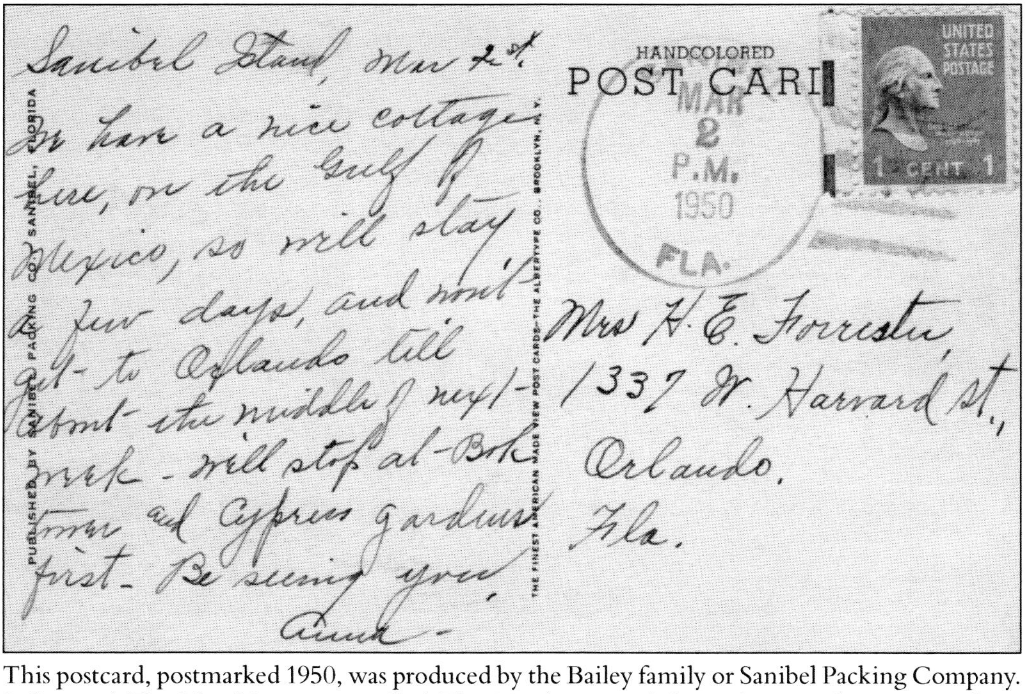
HANDCOLORED
POST CARI

UNITED STATES POSTAGE
1 CENT 1

MAR 2 P.M. 1950 FLA.

PUBLISHED BY SANIBEL PACKING CO., SANIBEL, FLORIDA

THE FINEST AMERICAN MADE VIEW POST CARDS—THE ALBERTYPE CO., BROOKLYN, N.Y.

Sanibel Island, Mar 2nd.
We have a nice cottage here, on the Gulf of Mexico, so will stay a few days, and won't get to Orlando till about the middle of next week - will stop at Bok tower and Cypress gardens first. Be seeing you
Anna -

Mrs H. E. Forrester,
1337 W. Harvard St.,
Orlando,
Fla.

This postcard, postmarked 1950, was produced by the Bailey family or Sanibel Packing Company. It featured The Island Inn, once called The Matthews, and the writer was fortunate to have a cottage there in March. The writer planned on later visiting then popular Bok Tower and Cypress Gardens, but only if she did not fall under the spell of Sanibel and Captiva. (Courtesy of Islander Trading Post.)

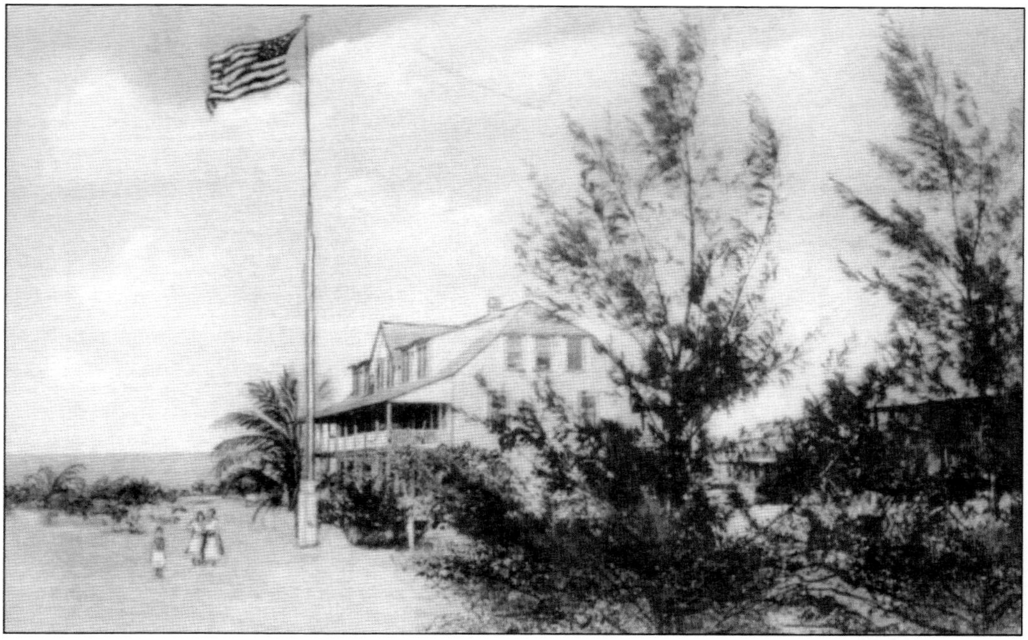

The Barracks was a three-story hotel constructed in 1914 after an earlier two-story building burned down. As part of The Matthews, it offered 30 double rooms with few amenities, but it was popular with those who liked rustic, dormitory-style lodging. It was demolished by Hurricane Donna in 1960. The historic Island Inn continues to offer meals and lodging today. (Courtesy of Alvin Lederer.)

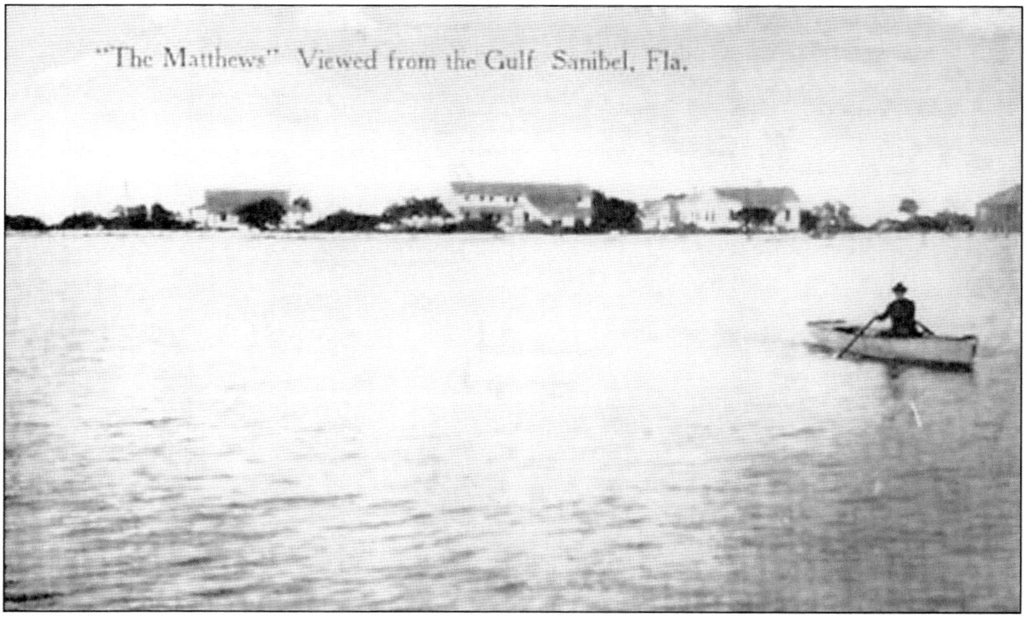

The Matthews grew, and neighbors built winter homes. More guests arrived to escape cold northern winters. Fishing, bird watching, and shelling were favorite pastimes for guests, and they held their first shell show there in 1916. Another inn, The Sisters, also held shell shows. Harriet Matthews and later her daughter Charlotta managed the inn, which survived through the hardships of World War I, the Great Depression, and World War II. (Courtesy of Alvin Lederer.)

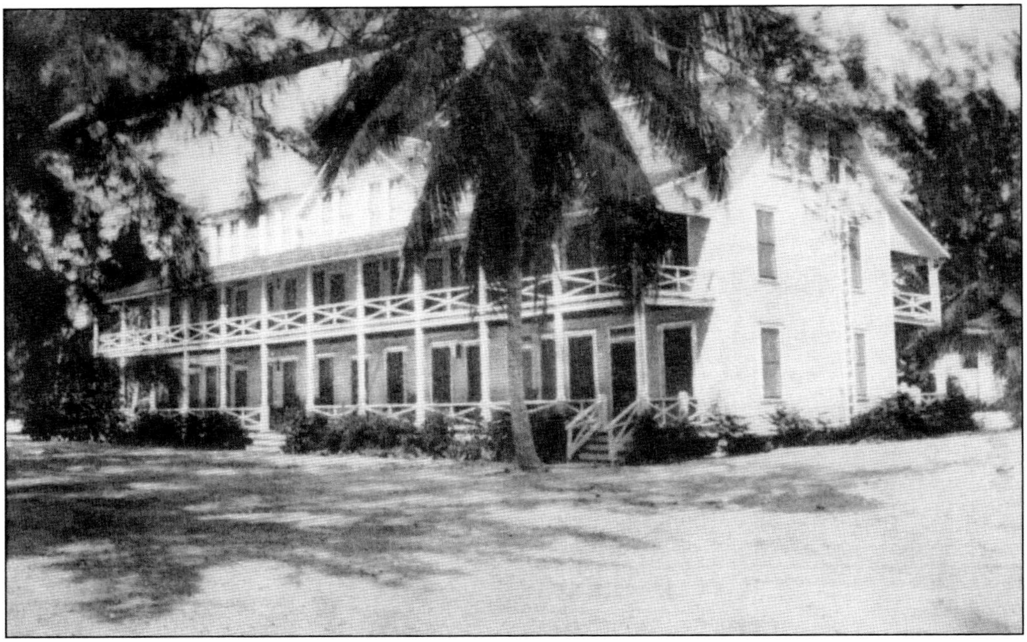

The Barracks at The Matthews was a rambling wood structure. In 1937, The Matthews name was changed to The Island Inn. After The Barracks demise in 1960, another large building was constructed of sturdier concrete block. The Island Inn was sold to a group of 150 guests in 1957, and positive changes continued under the management of Jack and Milbrey Rushworth from 1964 to 1990. (Courtesy of Islander Trading Post.)

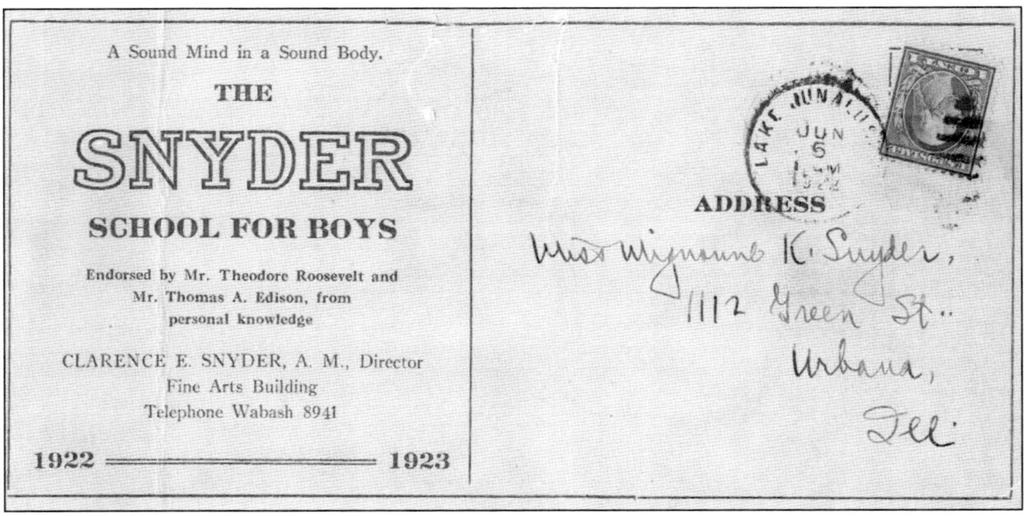

The Snyder School for Boys was the winter home of a northern private school. Boys often returned to the islands as adults after attending the outdoor school. (Student Bill Kimball returned to purchase part of The Island Inn and serve as its president.) In 1914, Clarence Snyder bought the Eyber House, once the Dickey Hotel, moved the school from Buck Key, and continued the school until 1926. The building burned down in 1935. (Courtesy Captiva Island Historical Society.)

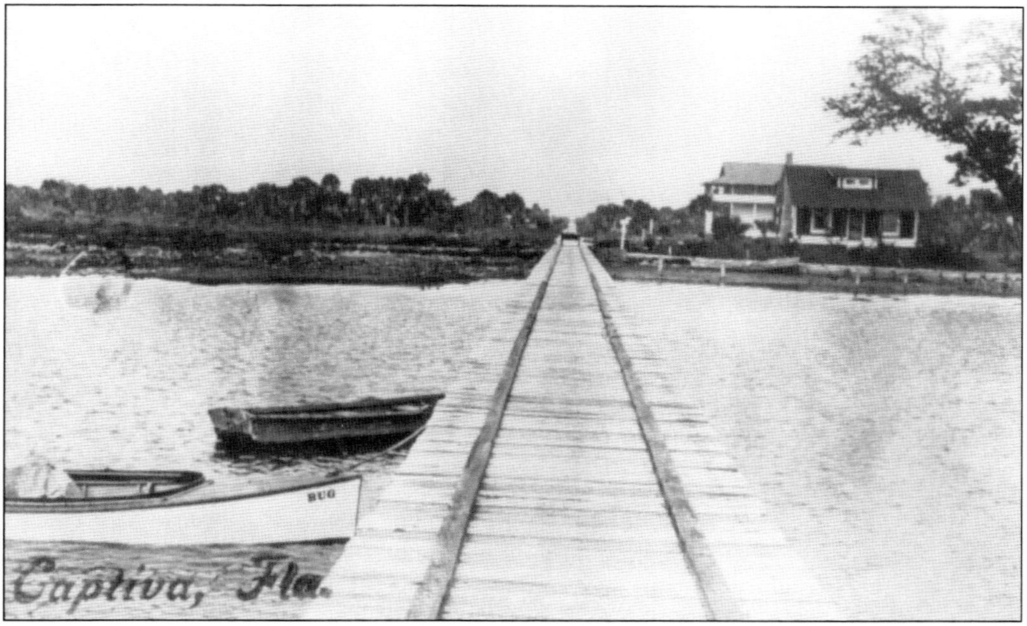

Docks played key parts in the history of Captiva, but none more than the Randall or "City Dock." There were buildings at the end of the dock where freight and ice were unloaded, and passengers embarked or disembarked via the steamships *Gladys* and *Dixie*. The wooden rails running down the dock planks directed a cart that moved freight and luggage. The building to the right was Miller's boardinghouse. (Courtesy of Captiva Island Historical Society.)

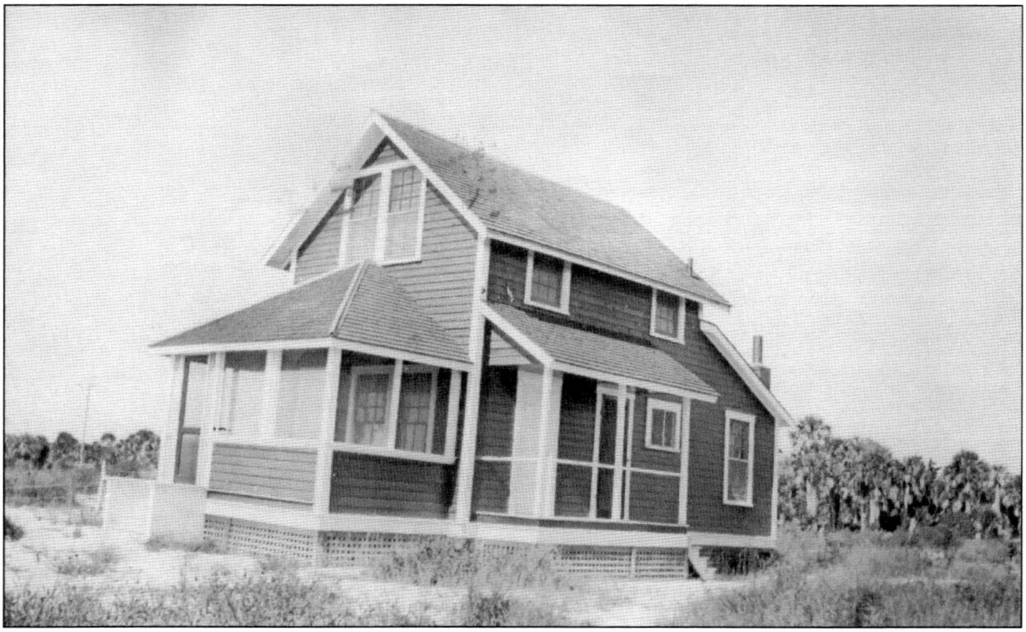

Captiva was first home to farming homesteaders but soon became popular with visitors wanting to spend the entire winter as islanders. This home photograph was made into a postcard by the proud new owner, Sarah Way. The home was built by F.A. Lane, an energetic early investor who also constructed his own home and the Bayview Hotel (1911–1915), where he filled in much of the low bay-front land. (Courtesy of Captiva Island Historical Society.)

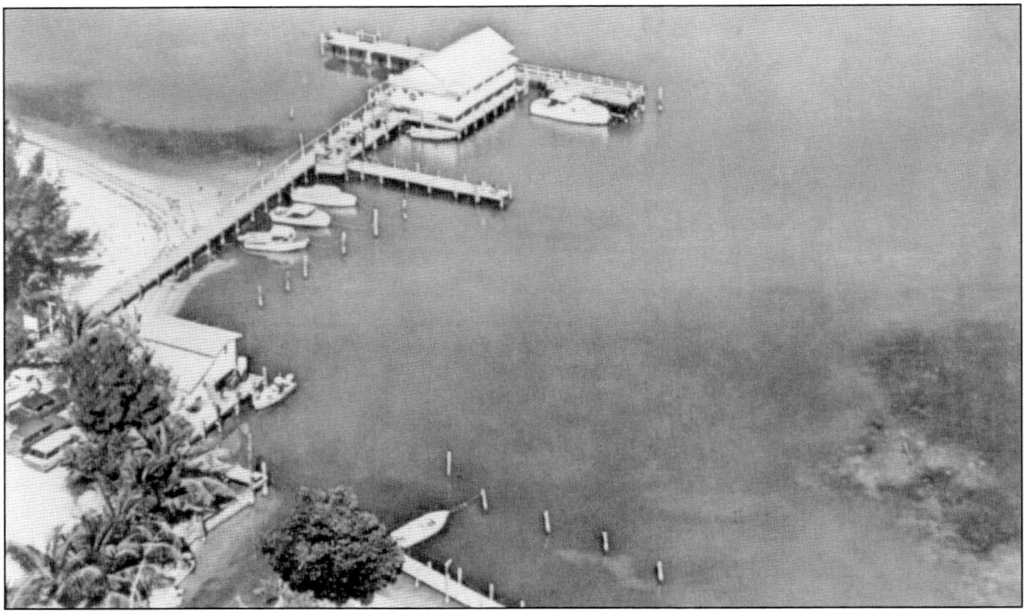

In 1935, Andy Rosse was a fishing guide at 'Tween Waters Inn. He bought the Randall dock, calling it Andy's Fishing Pier. Andy built a second dock (adjacent to the old dock) and his wife, Dessa, ran the restaurant at the end of that. It was the place to gas up a car or boat and have a cold cola or beer. Andy died in 1984; what had been Palm Avenue is now called Andy Rosse Lane. (Courtesy of Islander Trading Post.)

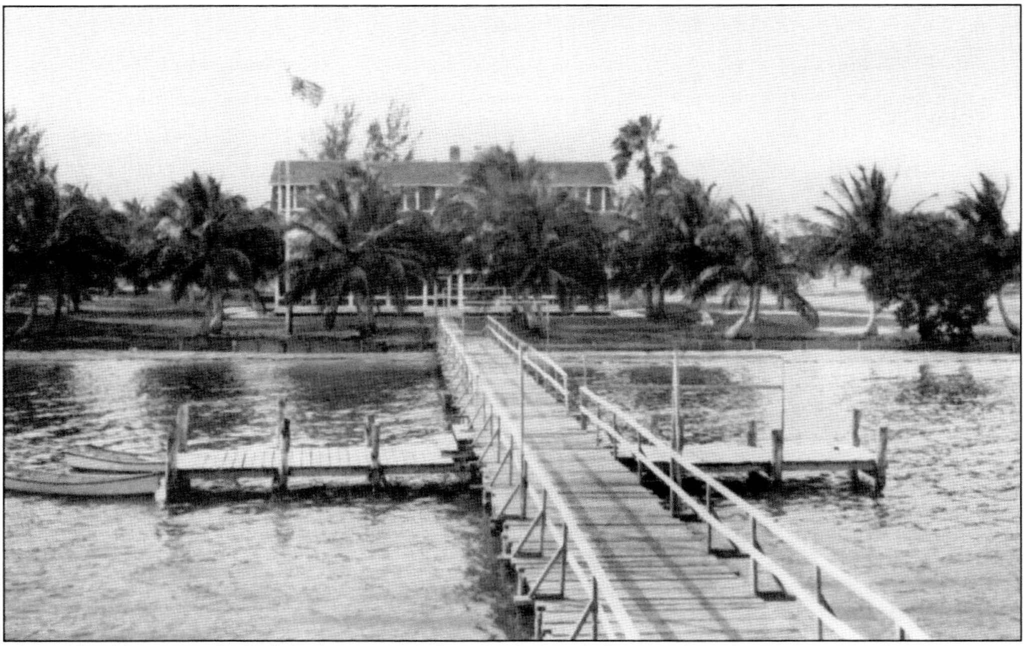

Captiva was fortunate to have several early inns and hotels. This attracted colorful travelers and adventurers from the north, who often chose to stay the entire winter. This postcard shows the Bayview Inn, Fisherman's Lodge, Captiva Hotel, or Captiva Lodge that prevailed through a multitude of owners, name changes, and hurricanes. The hotel was lost in 1948 to fire. (Courtesy of Captiva Island Historical Society.)

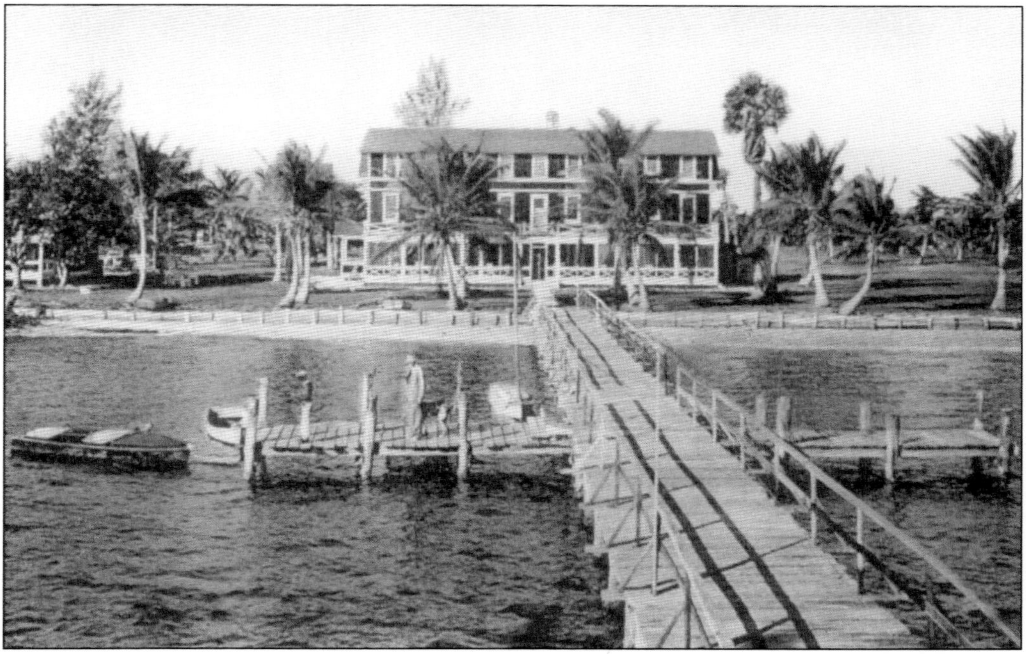

The Bayview Inn was built on lowland that was dredged and filled by Frank A. Lane of Connecticut. Adding rooms, including a barbershop, and stories every year, he completed the hotel complex in 1914, just before his death. His business partner, Dr. Franklin Miles, was left with the mortgage. (Courtesy of Captiva Island Historical Society.)

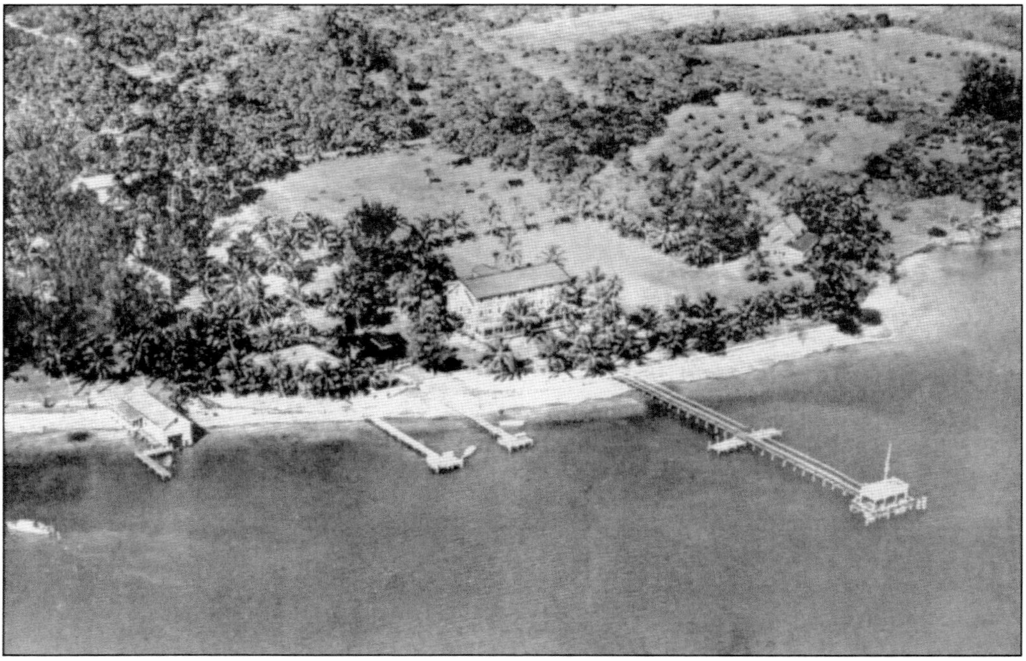

Postcard aerial views of Captiva Island show that agriculture flourished, whether it was citrus, vegetables, or coconut palms. Golf was an early sport on Captiva, with an eight-hole course behind the Bayview Inn that welcomed sport fishermen, vacationers, and businessmen. The Ellis house is on the left, and the Iredell house is on the right. (Courtesy of Islander Trading Post.)

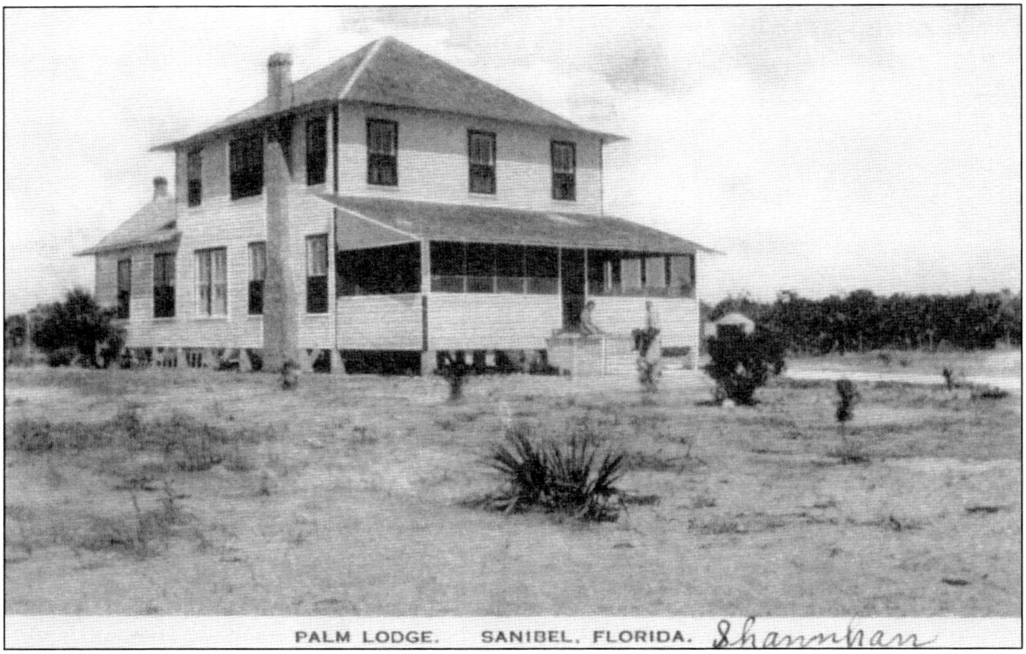

Palm Lodge or The Palms, near the lighthouse, was owned by past lighthouse keepers, the Shanahans. It was a successful inn until it burned down one early evening in 1936. Poet Edna St. Vincent Millay and husband had just checked into The Palms and gone for a beach walk when they saw the building in flames. She lost the only copy of her completed manuscript *Conversation at Midnight*, which she was able to reconstruct. (Courtesy of Sanibel Public Library.)

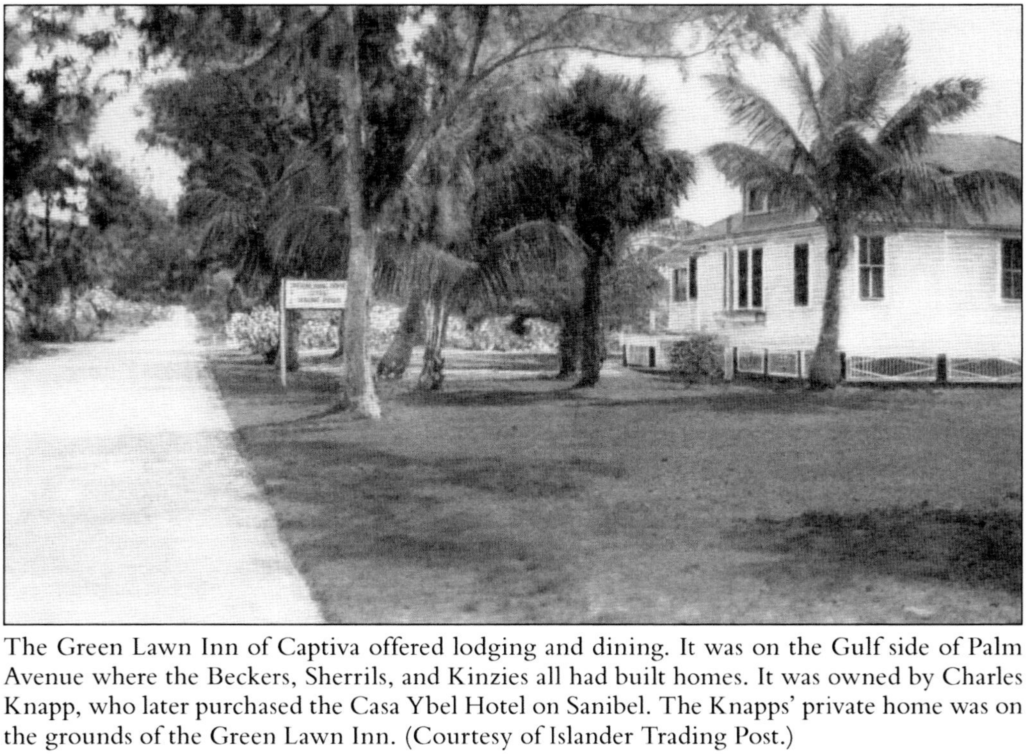

The Green Lawn Inn of Captiva offered lodging and dining. It was on the Gulf side of Palm Avenue where the Beckers, Sherrils, and Kinzies all had built homes. It was owned by Charles Knapp, who later purchased the Casa Ybel Hotel on Sanibel. The Knapps' private home was on the grounds of the Green Lawn Inn. (Courtesy of Islander Trading Post.)

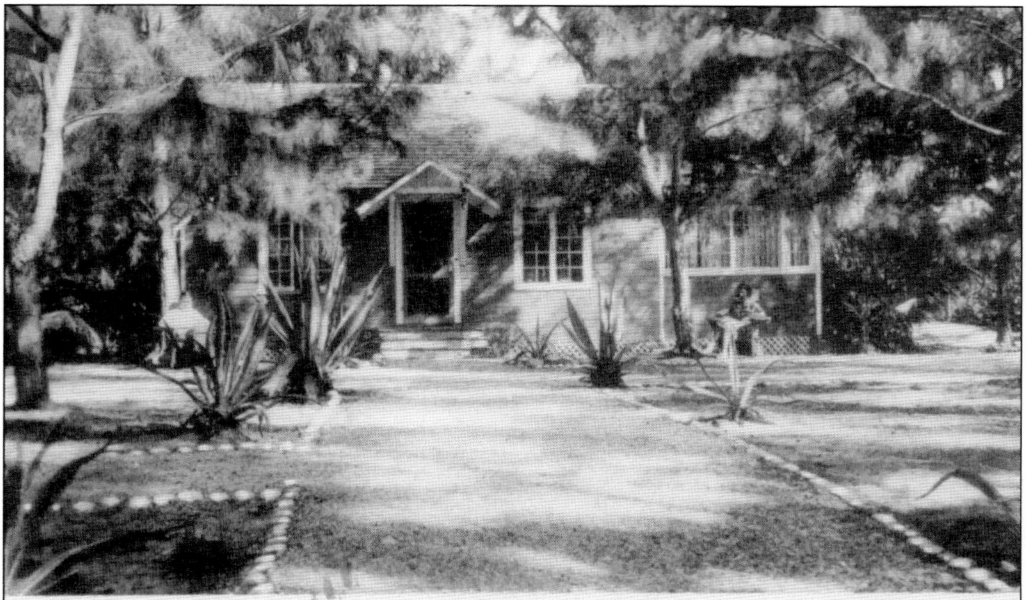

MAIN COTTAGE, 'TWEEN WATERS INN, CAPTIVA ISLAND, FLA.

'Tween Waters Inn was founded by Bowman and Grace Price in 1931. (Their daughter Dorothy Price Wakefield continued to live on Captiva until recently.) Reba Fitzpatrick owned the original building, which the Prices bought in 1925. To supplement their farming income, Grace took in boarders. They soon realized that being innkeepers was a fine life, and the legendary inn, restaurant, and marina were created. (Courtesy of Alvin Lederer.)

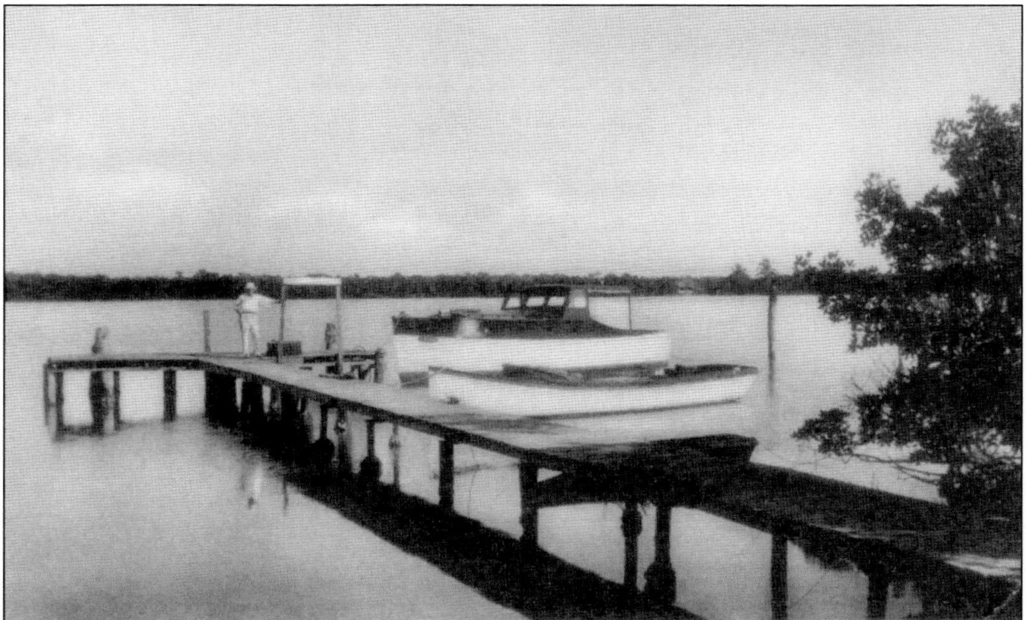

PRIVATE DOCK AND GUIDE BOATS, 'TWEEN WATERS INN, CAPTIVA ISLAND, FLA.

Much of the allure of 'Tween Waters Inn was the proximity to Gulf and bay waters. Many notables, including Charles and Anne Lindbergh and J.N. "Ding" and Penny Darling, came to enjoy excellent fishing, shelling, and socializing. Teddy Roosevelt was a visitor who preferred to stay on a barge in the bay channel that now bears his name. (Courtesy of Islander Trading Post.)

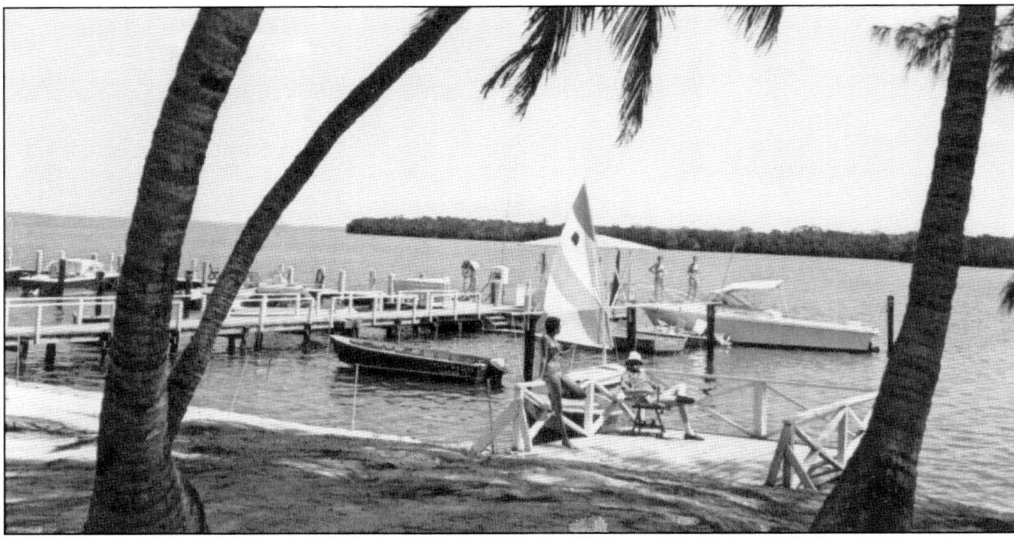

'Tween Waters Inn grew despite the Depression and World War II. With the addition of ferries, guests could bring their cars to Captiva. A seaplane landed and delivered daily newspapers. Captiva had the charms of being remote and casually sophisticated. The inn was later purchased by a group of guests who were businessmen from Rochester, New York. They continued to update and expand the cottages to the modern resort it is today. (Courtesy of Islander Trading Post.)

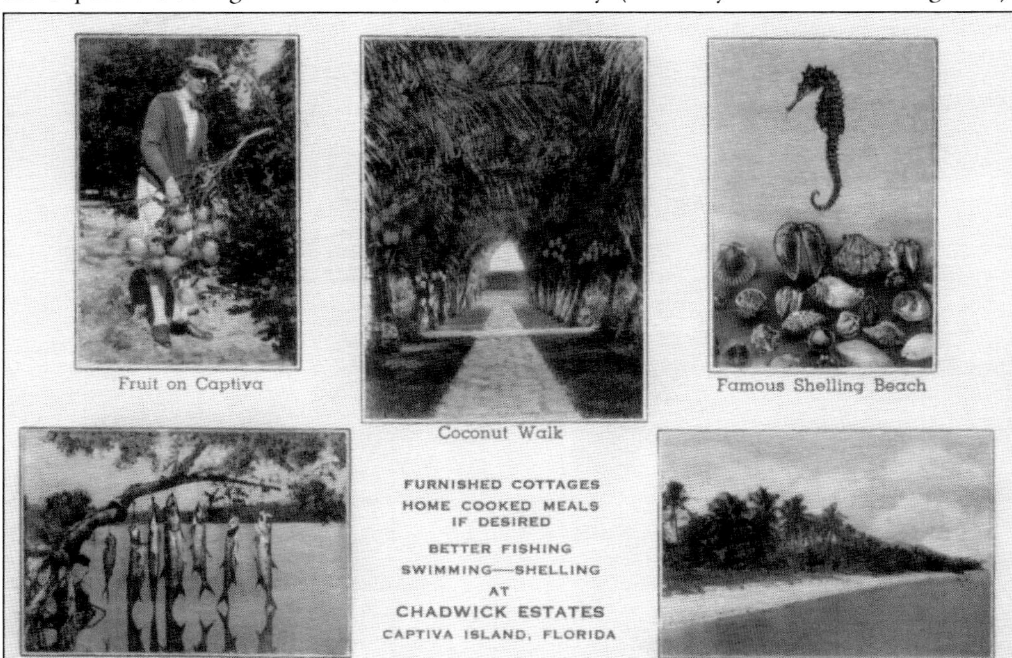

The Chadwick Estate was the dream of Clarence and Rosemont Chadwick. In 1923, they bought the old Carter and Bryant homesteads. In 1926, the hurricane damaged much of the farmland and tired landowners sold to the Chadwicks. Eventually, they owned 400 acres on Captiva and Sanibel and created a plantation, growing coconuts and citrus. Suffering from arthritis, Clarence eventually was forced to manage his plantation from a wheelchair. (Courtesy of Islander Trading Post.)

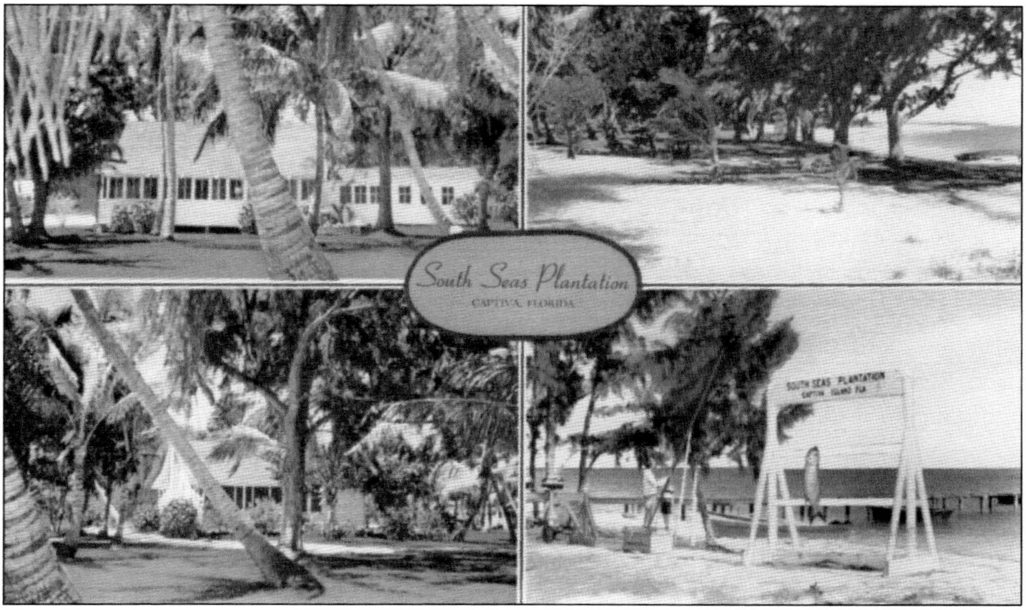

The Chadwicks renovated old homes, built cottages, and planted coconut palms on their many acres. During the war, they had numerous guests visit their plantation and some bought land and built homes. After the war, the American Hotels Corporation bought the plantation, and it became South Seas Plantation, still known today as an exclusive, all-inclusive resort. (Courtesy of Deborah Gleason collection.)

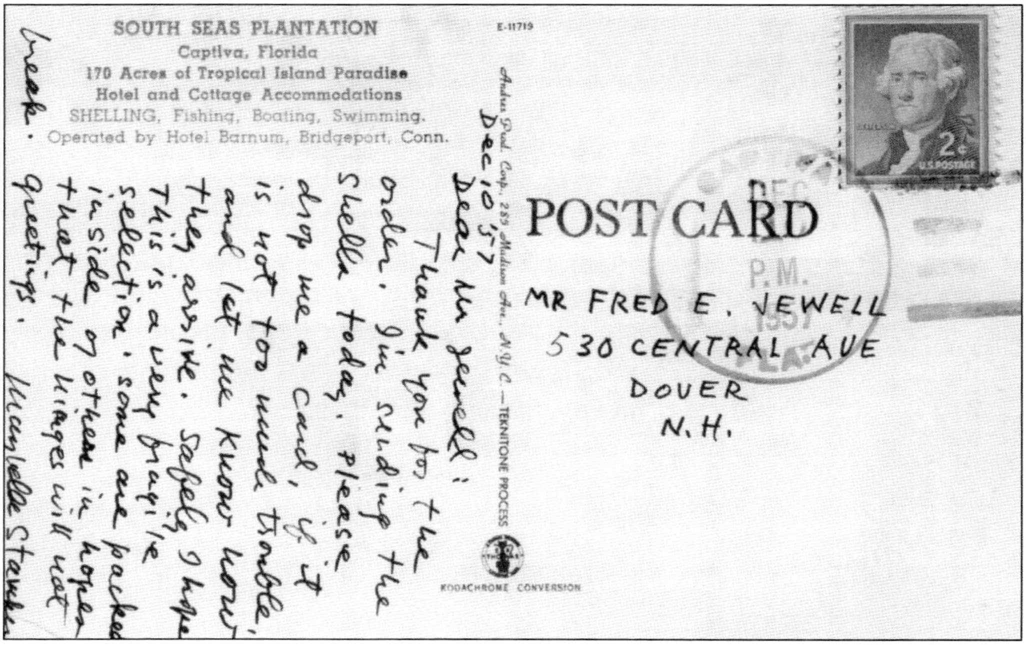

This ordinary postcard was written in 1957 from a Captiva resident who had sent a client some shell specimens, possibly sunray venus or tellin shells. That resident was the reclusive but accomplished artist Maybelle Stamper, who sold artwork and shells to feed herself and her cats. Her dislike for South Seas Plantation did not stop her from making good use of their postcards. (Courtesy of Deborah Gleason collection.)

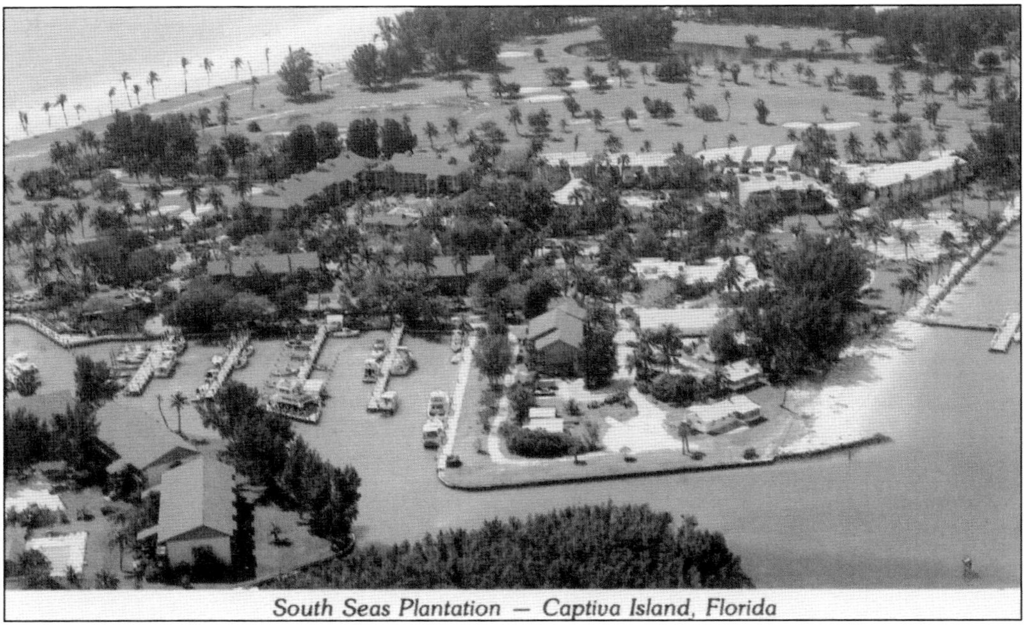

South Seas Plantation began with a nine-hole golf course and later expanded to 18 holes. In this 1970s postcard, the resort was owned by Mariner Corporation, and many of the waterfront condominiums were not yet built. In 2004, Hurricane Charley, with 150-mile-per-hour winds, destroyed much of the resort. Today, the LXR Luxury resort is totally rebuilt and known as a popular family vacation destination. (Courtesy of Deborah Gleason collection.)

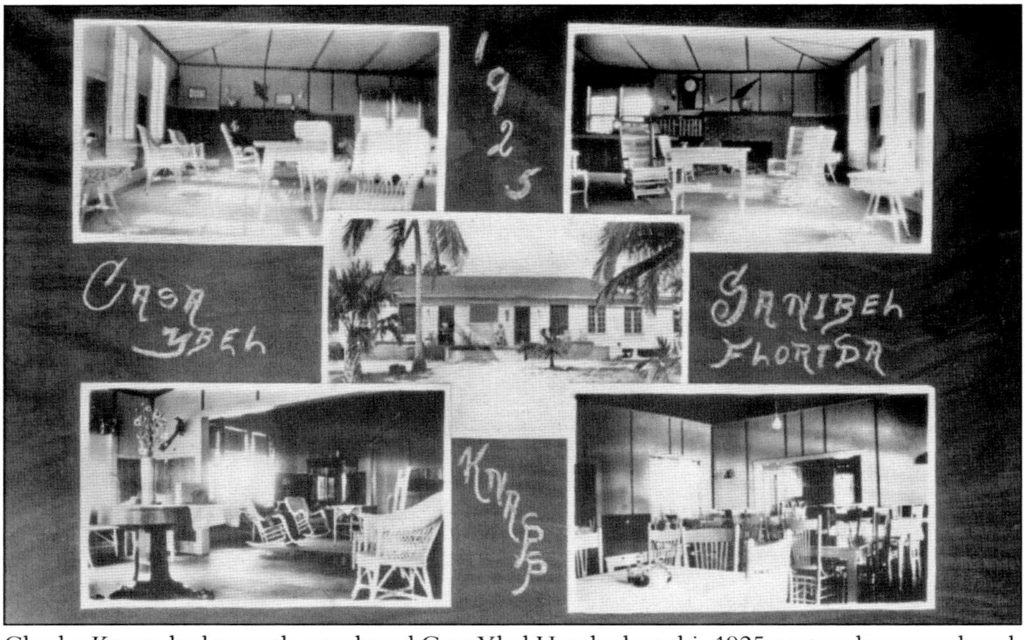

Charles Knapp had recently purchased Casa Ybel Hotel when this 1925 postcard was produced. Once named The Sisters, the Barnes family had been the original owners for over 30 years, building a church, cottages, and a grand home, Thistle Lodge. The hurricane of 1910 destroyed the Church of the Four Gospels, but the inn continued to attract sportsmen, adventurers, and shell collectors. (Courtesy of Islander Trading Post.)

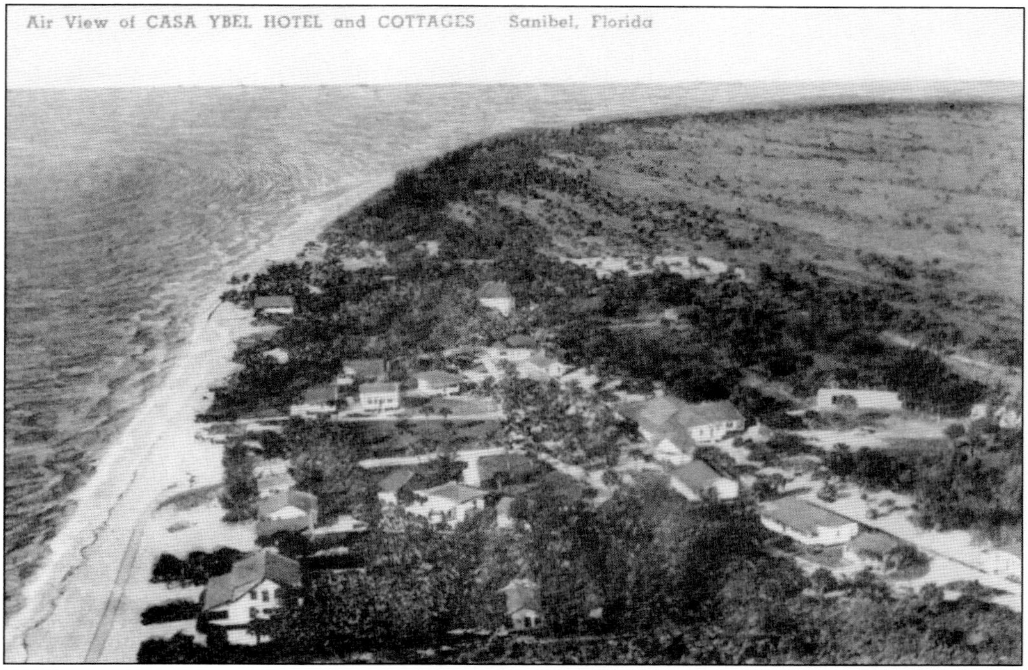

This aerial view of Casa Ybel Hotel shows the bend of the island known to some as Knapp's Point. The island was still relatively undeveloped at this time, with some farming still being attempted. The storm of 1926 had covered much of the island farmland with saltwater, making it unfit for commercial farming. The wagon trip from the bay-side docks across the island prairie to Casa Ybel sometimes took up to 40 minutes. (Courtesy of Charles LeBuff collection.)

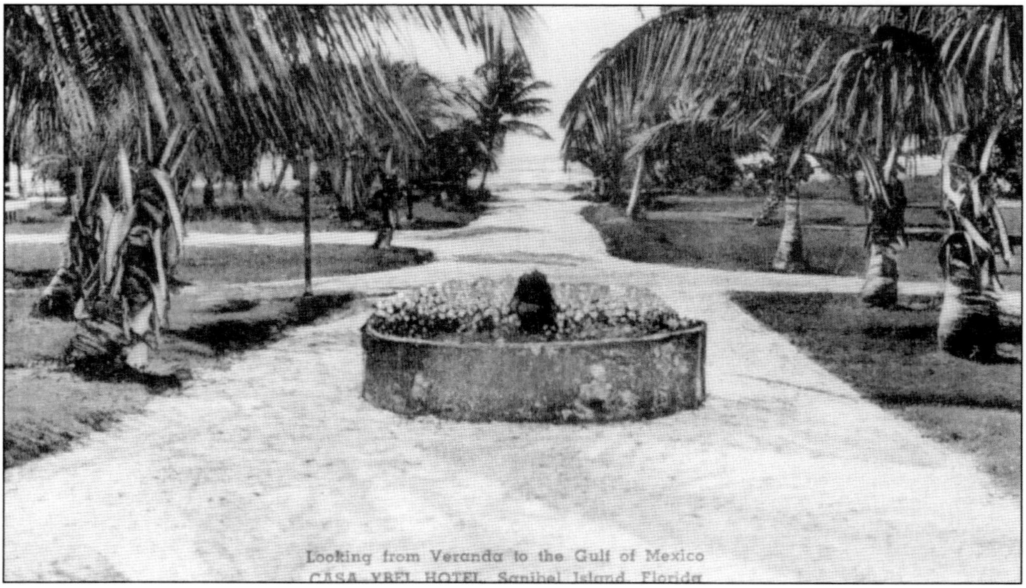

The Casa Ybel Hotel evolved with time and offered landscaped gardens, tennis, and even air service via seaplane. In the 1940s, Charlie Kohler offered the first seaplane service, and then Buddy Bobst brought Gulf Airways to shuttle passengers from Page Field to the shores of Casa Ybel. In the 1930s, the daily newspapers were also delivered via plane by Carl Dunn. (Courtesy of Islander Trading Post.)

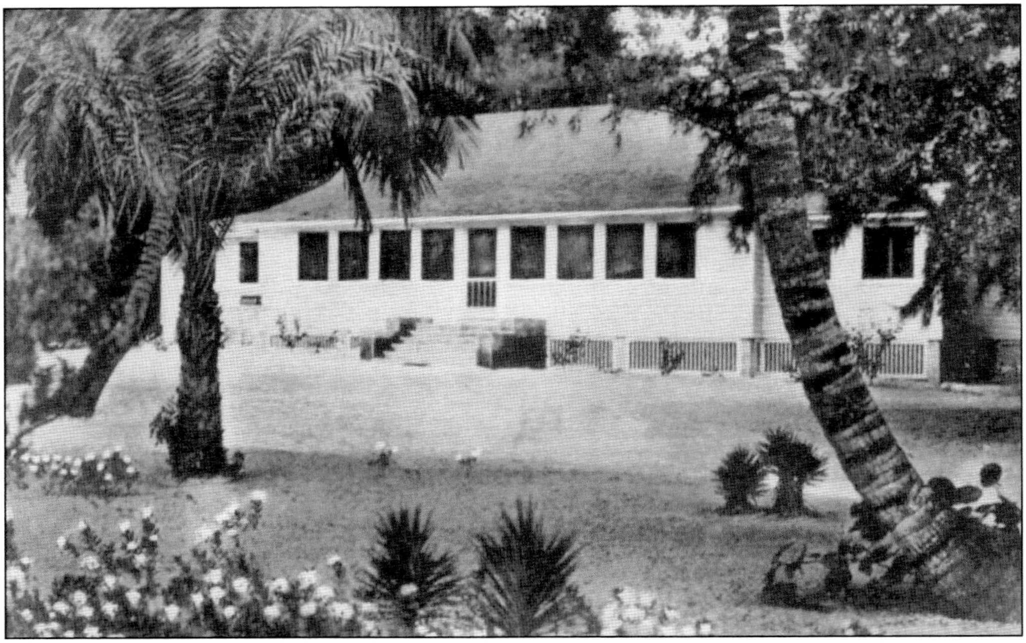

Cottages and other buildings at Casa Ybel were wisely raised up to allow tidal surge to pass under. The easiest plants to landscape with were the colorful periwinkles and dependable palms that lent an exotic feel to the grounds. In the 1940s, the joys of island life were vividly illustrated in publications like the *Saturday Evening Post* and *Life* magazine. (Courtesy of Alvin Lederer.)

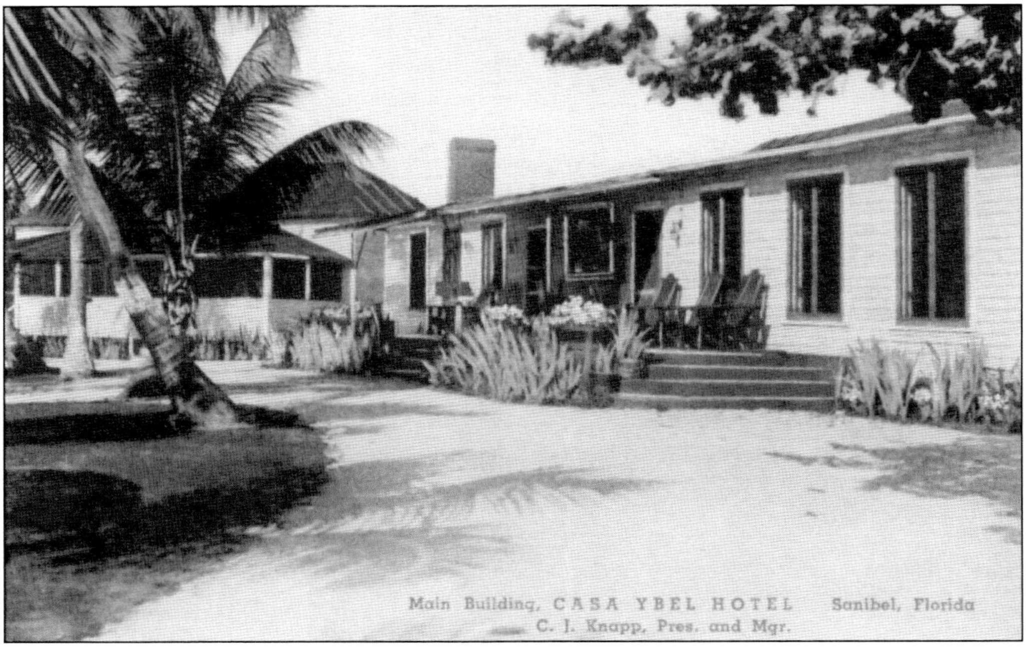

After leaving his Captiva Green Lawn Inn, Casa Ybel president and manager Charles Knapp put his heart and soul into his Gulf-front resort. During World War II, two of the cottages were renovated to be military quarters for those stationed on Sanibel, and practice targets were set up on the beach for planes. Sentries were in place to warn unsuspecting islanders of scheduled target practice. (Courtesy of Ralph Curtis.)

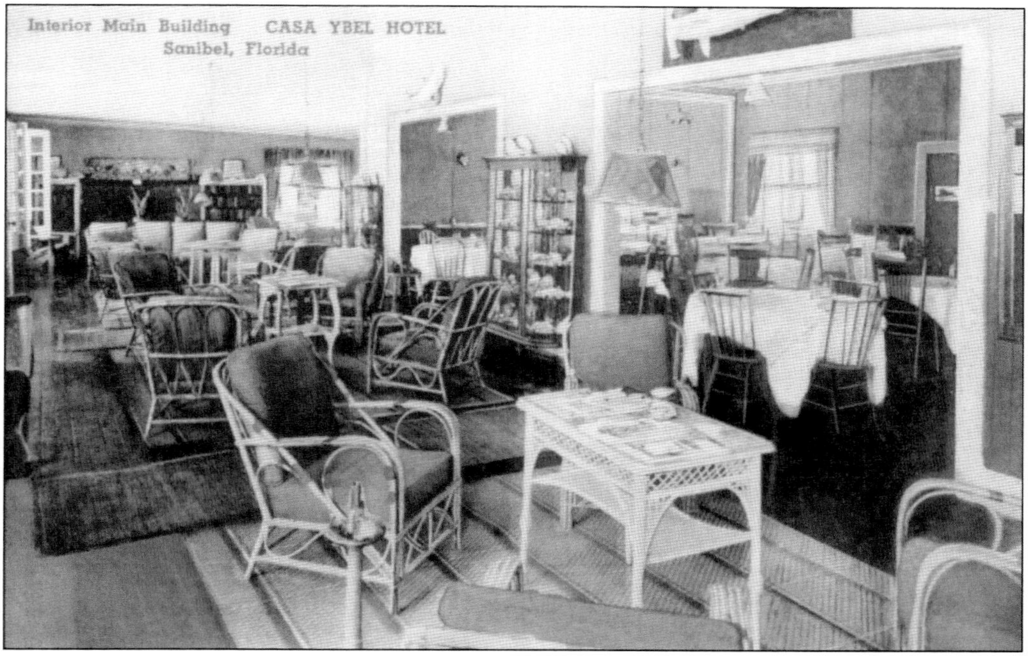

The interiors of Casa Ybel and The Island Inn were very similar, with wicker and rattan furniture being the practical choice. Guests gathered together for dining, socializing, and entertainment. The first shell show is said to have been at The Sisters, or Casa Ybel. The Matthews also had such shell shows, and in 1931, they were combined as an island-wide event at the Sanibel Community House. (Courtesy of Islander Trading Post.)

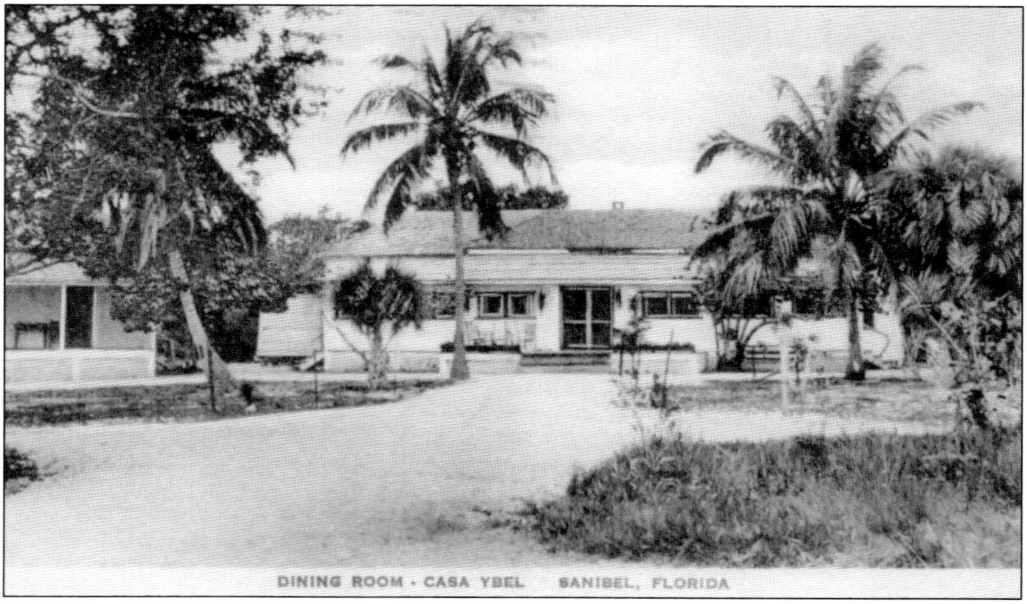

The buildings at Casa Ybel were wisely built with hip rooflines, increasing their chances of survival in the summer storm season. The cistern shown to the left of the dining room was for the collection of rainwater, the preferred drinking source. Many inns had wells to produce water for bathing and other uses, but the sulfur smell was usually too strong for even making lemonade. (Courtesy of Islander Trading Post.)

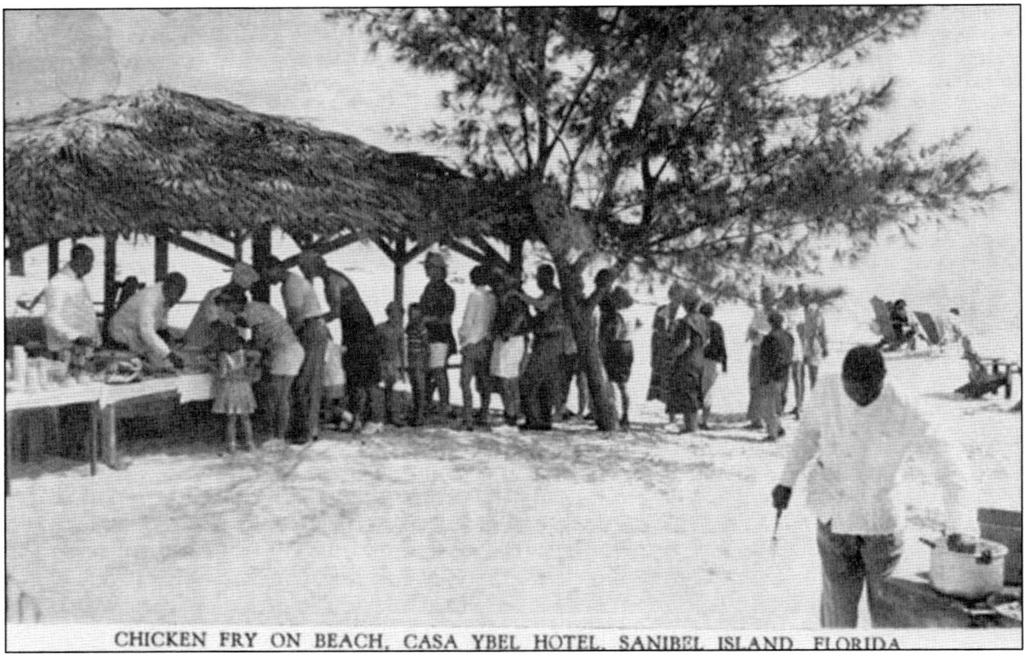

Beachside dining was a favorite at Casa Ybel after the Howard Dayton Hotel chain purchased it in 1946. There were palm frond pavilions and outdoor barbecue pits for food preparation and serving. The competent kitchen staff always wore white, bringing a touch of sophistication to the outdoor feast. (Courtesy of Islander Trading Post.)

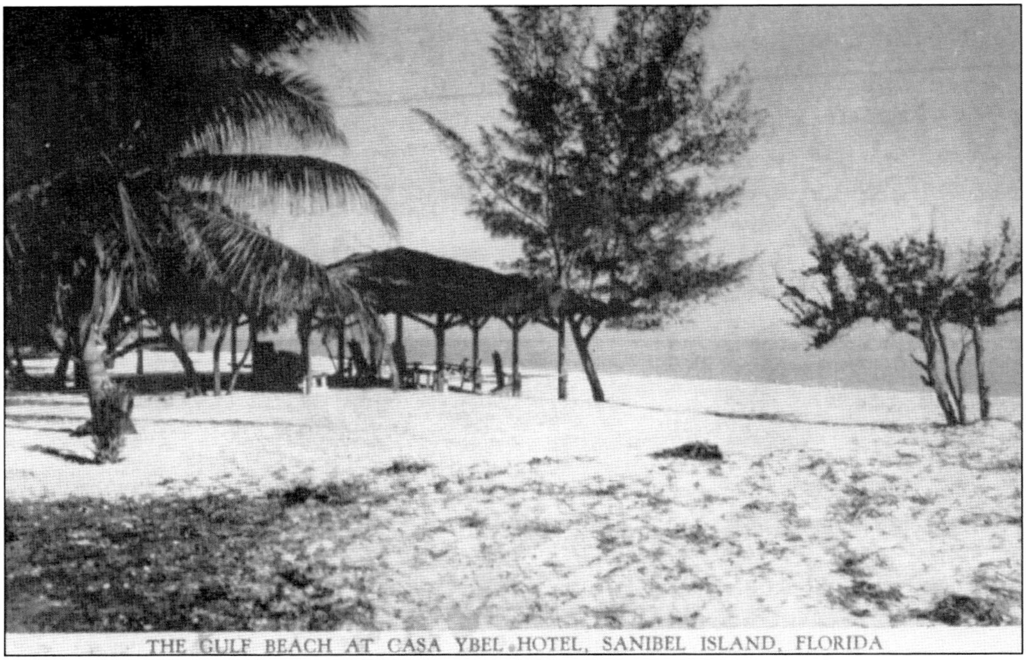

The palm frond pavilion, or hut, was a favorite at all island motels and inns. It gave shelter to those with sunburnt shoulders and offered a cool spot to nap while enjoying the Gulf breeze. Those huts, often built close to the high-tide mark, are now prohibited as they present obstacles to the many sea turtles that nest on the beaches in the summer. (Courtesy of Islander Trading Post.)

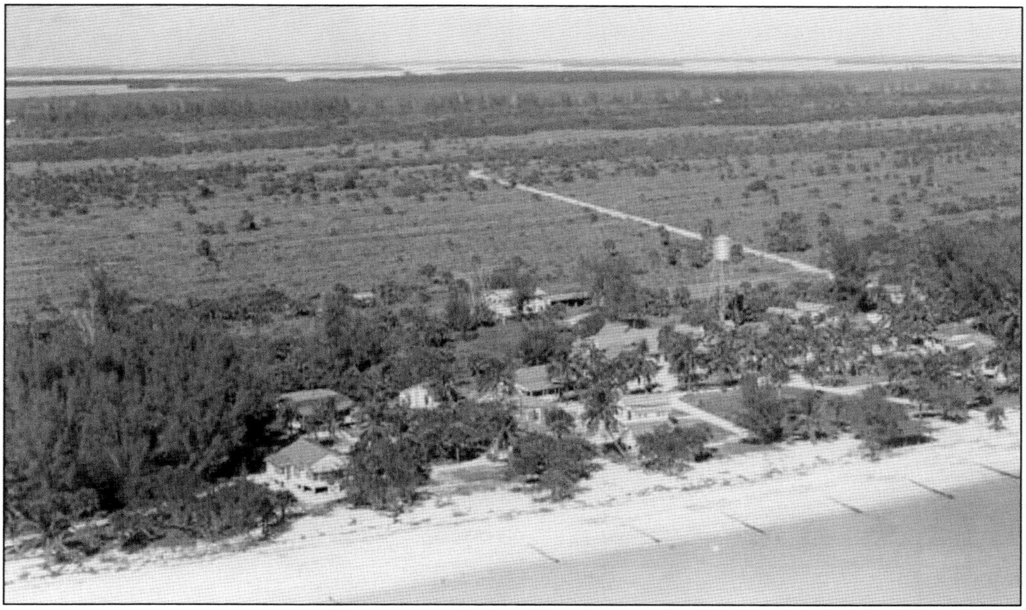

Casa Ybel is the oldest continually operating inn on the islands, and the collection of buildings grew with each new owner. The water tower shown was necessary to bring plumbing into the main buildings and cottages. Central water was not offered on Sanibel until after 1965. The isolation of Casa Ybel Hotel is notable as no other buildings are visible on the vast island prairie and wetland landscape. (Courtesy of Alvin Lederer.)

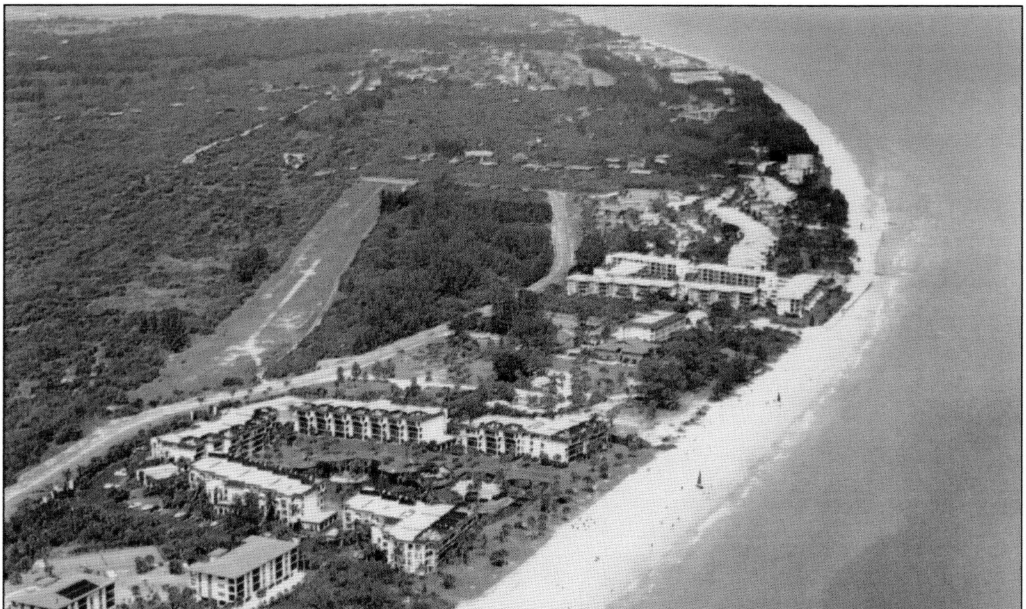

This late-1970s postcard shows the final days of the Casa Ybel airstrip. Howard Dayton, the third owner of Casa Ybel, astutely developed a grass landing strip behind the hotel, bringing many airborne, adventurous, and usually wealthy visitors. The Pointe Santo Condominium project was built without concern for the safety of the airstrip, and in 1979, the FAA shut down all usage of it. (Courtesy of Deborah Gleason collection.)

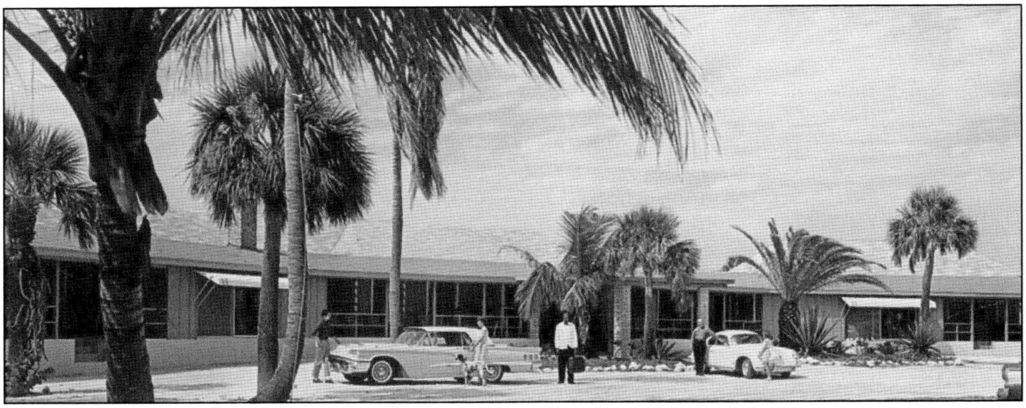

Casa Ybel was brought into the world of more glamorous hotels when it became part of the Howard Dayton Hotel chain. Electricity came to the islands in 1941, household telephone service 20 years later, and during the 1950s, the hotel offered a landing strip and marina facilities at Tarpon Bay. The hotel was sold to the Mariner Corporation in 1977. They introduced time-share ownership and sold the restaurant and common areas in 1990. (Courtesy of Sanibel Historical Museum and Village.)

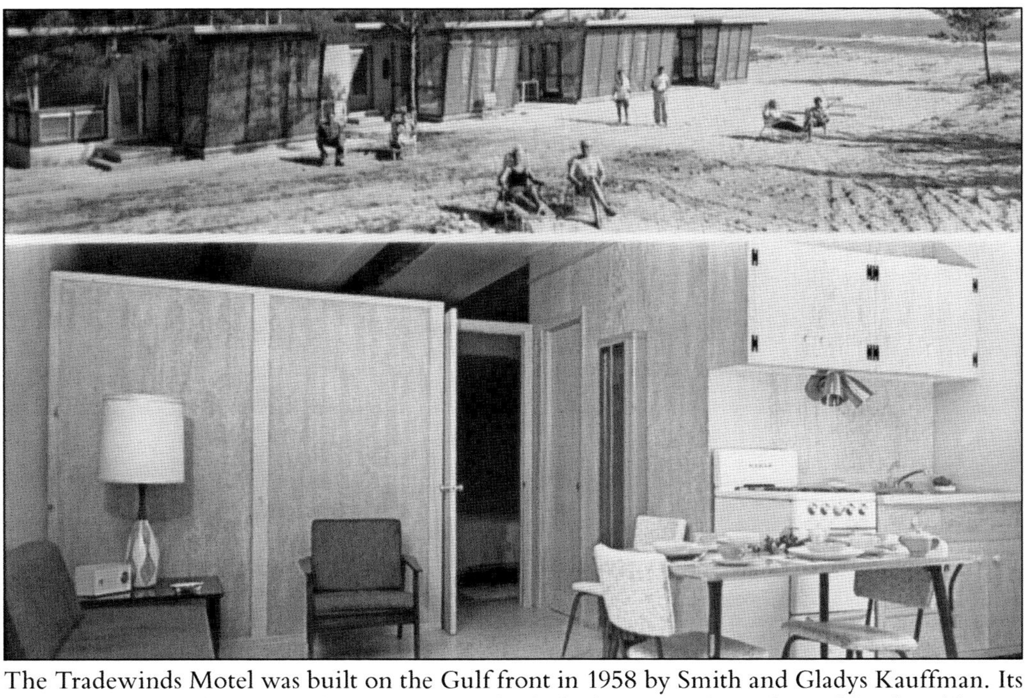

The Tradewinds Motel was built on the Gulf front in 1958 by Smith and Gladys Kauffman. Its modern design offered a kitchenette, private bath, bedroom, and porch. Unlike the old inns, guests were not expected to participate in social activities. The motel is known today as the Tropical Winds Motel. (Courtesy of Deborah Gleason collection.)

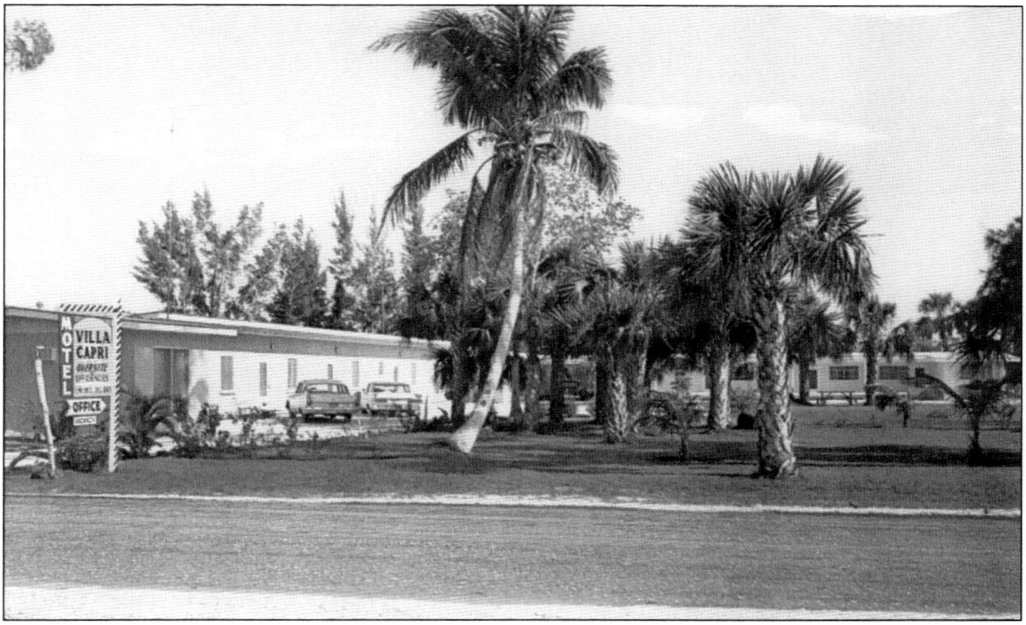

The Villa Capri Motel was a popular Periwinkle Way motel that offered rooms and efficiencies at a modest price. Built in 1958 by Marshall and Hazel Tabacchi of St. Louis, it appealed to those travelers not requiring a Gulf view. Marshall was an island character the day he arrived, and after retiring, he was an active island volunteer. The motel is now called the Anchor Inn. (Courtesy of Deborah Gleason collection.)

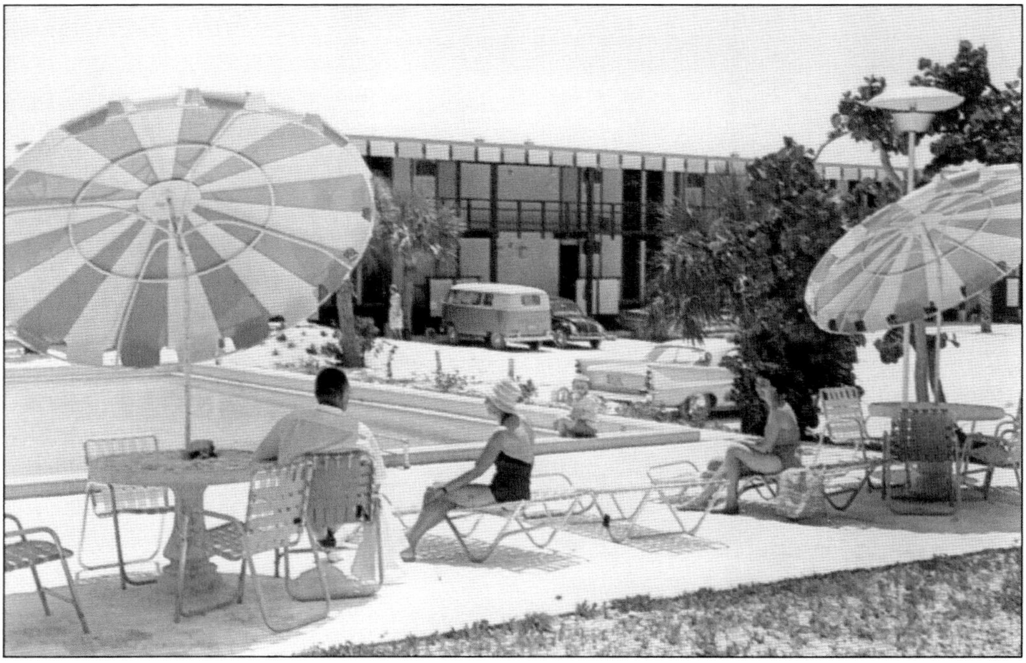

The Reef Motel was one of the last to be built on an island destined for condominiums. The motel was built by Finley Matthiessen in the early 1960s. The two-story multiunit buildings were considered progressive for Sanibel. But the owners knew the new causeway would bring more and more vacationers to Sanibel's once-quiet shores. (Courtesy of Deborah Gleason collection.)

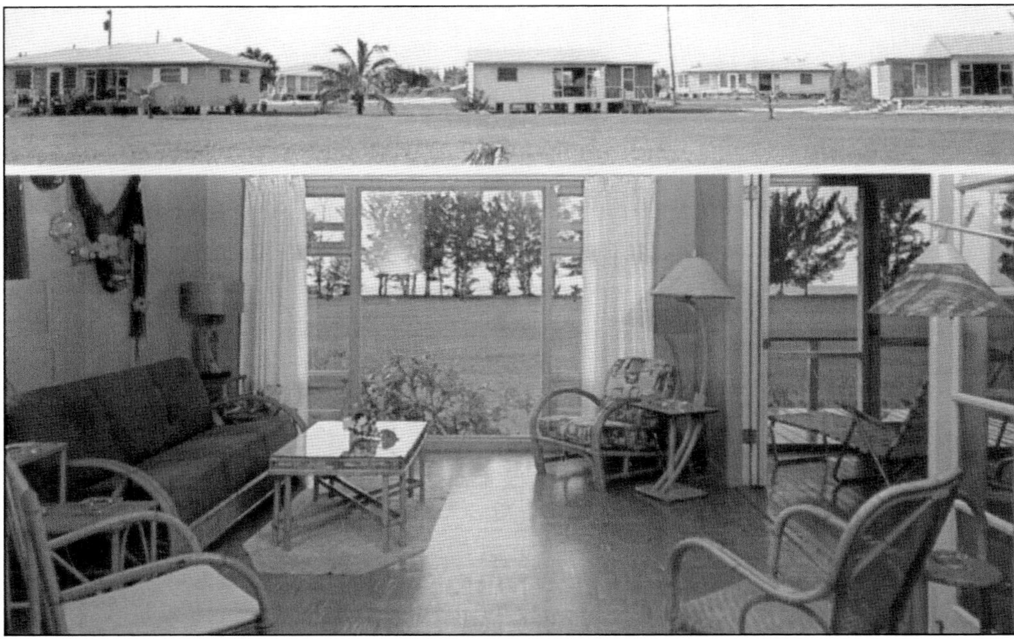

The Shell Basket was a group of cottages in the Las Conchas subdivision, built in the 1940s and 1950s. Most were used as seasonal homes and rentals. Typical for the day, they were elevated only three feet, enough for utility access and an occasional tidal surge. Several of them exist today and are used as private homes or as monthly rental homes. (Courtesy of the Islander Trading Post.)

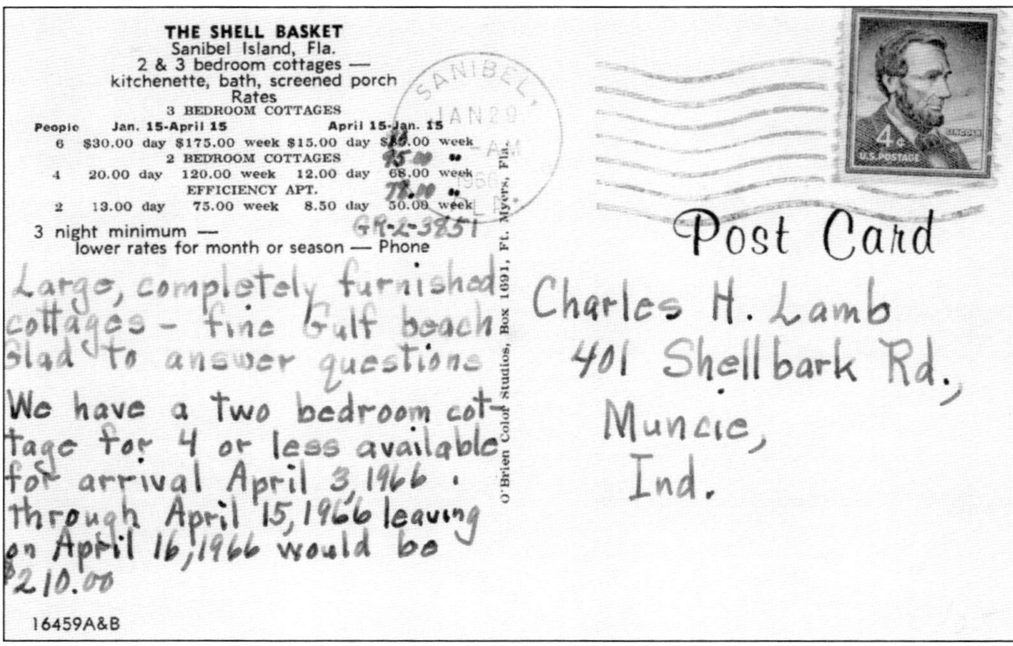

THE SHELL BASKET
Sanibel Island, Fla.
2 & 3 bedroom cottages —
kitchenette, bath, screened porch
Rates

People	Jan. 15-April 15		April 15-Jan. 15	
	3 BEDROOM COTTAGES			
6	$30.00 day	$175.00 week	$15.00 day	$80.00 week
	2 BEDROOM COTTAGES			
4	20.00 day	120.00 week	12.00 day	68.00 week
	EFFICIENCY APT.			
2	13.00 day	75.00 week	8.50 day	50.00 week

3 night minimum —
lower rates for month or season — Phone GR-2-3251

Large, completely furnished cottages - fine Gulf beach Glad to answer questions
We have a two bedroom cottage for 4 or less available for arrival April 3, 1966 through April 15, 1966 leaving on April 16, 1966 would be $210.00

O'Brien Color Studios, Box 1691, Ft. Myers, Fla.

SANIBEL JAN 29 1966

Post Card

Charles H. Lamb
401 Shellbark Rd.,
Muncie,
Ind.

16459A&B

The addressee had most likely inquired as to the availability of a cottage in April 1966. Three-bedroom rental cottages were uncommon, and the weekly rate of $175 for a three-bedroom and $120 for a two-bedroom would be less than a daily rate today. The phone number started with GR, the GReenleaf exchange on Sanibel before 472 and the additional 395 and 579 exchanges, which came much later to keep pace with growth. (Courtesy of the Islander Trading Post.)

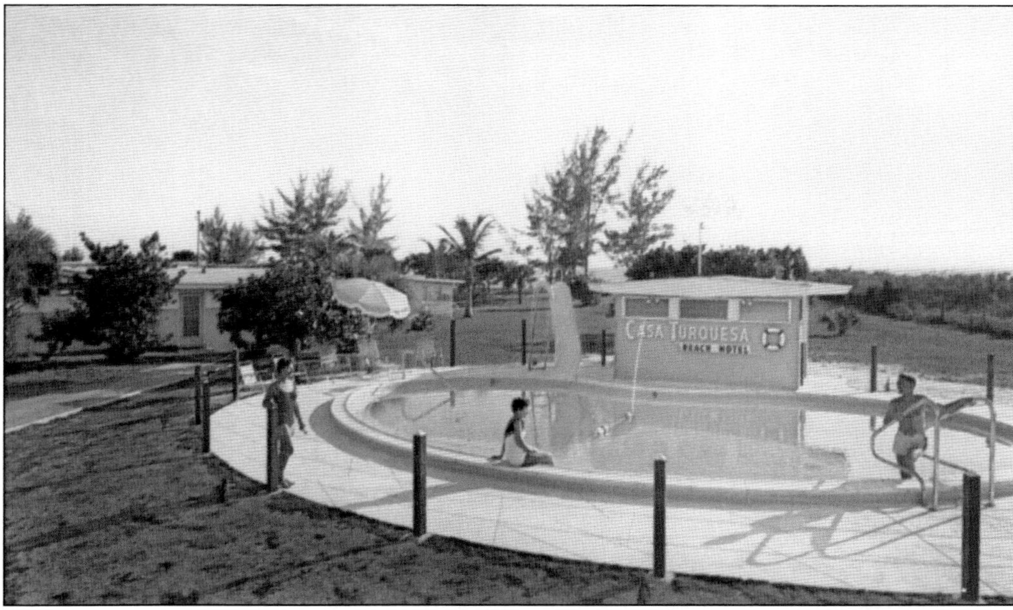

Casa Turquesa, a West Gulf Drive motel, was built in 1953 by Jim and Jeane Jack, who moved from Michigan with their children, Linda and Jim. The Jacks were active community volunteers, and Jim Sr. was a charter member of the pre-incorporation Sanibel Island Planning and Zoning Authority. They sold their property in 1970, and it exists today as Forty/Fifteen, still a motel. (Courtesy of Deborah Gleason collection.)

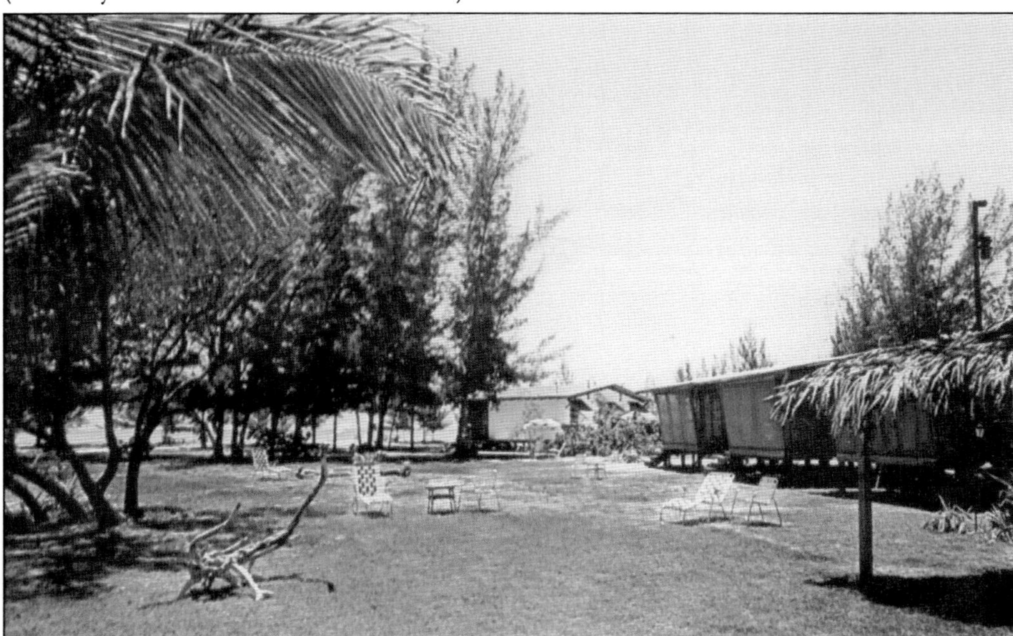

Mike and Dorothy McQuade and their children, Judy, Mark, and Debbie (coauthor Deb Gleason), traveled from Baltimore, Maryland, to buy five acres of Sanibel Gulf-front property in 1957. Over the next 15 years, Mike built 12 cottages before selling his property to a group of investors. Within two years, they had started removal of the cottages and the building of today's Sanibel Siesta Condominium. (Courtesy of Deborah Gleason collection.)

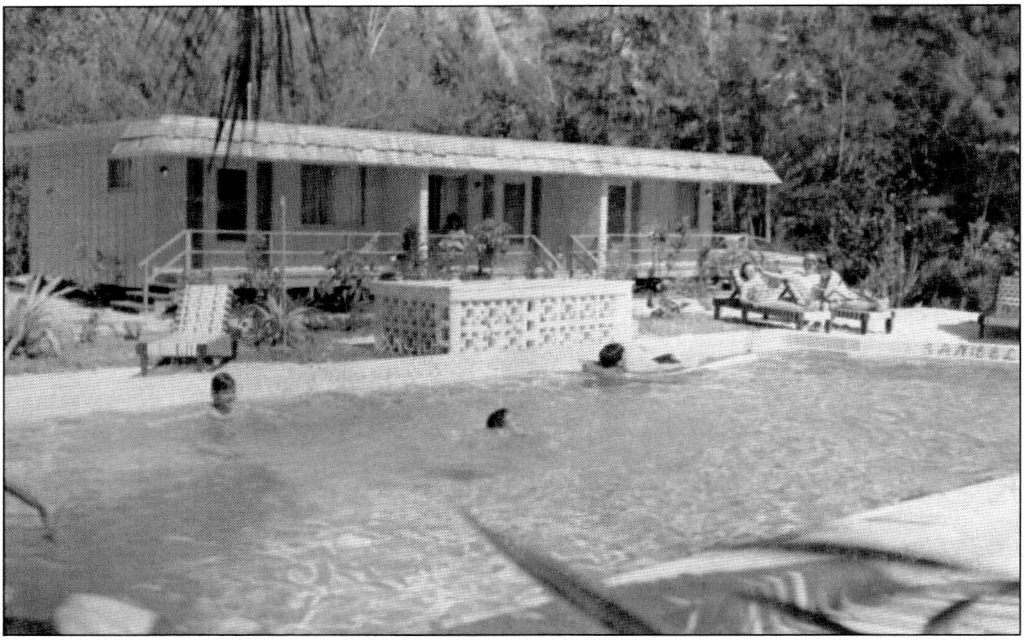

Like many other mom-and-pop motels of the 1950s and 1960s, the Sanibel Siesta motel thrived during the winter season and strived to make ends meet in the summer. The pool was a 1965 improvement that appealed to vacationing families, but many early motels offered just the simple joys of sun, surf, and shuffleboard. This motel also offered the islands first bike and beach equipment rentals. (Courtesy of Deborah Gleason collection.)

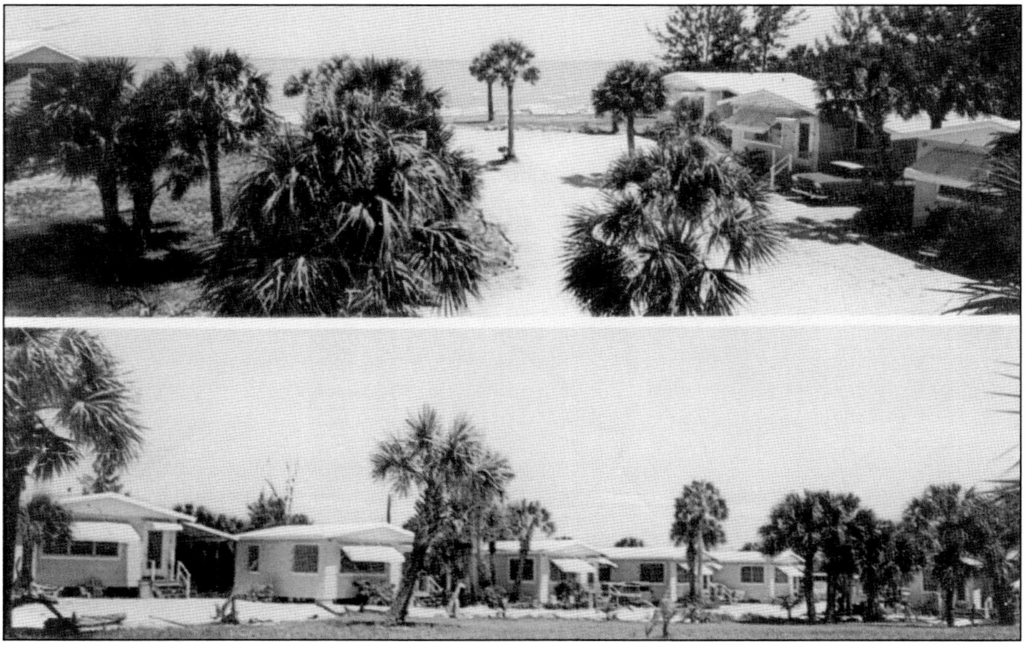

Sanibel Cottages, located on the Gulf at Knapp's Point, were owned by Floyd and Blanche Pflough. They arrived in 1957 and grew their two existing cottages to 12. The motel sold in 1971, and the Pfloughs retired for the third time. The cottages were removed, and a time-share condominium project using the same name was built. (Courtesy of Deborah Gleason collection.)

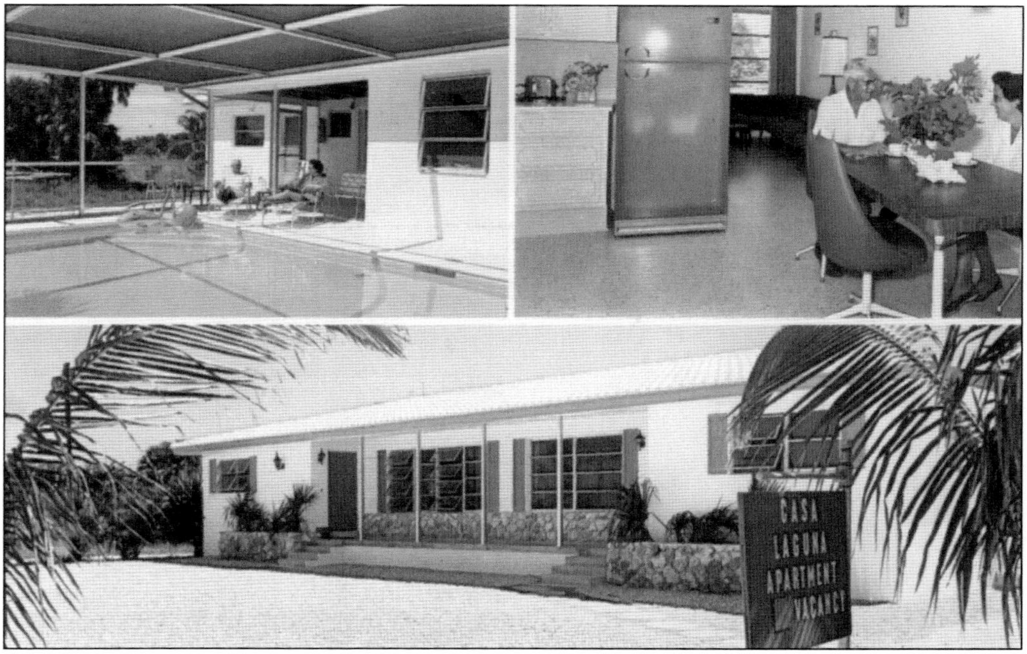

Casa Laguna offered rental duplex apartments on Sanibel's eastern end in the 1960s. While they were not Gulf front, they were canal front and only a short walk to the beach. Owned by the Walthers family, they were sold in the 1970s and are now owned and used as a private home. (Courtesy of the Islander Trading Post.)

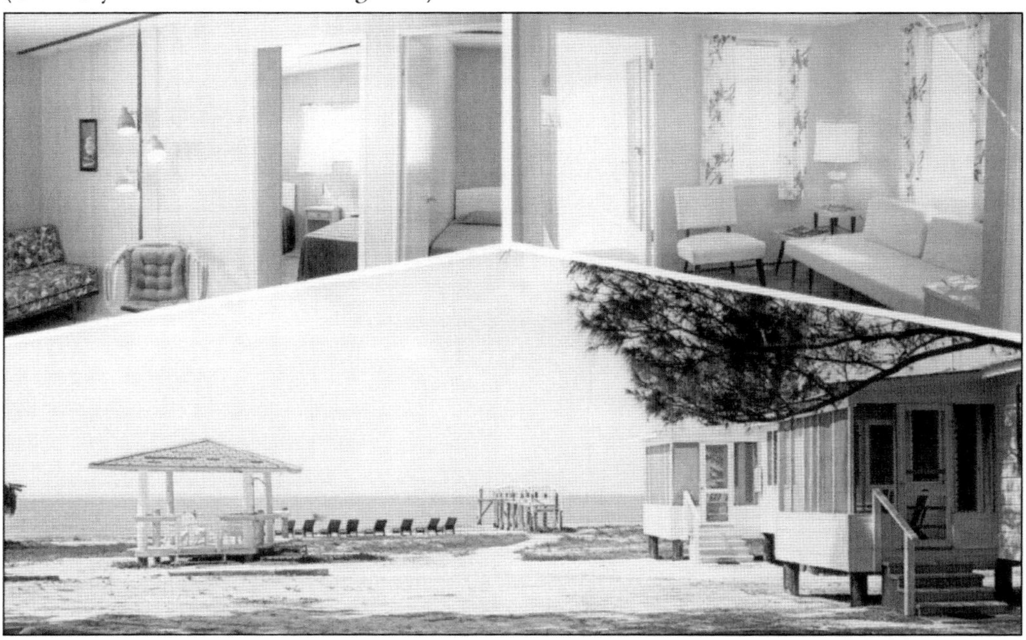

Buchanan's Surf 'n Sand cottages were tucked away at the end of Shell Basket Lane. Fishing piers like Buchanan's were built over the years, and hurricanes routinely destroyed them. This one was largely ineffective, as it only went into five feet of water on high tides. The remaining pilings were removed after the Zajicek family bought the property. They later sold to a condominium project known as Plantation Village. (Courtesy of the Islander Trading Post.)

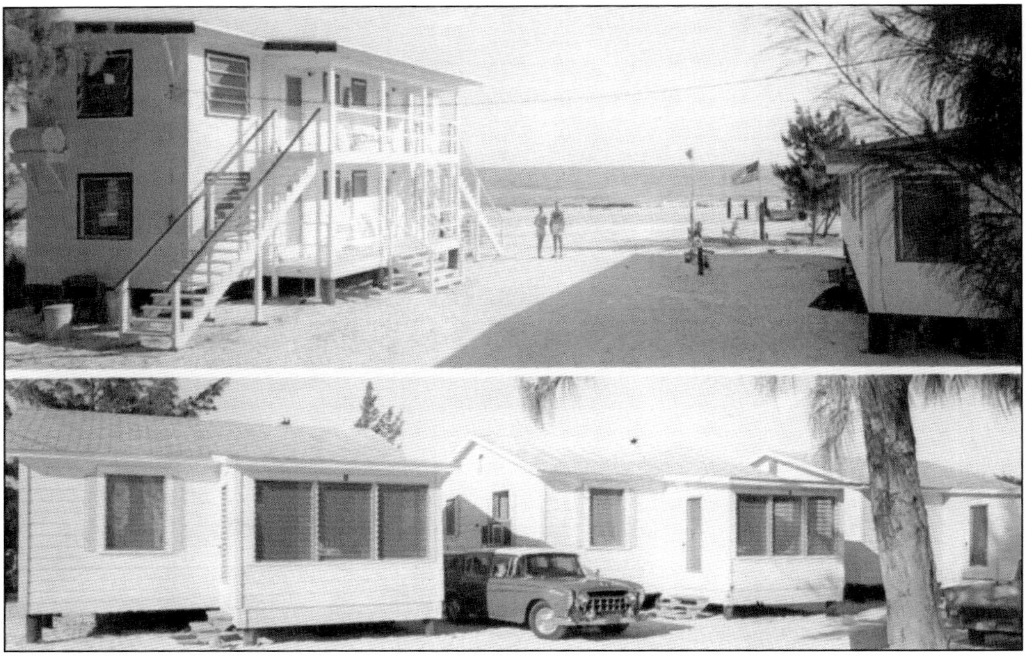

Funk's Gulf Breeze Cottages were located next to Buchanan's Surf 'n Sand on the Gulf beach. They were owned and operated by Lew and Mary Funk and their son Jerry. The motel was sold in the 1970s, and it is one of only a few vintage motels still operating today, as Gulf Breeze Cottages and Motel. (Courtesy of Deborah Gleason collection.)

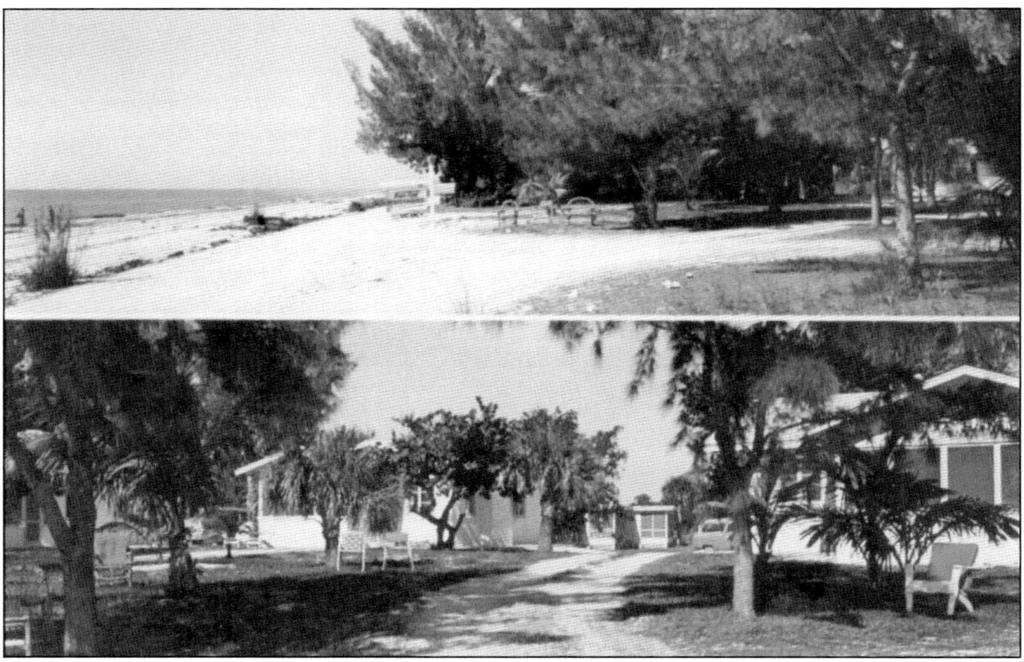

Tom and Barbara Billheimer and their three sons, Jon, Michael, and Kimball, came to join family members on Sanibel in 1956. They opened the High Tide Motel when Gulf Drive was beachside. They sold their motel in 1971, and it too became a condominium project. Michael now owns Lighthouse Café on Sanibel's east end. (Courtesy of Tom Hoopes.)

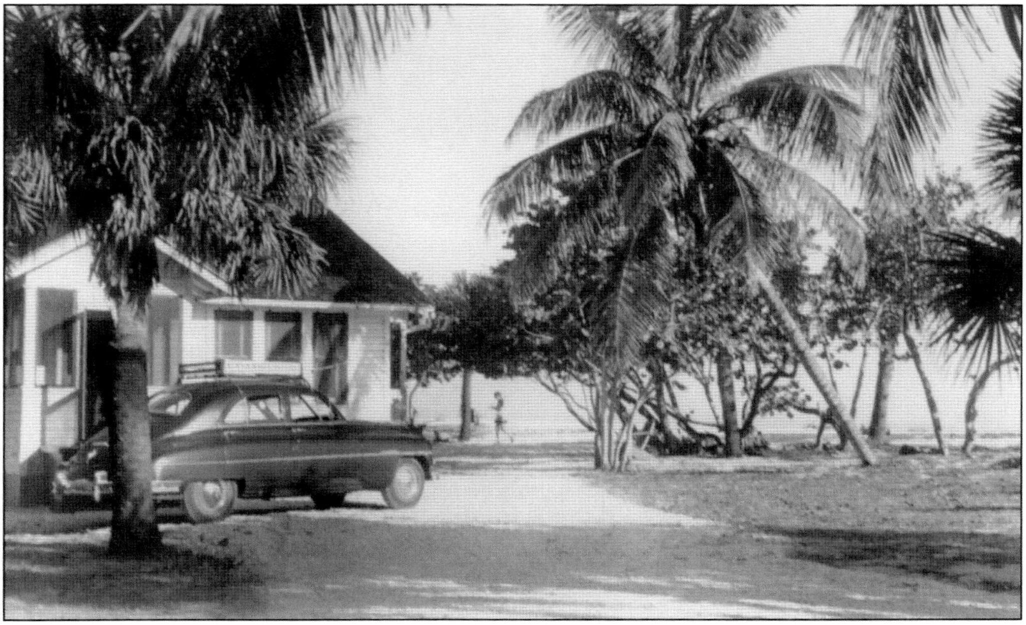

This island cottage is not identified, but it could easily be on either island. Francis Bailey, native son and kin to the owners of The Island Inn, said, "The best we could offer folks was nothing." It was indeed the simple cottages and natural surroundings that attracted guests like Anne Morrow Lindbergh, who wrote *Gift From The Sea* during her many stays on Captiva. (Sanibel Public Library.)

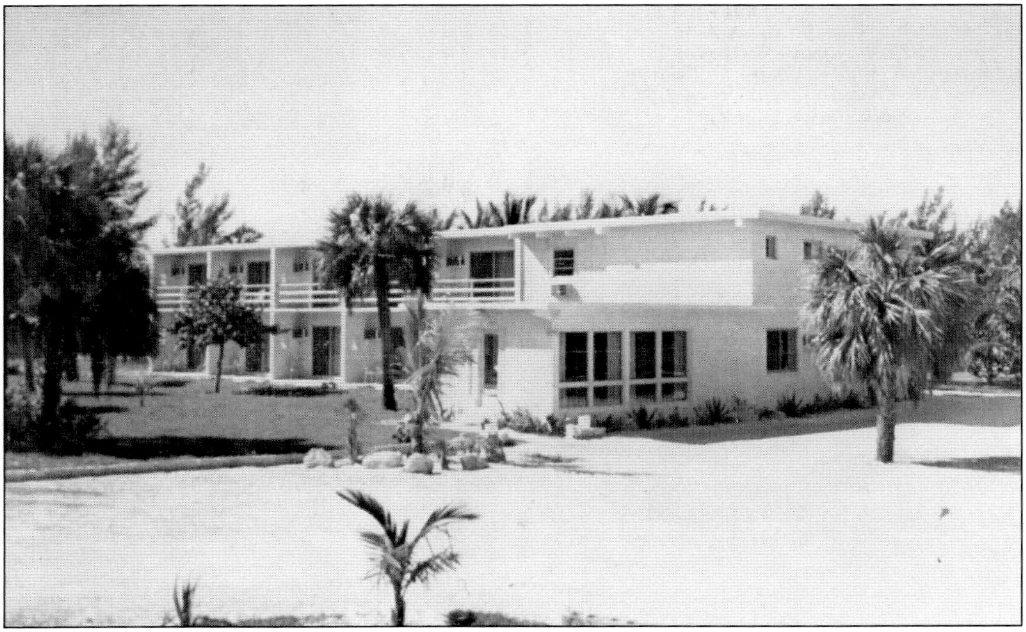

The Caribe Adventure was a West Gulf Drive motel that John Wright opened in the 1960s. The fill for the building site was dug out on the beach with a dragline and moved inland to bring the property to grade for construction—a common practice back in those days but now illegal. It was sold and eventually became a time-share property. It continues to operate today as The Caribe. (Courtesy of the Islander Trading Post.)

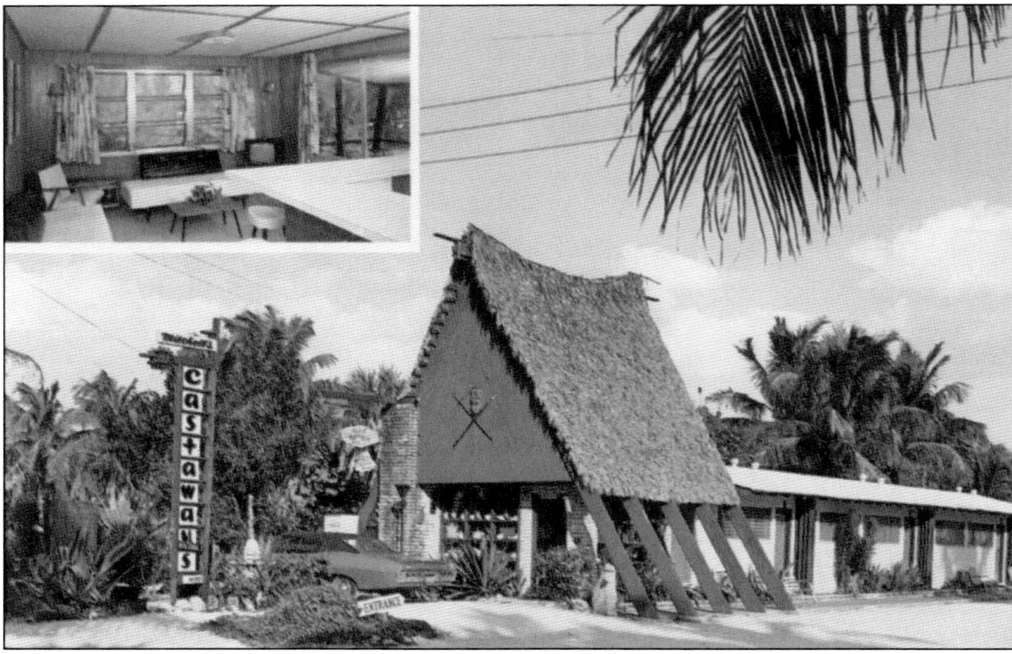

Around 1920, William and Stella Mitchell moved their family to Sanibel. The Mitchell's two-story home still stands on Sanibel near the Blind Pass Bridge. Their son Dean Mitchell opened Castaways Motel and Marina in the early 1950s and Mitchell's Sand Castles in the 1960s. The property is now owned by Rochester Resorts. (Courtesy of Ralph Curtis.)

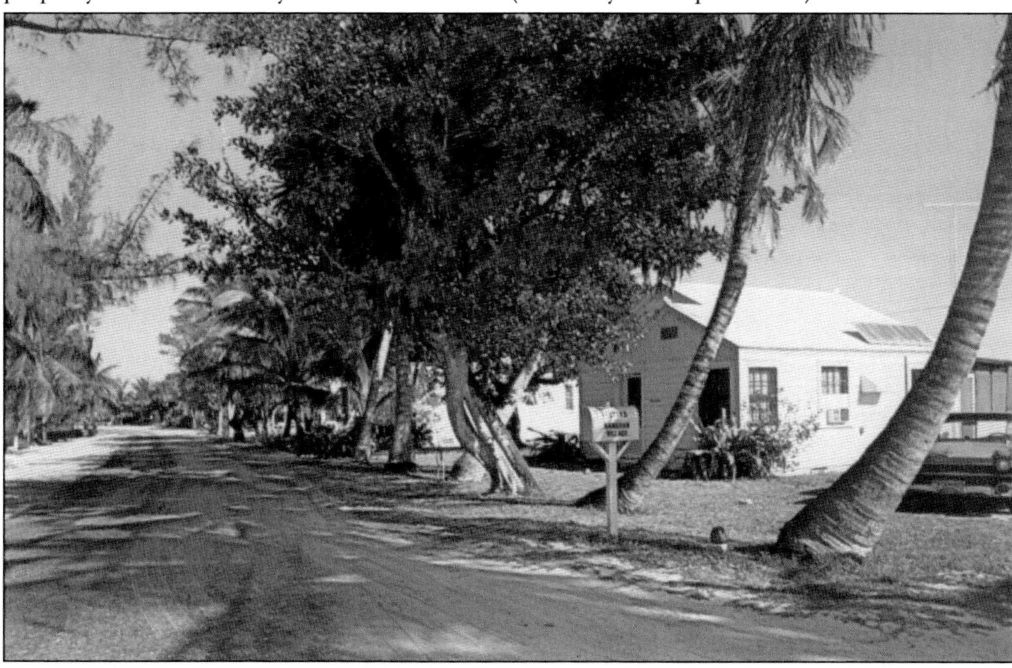

Betty's Hawaiian Village was a group of bay-front cottages and a small marina on Sunset Bay, a waterway that connected to Blind Pass adjacent to the Castaways Motel. Owned and managed by Betty Clements in the 1960s, it had previously been named Lowe's Cottages. The cottages are now part of Castaways Beach and Bay Cottages. (Courtesy of Islander Trading Post.)

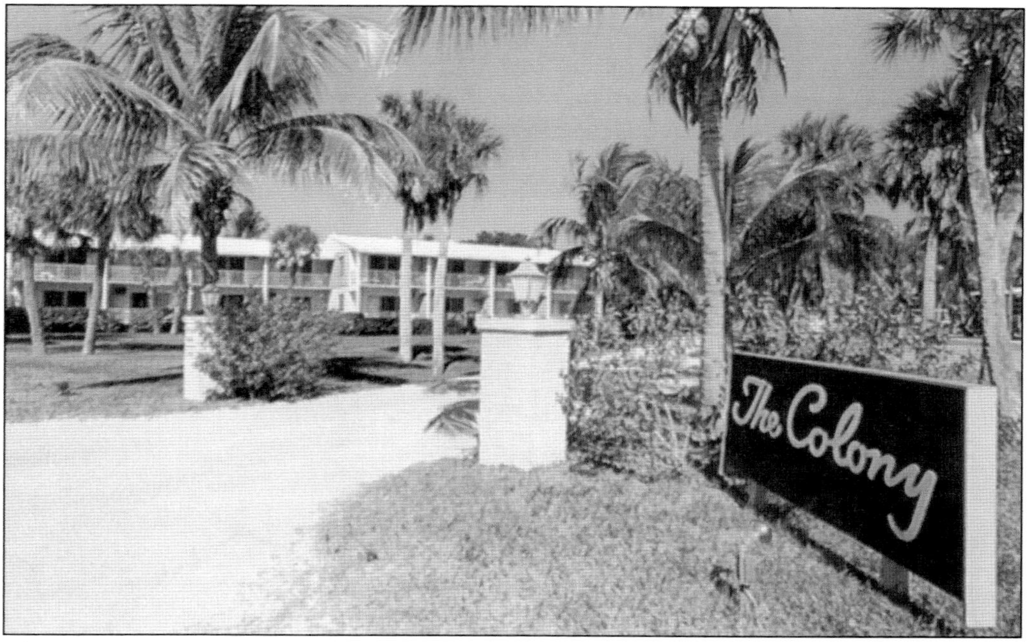

The Colony on Sanibel's eastern Gulf front was owned and operated by Bob and Kay Montieth. The property included housekeeping cottages and motel rooms. The property continues today, although many of the cottages have been privately sold and the motel rooms have been sold as condominiums. (Courtesy of Islander Trading Post.)

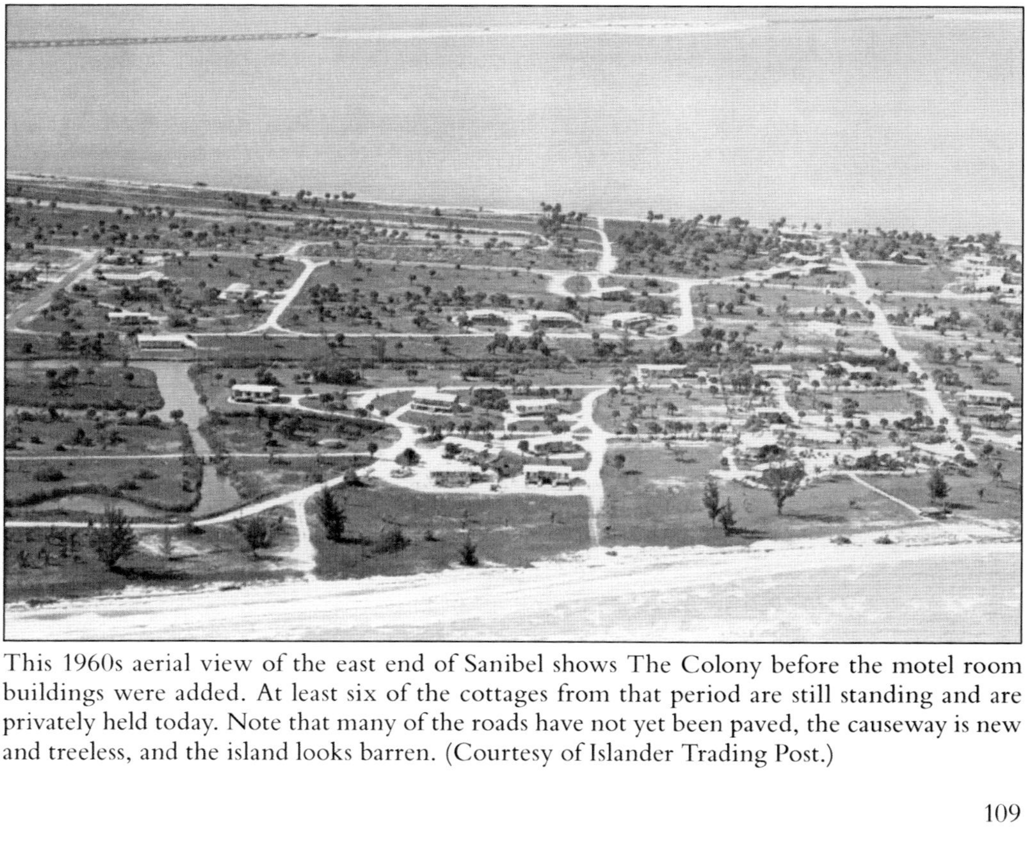
This 1960s aerial view of the east end of Sanibel shows The Colony before the motel room buildings were added. At least six of the cottages from that period are still standing and are privately held today. Note that many of the roads have not yet been paved, the causeway is new and treeless, and the island looks barren. (Courtesy of Islander Trading Post.)

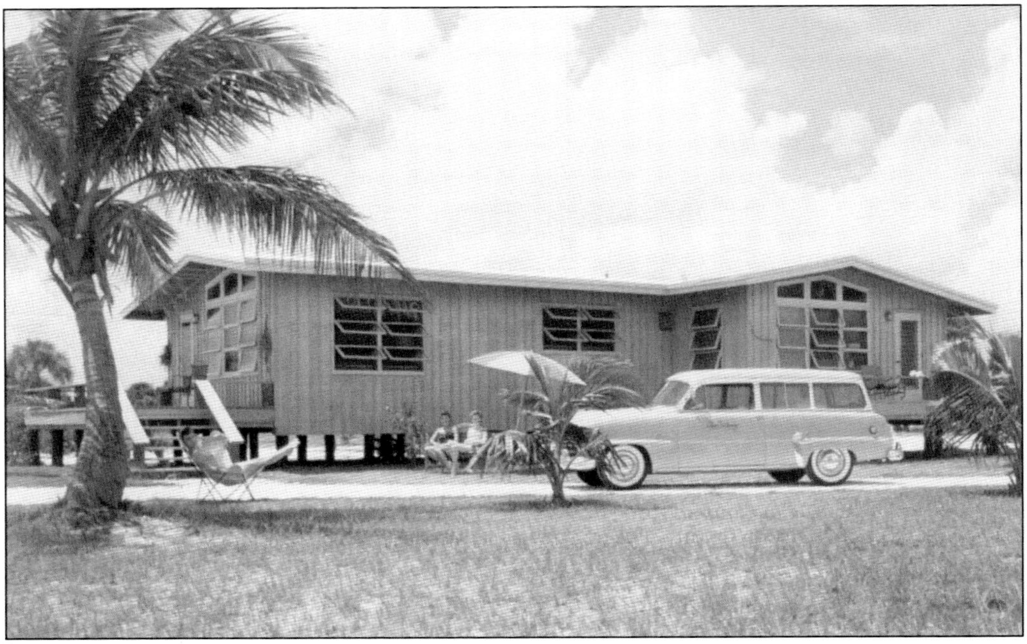

This classic cottage at The Colony was not Gulf front but was within easy walking distance to the beach. Many cottages of that day did not have air-conditioning or even television. People came to Sanibel for a simple escape from the mainland. (Courtesy of Islander Trading Post.)

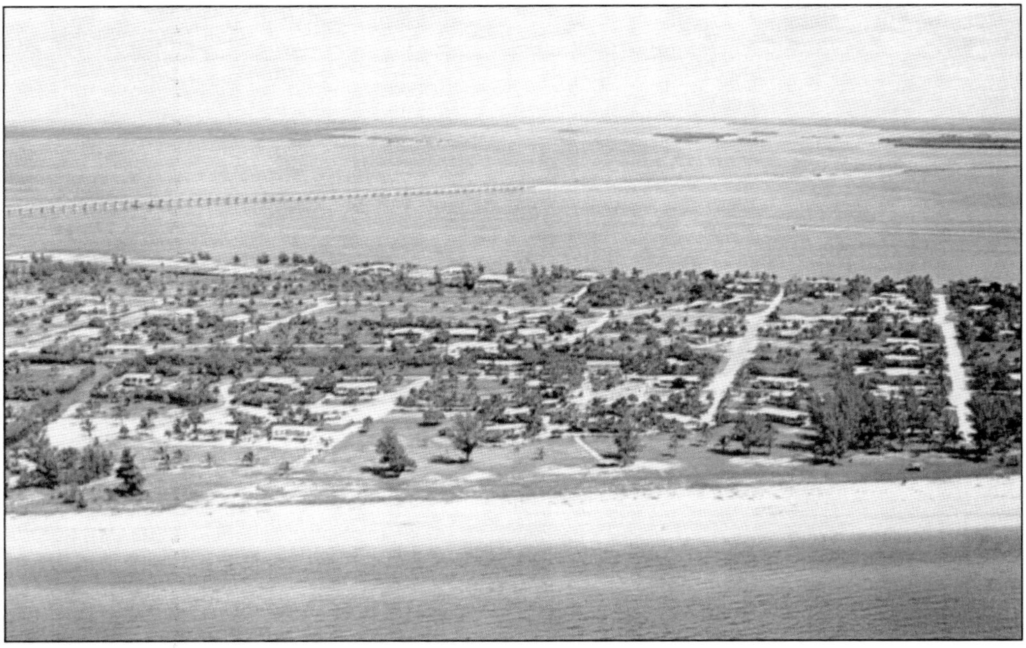

Another 1960s aerial view of the east end of Sanibel includes Buttonwood Lane. Today's Gulf-front and bay-front mansions are not yet imagined, much less constructed. The island's simple ambiance survived through much of the 1960s, but developers like Hugo Lindgren were busy digging canals and selling scores of residential lots. (Courtesy of Deborah Gleason collection.)

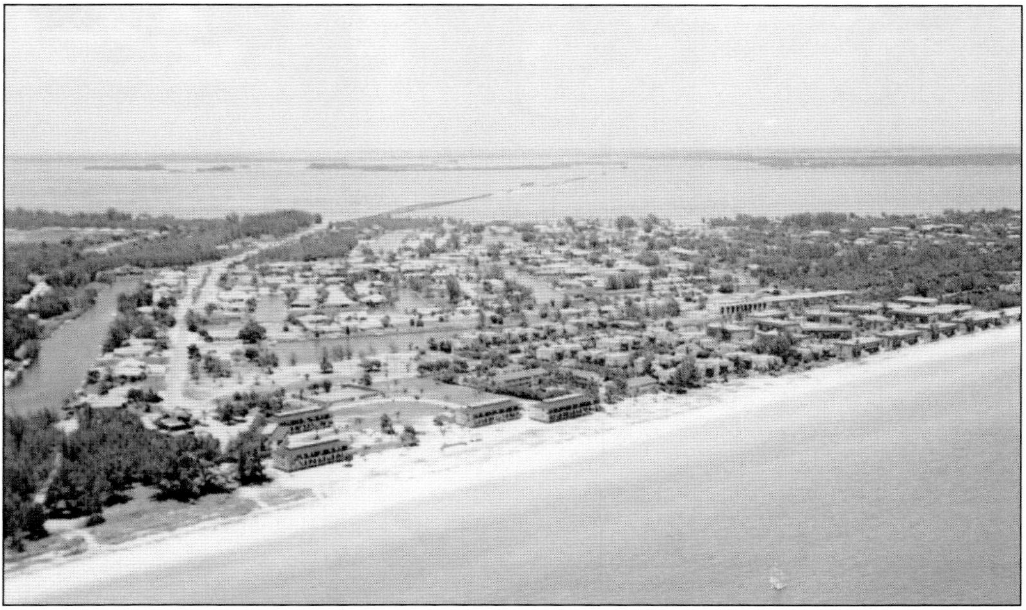

The 1970s were years of shocking change for many islanders. The Shell Harbor Inn was built, as was the Sanibel Arms and Sanibel Moorings condominiums. Shell Harbor subdivision was progressing quickly, and some old-timers worried that the new, complex canal system would weaken the east end of the island in a large hurricane. (Courtesy of Deborah Gleason collection.)

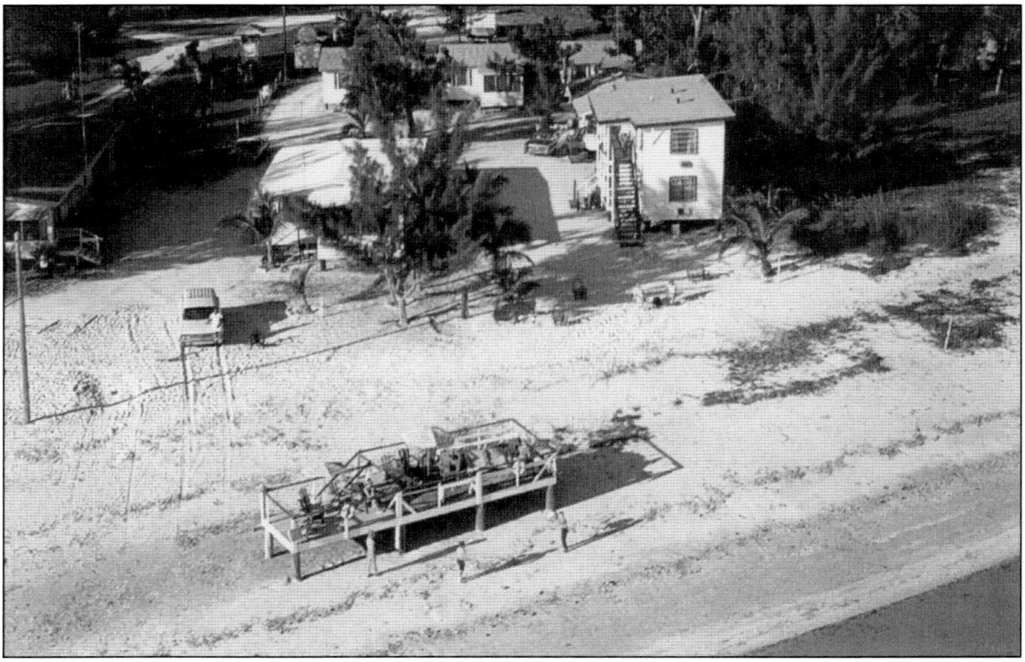

Funk's Gulf Breeze Motel was an assortment of frame cottages with a beachfront sunning platform. Perhaps it did keep some of the no-see-ums off sunbathers while the breeze circulated under the porch. Gulf Breeze Cottages is still operating today, offering vintage cottages and efficiency accommodations. (Courtesy of Deborah Gleason collection.)

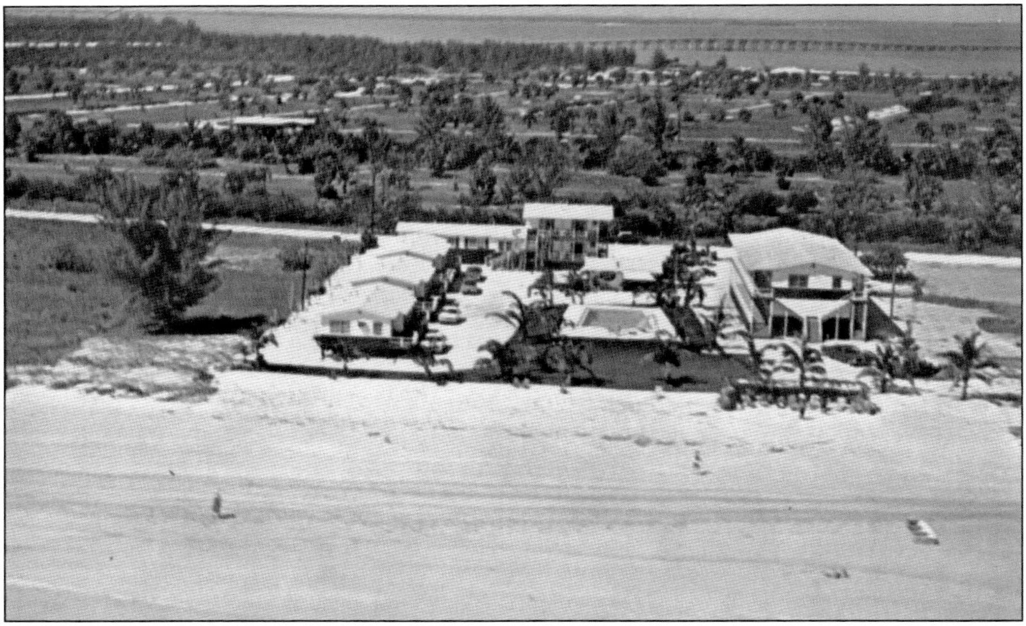

The Gallery Motel was established in 1960 by Dave and Rudy Holtzman. This motel is known today as the Seaside Inn. The Holtzmans came from New York with their children, Pam and Gary, and after the motel, they built the Shell Harbor Inn. The latter has since become the Sanibel Inn. The Holtzmans moved from Sanibel in the 1980s but kept a house on Captiva. (Courtesy of Sanibel Historical Museum and Village.)

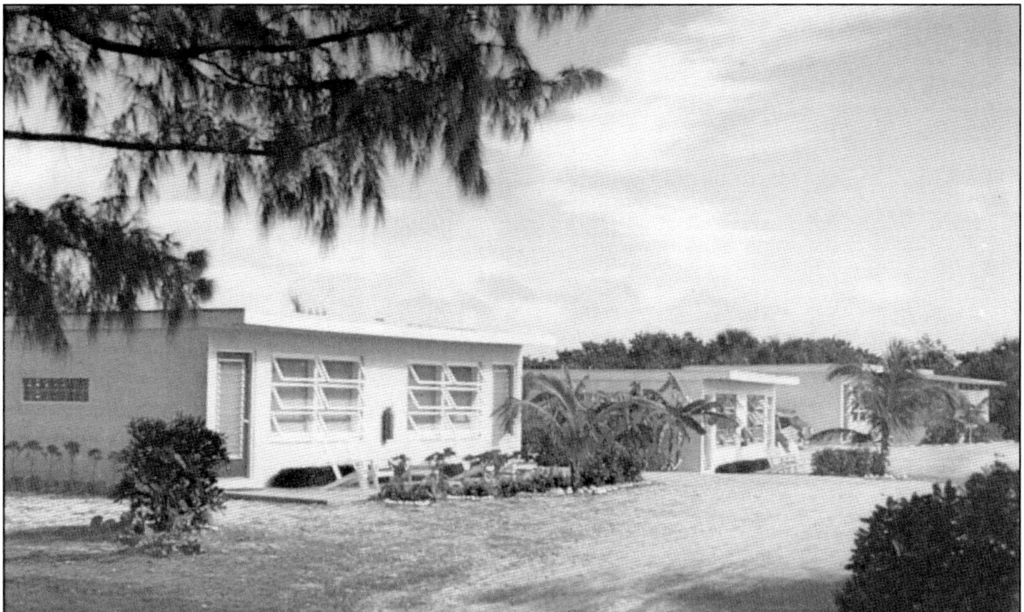

The Captiva Beach Motel and Apartments were located on the Gulf beach with the bay and a dock in the back. It was built and operated by H.K. "Jerry" and Dorothy Jeremiassen. The property was sold and became part of 'Tween Waters Resort in the 1970s. Many of the apartments were later demolished to make way for newer buildings. (Courtesy of Tom Hoopes.)

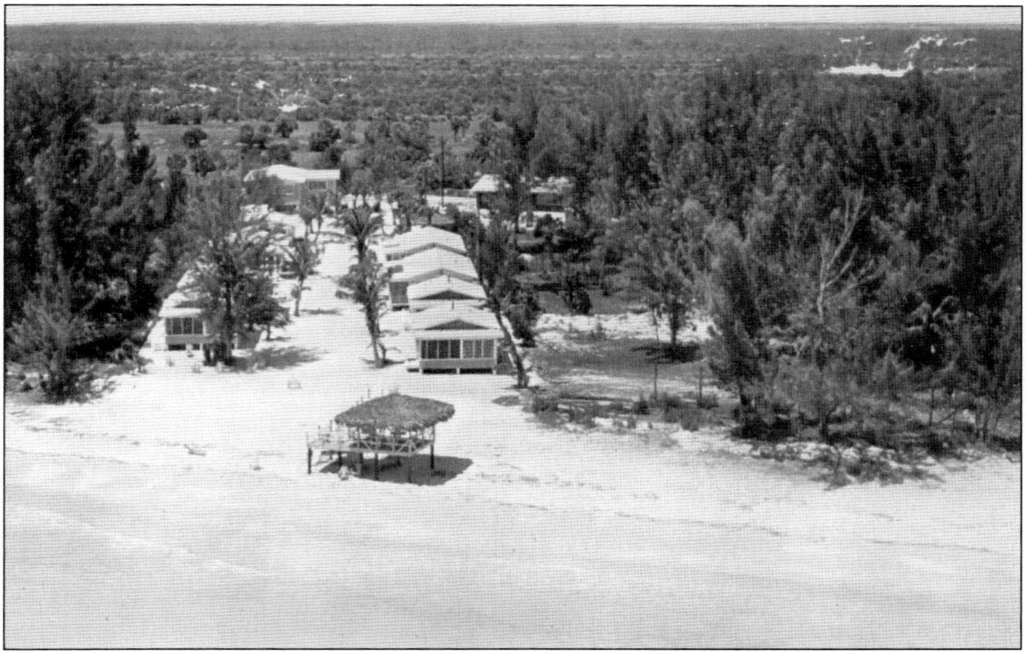

The Beachview Cottages were built and managed by Dave and Marge Wooster. They raised their family here, kids Bob, Linda, Janet, and Jeannie, and opened another island business, Wooster's TV. Both Beachview Cottages and Wooster's TV are still in business today under new ownership. (Courtesy of Deborah Gleason collection.)

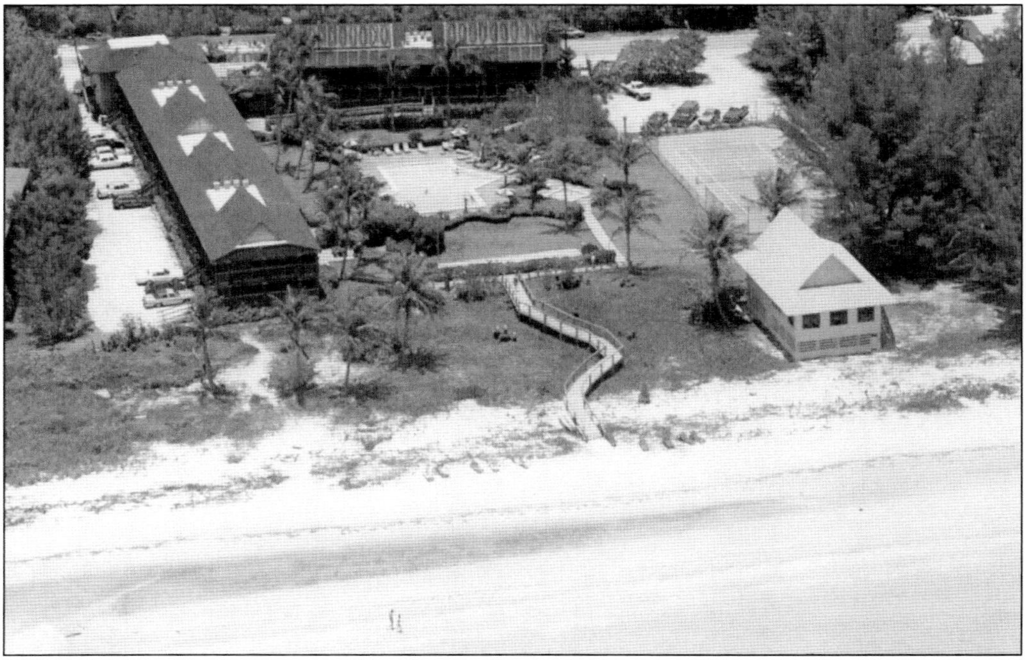

The Surfrider was a motel owned by Bill Such. It was built in the 1970s by Donald Hiers, who grew up on Sanibel and became a high-end builder. It was purchased by Captran Interval Resort in 1981 and continues as one of the remaining original time-share properties on Sanibel. (Courtesy of the Islander Trading Post.)

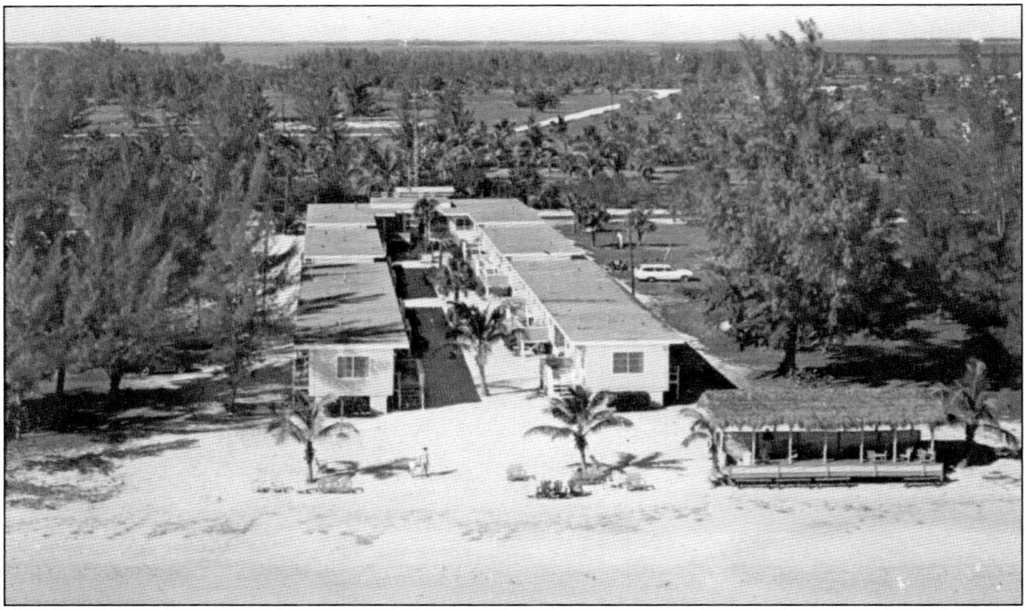

The Beachcomber Resort was an East Gulf Drive motel owned and operated by Carl and Myrtle Almas and Roly Frenette. Carl, concerned about limited access to his property, constructed a wooden bridge over Anchor Drive so vacationers would have a direct route to his motel. They sold the property in the 1980s, the cottages were removed, and Beachcomber Condominium was built in 1985. (Courtesy of Deborah Gleason collection.)

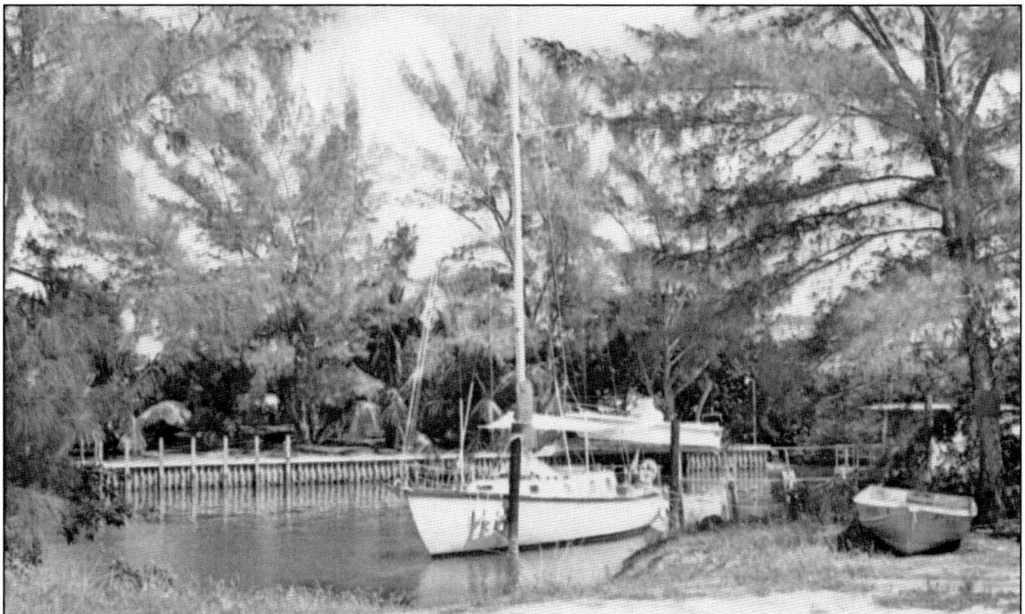

Sanibel Marina was built by Bill Way in 1959. Although the sloop pictured on this postcard portrays tranquility, the marina was the site of a tragedy in October 1960. An unusual tornado crossed over eastern Sanibel without damage until it touched down on the edge of the bay and picked up the marina building, which disintegrated over the water, killing Bill's employee, Freddie Purnell. (Courtesy of Deborah Gleason collection.)

Nine

A Refuge for Wildlife . . . and People

By 1900, the words "Sanibel-Captiva" were part of the American lexicon. Prosperous sportsmen and warmth-seekers had discovered the islands. The islands' reputation for seashell collecting, tarpon fishing, and solitude attracted affluent visitors. As on islands everywhere, the quality of life was different.

The wetlands, known as the Sanibel Slough, were unique. The grass-dominated marshes supported populations of resident and migratory wildlife—notably migratory birds. In the 1930s, an influx of conservation-inclined northerners joined with like-minded island residents and moved to protect wildlife and its habitat. During that decade, Jay Norwood "Ding" Darling, a nationally known conservationist and political cartoonist, visited from Iowa and became a Captiva Island property owner and winter resident. Darling used his high-level connections in government to get things done locally in the fields of land protection and wildlife conservation. By 1939, local efforts proved fruitful, and Sanibel and part of Captiva were designated as a State Wildlife Refuge by the Florida Legislature. Residents continued the fight, working toward federal involvement, and in 1945, Sanibel National Wildlife Refuge was established. Over time, the refuge grew, and in 1967, it was renamed J.N. "Ding" Darling National Wildlife Refuge to memorialize Darling's contributions nationally.

In the late 1960s, the US Fish and Wildlife Service made a commitment to connect wildlife values with outdoor recreation. Today, the facilities and public outreach programs at the refuge, including the privately funded Education Center and the concession operation at Tarpon Bay, continue this dual-purpose policy. Over 700,000 people now visit the refuge every year.

By the early 1970s, Lee County proposed zoning that would allow a population of 90,000 persons to inhabit and crowd the islands and stress invaluable natural systems. The people of Sanibel objected and voted to incorporate as a city so residents could choose their own dwelling unit density levels and their own future. In November 1974, voters unanimously broke from Lee County and the City of Sanibel was created. Captiva Island had earlier opted not to become part of a barrier island city and continues to be regulated by Lee County. Sanibel was saved by the wise citizens of that era.

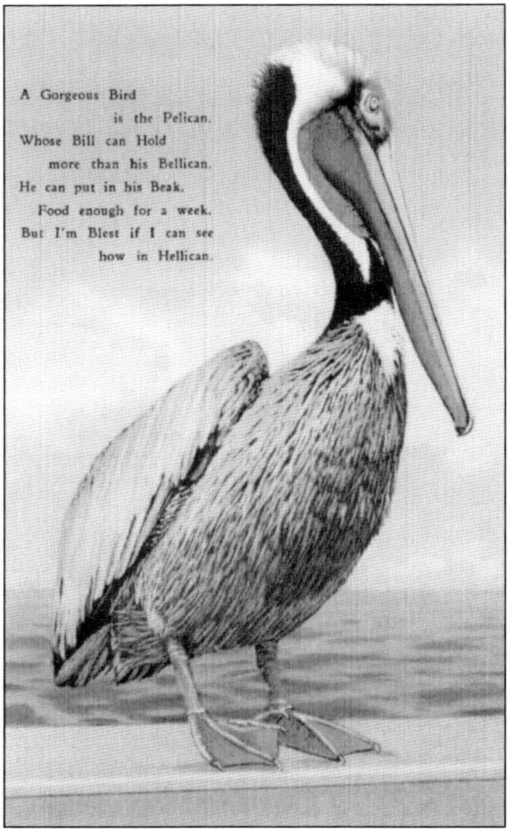

Over 250 species of birds have been recorded on Sanibel and Captiva Islands. For generations, the islands have been recognized as a "birders paradise." This reputation attracts tens of thousands of visitors to the islands each year. This postcard features the brown pelican and the ageless poem that best describes this strange-looking bird. (Courtesy of Deborah Gleason collection.)

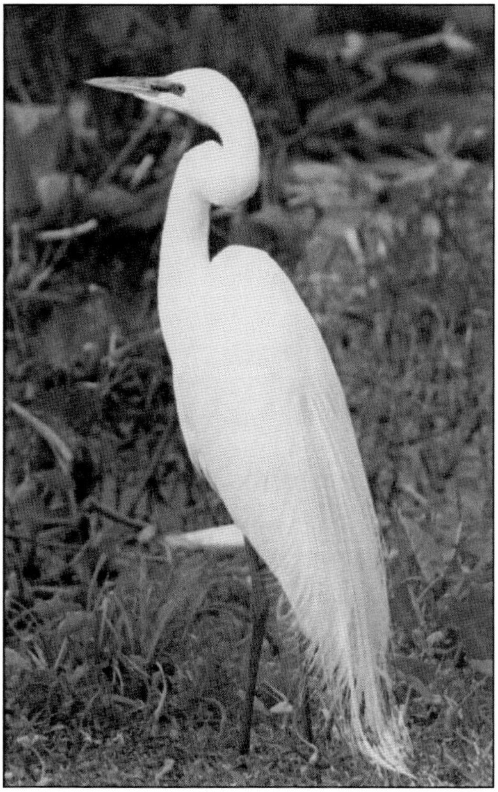

Once hunted to the brink of extinction for their lacelike plumes, the great egret pictured in this postcard is now a common bird on the islands. The plumes, or aigrettes, are part of their seasonal breeding plumage and are flowing over this bird's tail. Some great egrets, and their shorter relative the cattle egret, are often apt to stop traffic as they stalk Cuban anoles (common brown lizards) along island road shoulders. (Courtesy of Tom Hoopes.)

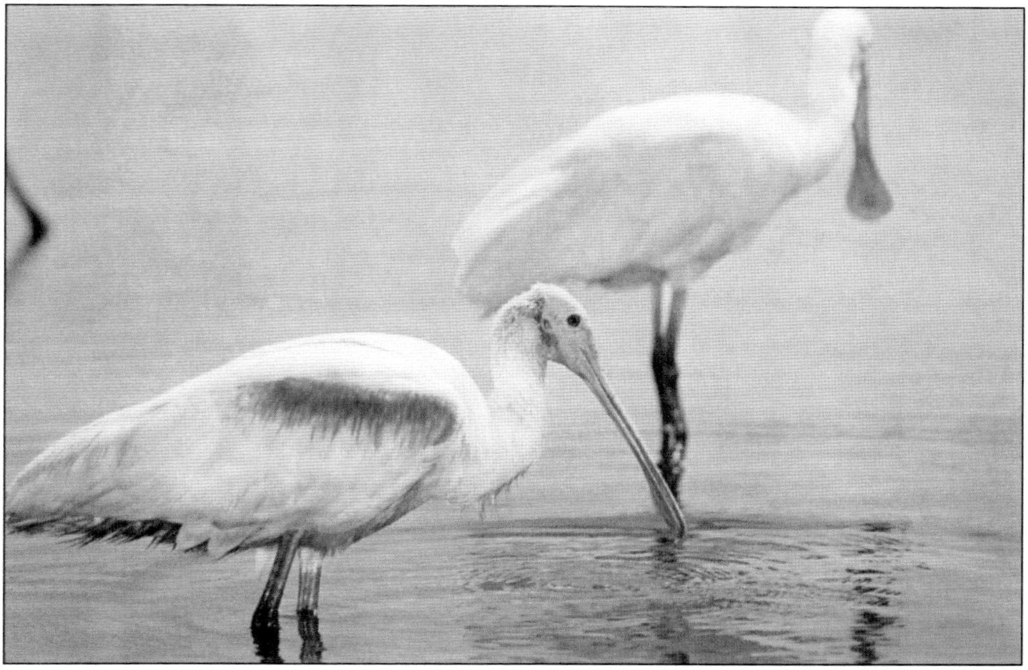

When first seen by bird identification novices, the roseate spoonbill (an adult and juvenile are pictured on this postcard) is often misidentified as a flamingo. Flamingos are not unknown on the islands, but they are considered extremely rare. The adult in the foreground is generally pink, has a crimson wing bar, and its head is completely bald. Spoonbills are quite common around the islands. (Courtesy of Deborah Gleason collection.)

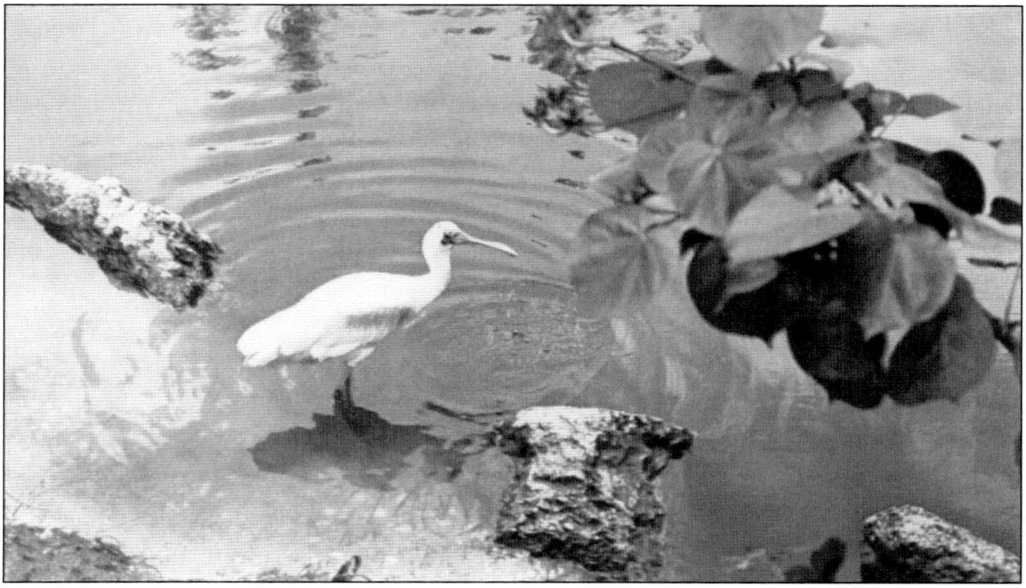

Although postcard photographers often take excellent photographs, they are not always as good or as special as they appear to be. This roseate spoonbill is a fine example of an adult, but it is not a wild bird. Since the 1960s, Sanibel's Periwinkle Park and Campground has exhibited a variety of captive birds, and this spoonbill was photographed there in the early 1970s inside one of their fenced ponds. (Courtesy of Ralph Curtis.)

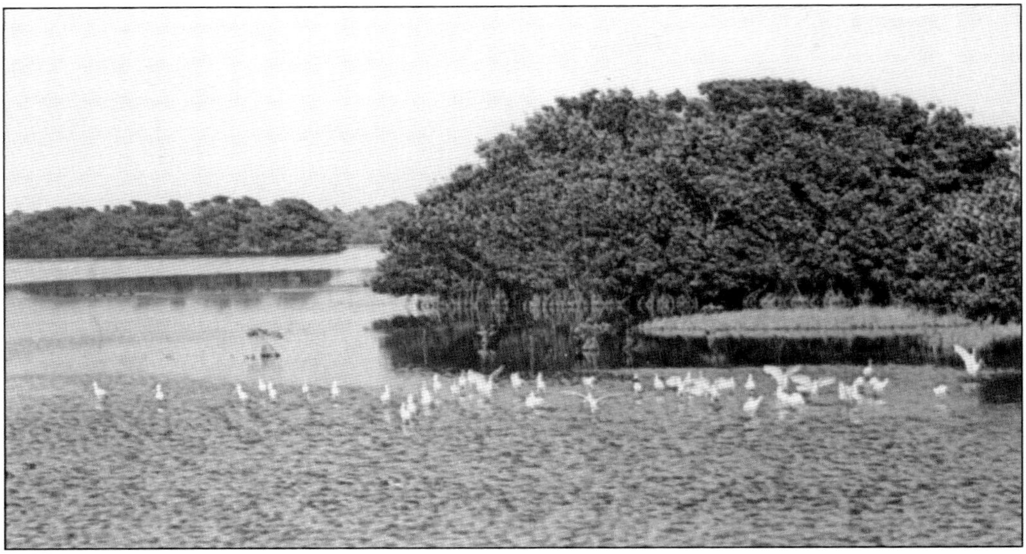

Spoonbills rest and forage on the tidal flats at J.N. "Ding" Darling National Wildlife Refuge on this postcard. Like the egrets, spoonbills were hunted close to extinction in the early 20th century for their feathers. They made a comeback and use the refuge year-round. Their unique feeding habits, displayed as they wade and swing their spatula-shaped bills from side to side, attract many serious and newcomer birdwatchers to the fast-growing hobby. (Courtesy of Ralph Curtis.)

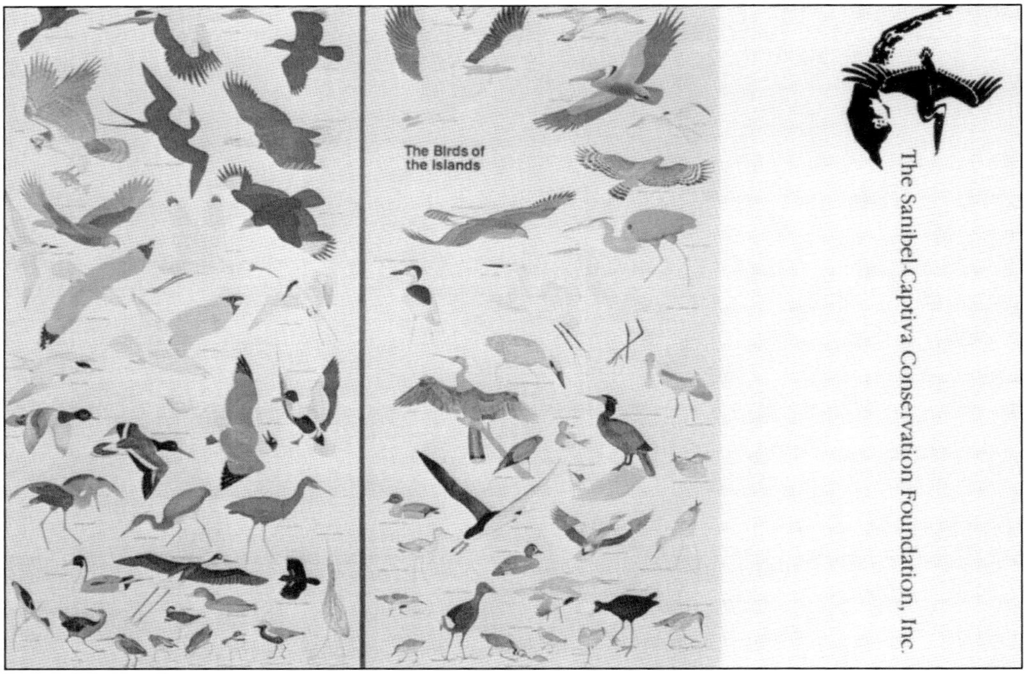

This bird-identification postcard was produced by the Sanibel-Captiva Conservation Foundation. This organization was formed in 1967 and continues to spearhead land acquisition on and around the islands for habitat protection and wildlife conservation purposes. In 2012, their most recent acquisition was Sanibel's Bailey Homestead. Their Nature Center and walking trails on Sanibel-Captiva Road offer visitors a quality experience and a better understanding of what these barrier islands are all about. (Courtesy of Tom Hoopes.)

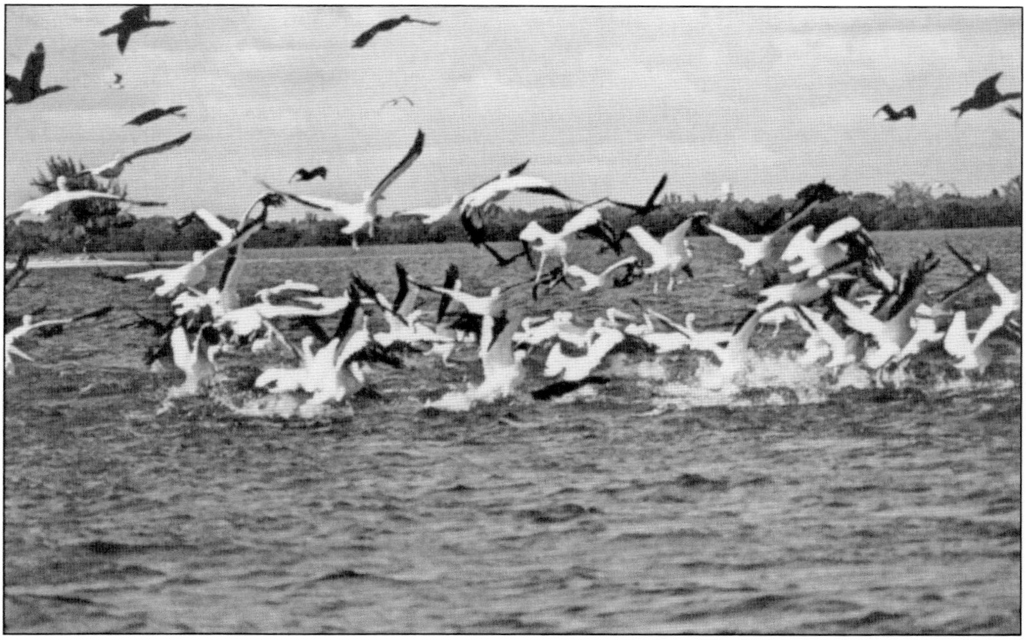

Migratory white pelicans are featured on this postcard. The original photograph was taken in upper Pine Island Sound. The Cabbage Key water tower is visible just above the mangroves. The wintering population of white pelicans around the islands has continued to grow through the years. In the spring, they migrate diagonally back across the United States to breed in the Northwest. (Courtesy of Sanibel Historical Museum and Village.)

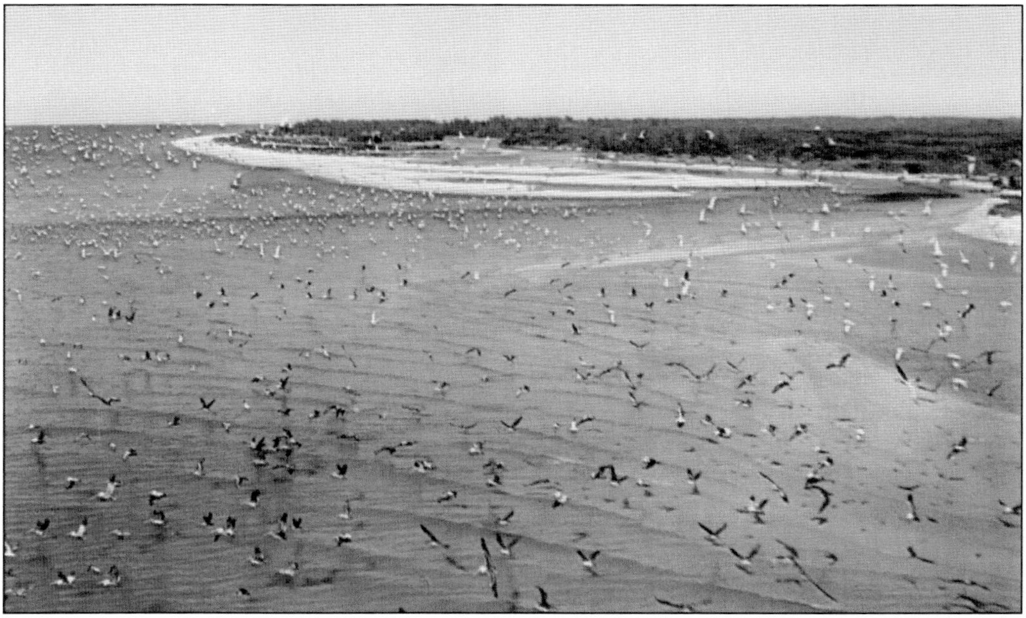

This postcard photograph was taken at the mouth of Blind Pass in the late 1950s, when the opening was located three miles south of the Blind Pass Bridge. Few people walked this beach in those days, and it provided undisturbed resting and nesting habitat for a multitude of bird species. Today, this area is called Bowman's Beach, and it is routinely crowded by people to the detriment of birdlife. (Courtesy of Charles LeBuff collection.)

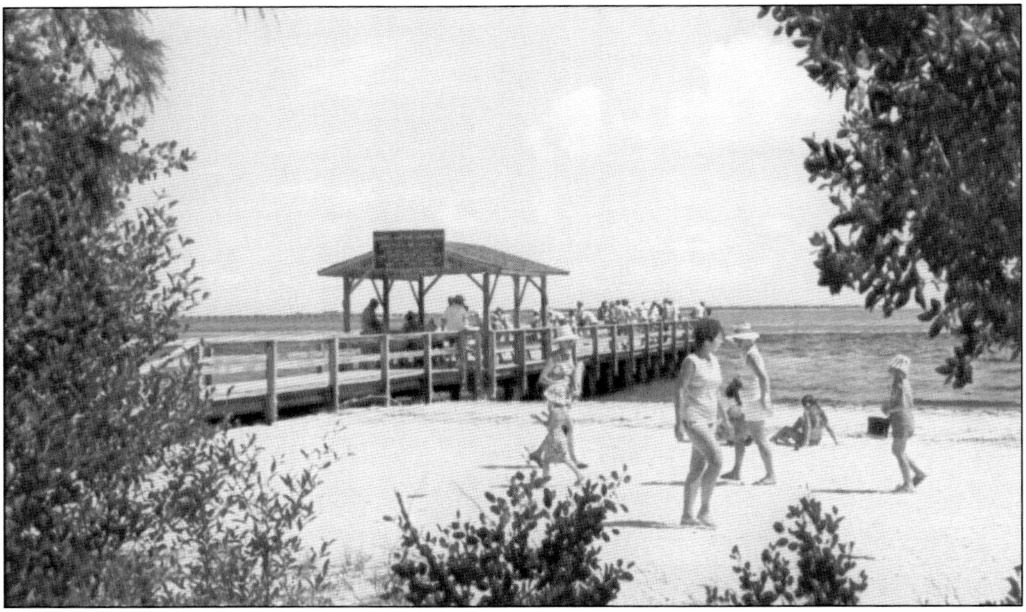

One of the refuge's amenities, when its headquarters was at Point Ybel, was the public fishing pier. This postcard features the new pier after construction in 1972. Today, the popular pier remains a fine example of outdoor recreation and attracts anglers from all over Southwest Florida. It provides a great spot for winter visitors to test their skill and sample the area's fisheries. It has since been rebuilt by the City of Sanibel. (Courtesy of Deborah Gleason collection.)

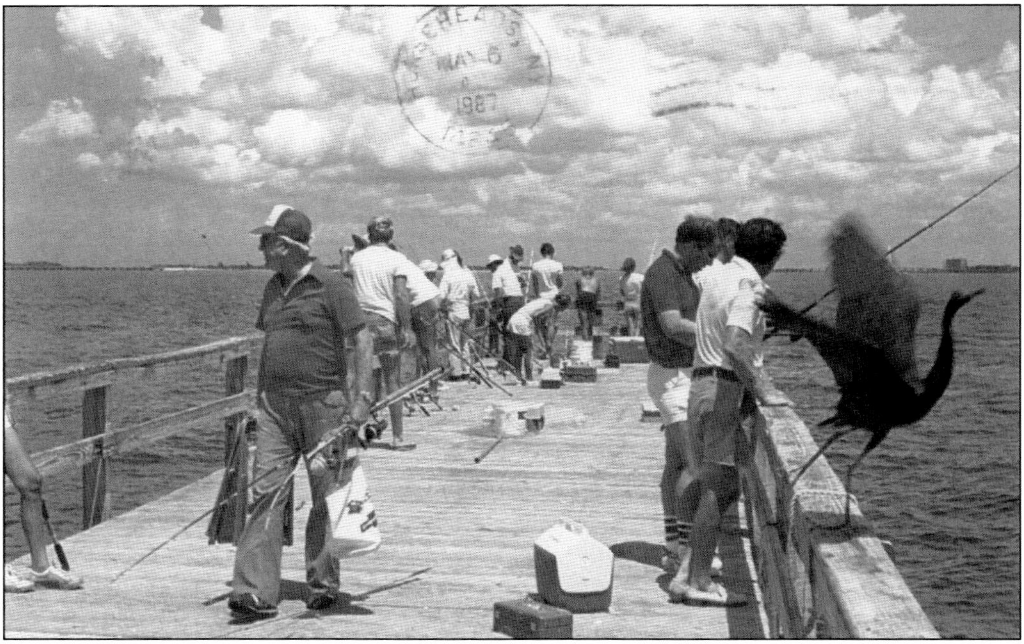

The Sanibel pier also attracts wildlife, as attested by this little blue heron flying away from the handrail. Some birds learned early that by hanging around the pier they could get handouts of fish scraps or unused bait. Bird entanglements with monofilament fishing line remain a serious problem; fishermen are expected to be responsible and should safely dispose of line to reduce unnecessary bird injuries. (Courtesy of Ralph Curtis.)

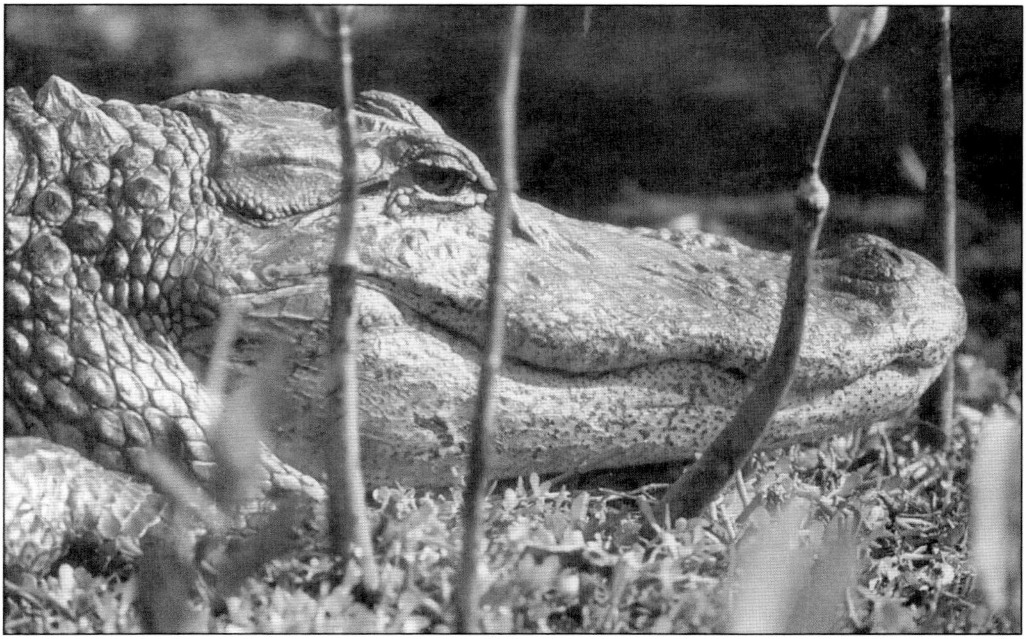

This postcard features a resting American alligator along Wildlife Drive in J. N. "Ding" Darling National Wildlife Refuge. Alligators are dangerous. Never approach them closely. There have been two fatalities on Sanibel in recent years because of alligator attacks. Alligators must never be fed because they lose their fear of man. (Courtesy of Sanibel Historical Museum and Village.)

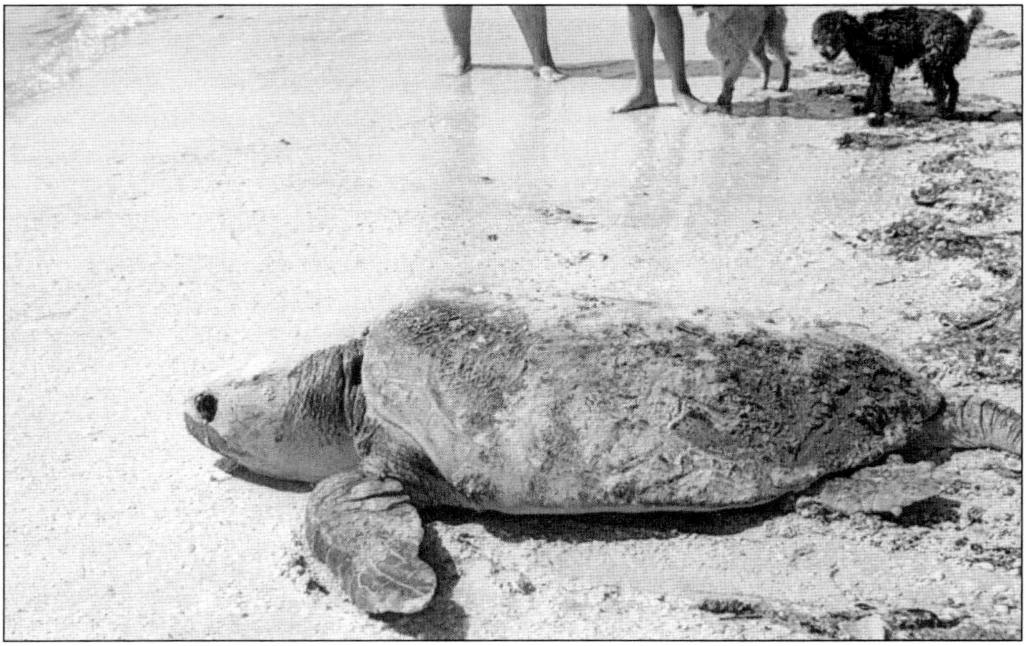

This adult male loggerhead sea turtle was rescued in 1969 by coauthor Charles LeBuff and brought to the lighthouse, tagged, and released (the legs on the right are his wife Jean's and the soggy poodles were theirs). A photographer happened on the release and snapped this photograph. A few years later, this postcard was being sold in island shops. Sea turtle conservation activities have been ongoing on the islands for decades. (Courtesy of Charles LeBuff collection.)

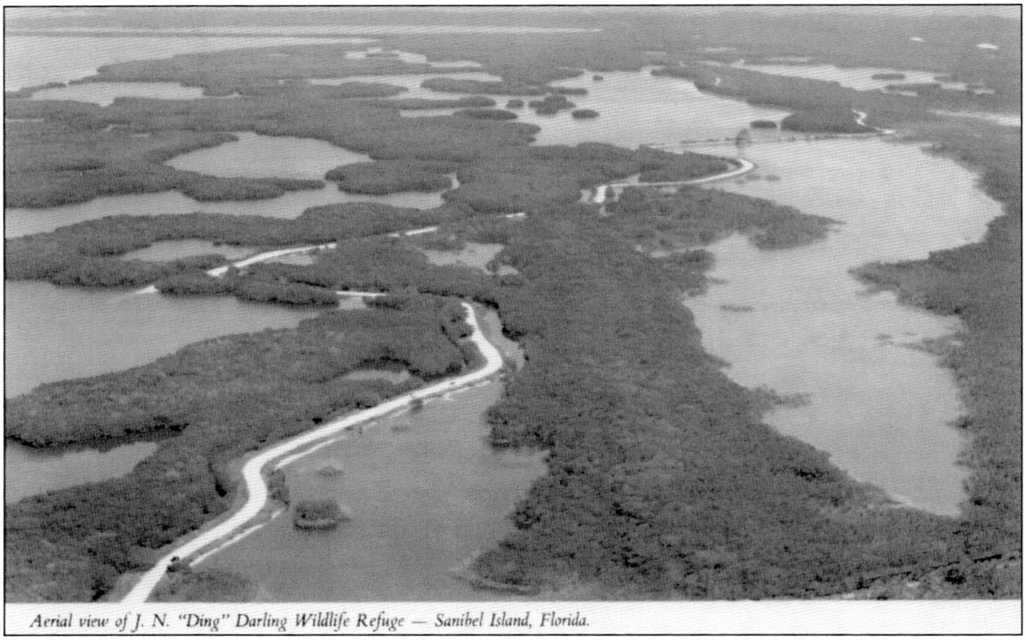

An aerial view faces east over J.N. "Ding" Darling National Wildlife Refuge in this 1970 postcard. This popular drive was originally designed as a mosquito control dike with the purpose of flooding wetlands to help prevent salt marsh mosquitoes from depositing their eggs on the sand. The white speck of beach, to the left of the center, is Colon's Point. The West Impoundment is to the right. (Courtesy of Tom Hoopes.)

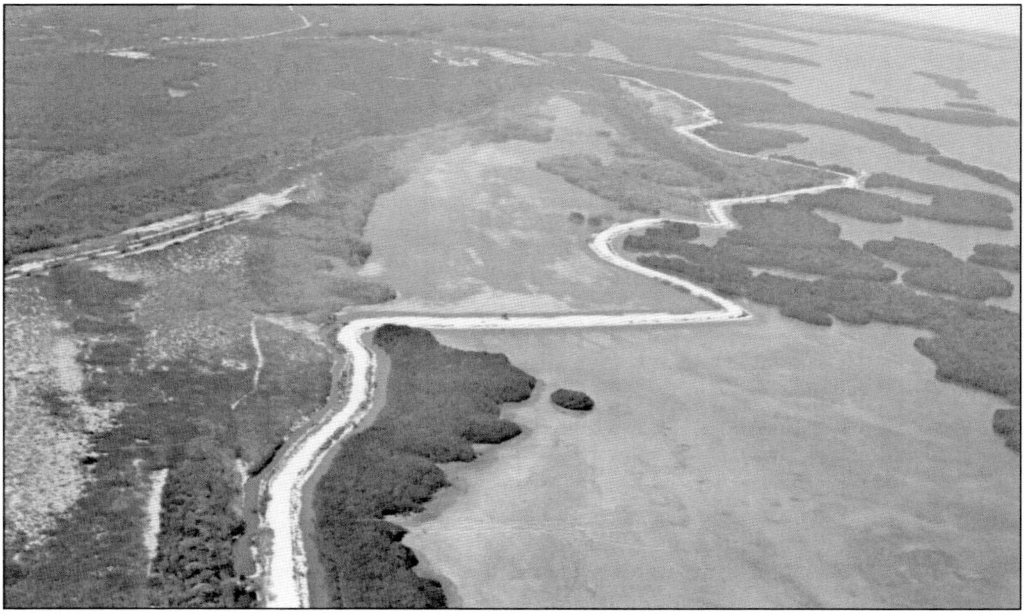

This west-facing aerial postcard shows the refuge drive at a time when the edges of the dike were routinely trimmed with machinery. By the mid-1970s, this management technique used by the refuge was changed, and thereafter, woody vegetation was allowed to prevail. Today, the berms of the dike are densely vegetated except for the limited number of observation windows that are kept trimmed for wildlife viewing. (Courtesy of Tom Hoopes.)

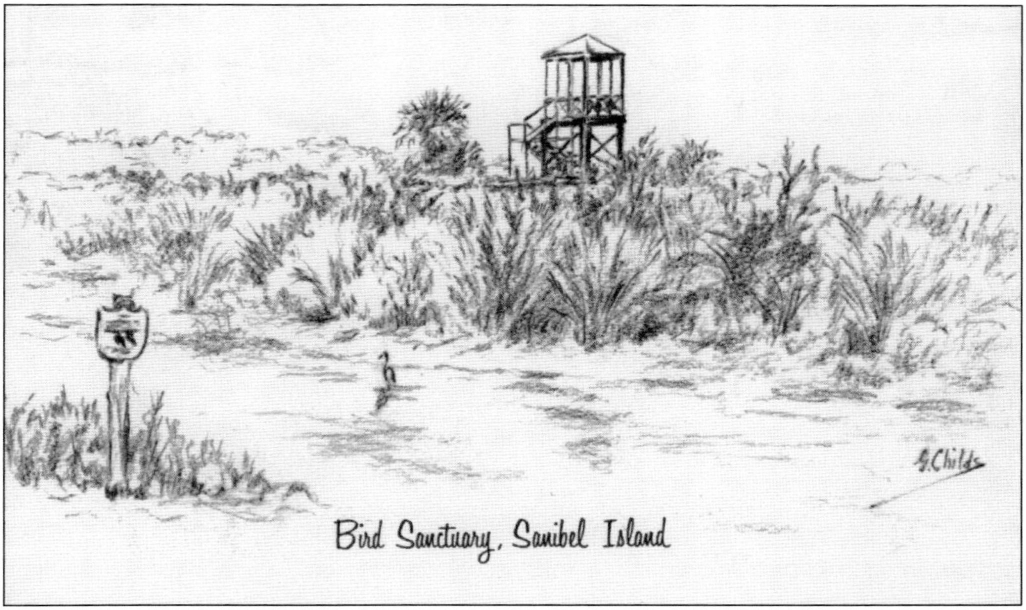

Gladys Childs captured the essence of the refuge's 100-acre Bailey Tract with this rendition. This observation tower, called the Bird Tower, was built by the US Fish and Wildlife Service in 1954 and provided a panorama of the Sanibel Slough. Before tall Australian pines blocked the vista, one could stand on the top platform of this tower and see the lighthouse four miles to the east. The tower was demolished in 1976. (Courtesy of Deborah Gleason collection.)

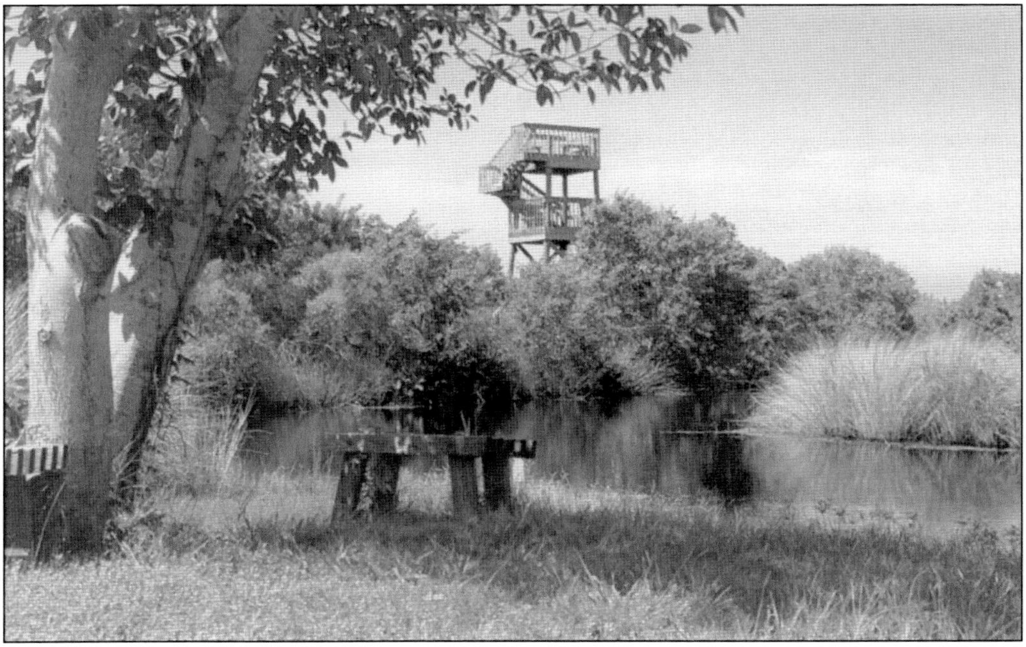

The observation tower near the Sanibel-Captiva Conservation Foundation's Visitor Center stands beside the Sanibel River and provides an overlook of the waterway. Originally, this "river" flowed into the Gulf of Mexico when the interior wetlands of Sanibel were flooded by rainfall to overflow capacity. The water would break through the beach at the island's eastern end and drain away. (Courtesy of Deborah Gleason collection.)

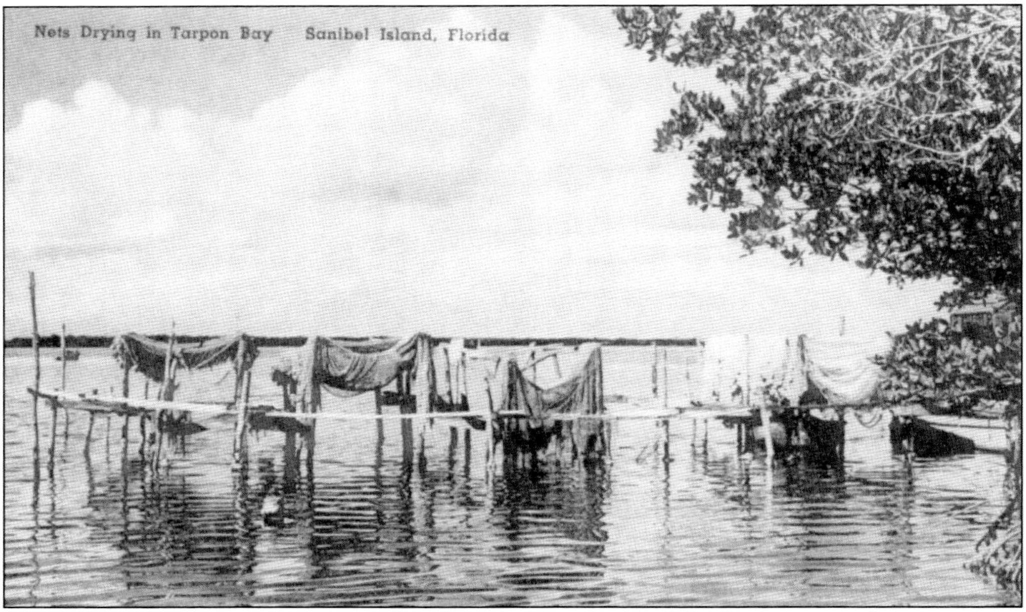

Tarpon Bay was a once a center for agricultural shipments and a base for commercial fishing. This early-1930s postcard shows net drying racks. Gill nets in that day were made of cotton and linen, covered with lime, and air-dried to avoid rot. When gill-netting was banned in Florida in 1995, nets were made from rot-resistant nylon and monofilament. (Courtesy of Sanibel Public Library.)

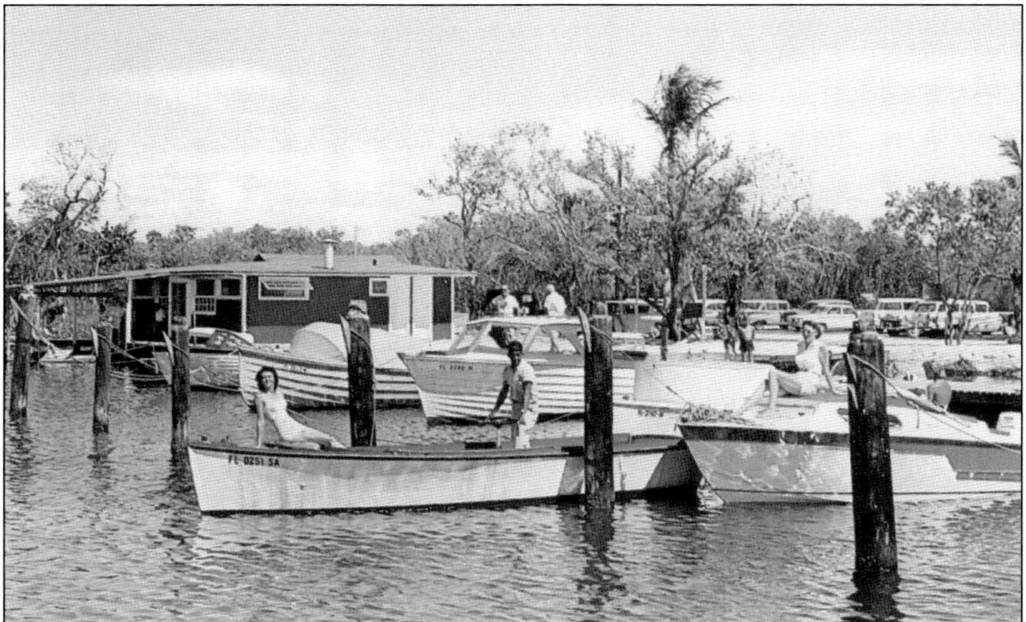

This postcard from the early 1960s depicts the Casa Ybel Marina on Tarpon Bay. The man standing in the boat is marina manager Dewey Miller. Soon after this photograph was taken, Dewey bought land from Clarence Rutland and opened his own marina a few hundred yards east of where this picture was taken. Eventually the US Fish and Wildlife Service bought both marinas and closed Dewey's. (Courtesy of Charles LeBuff collection.)

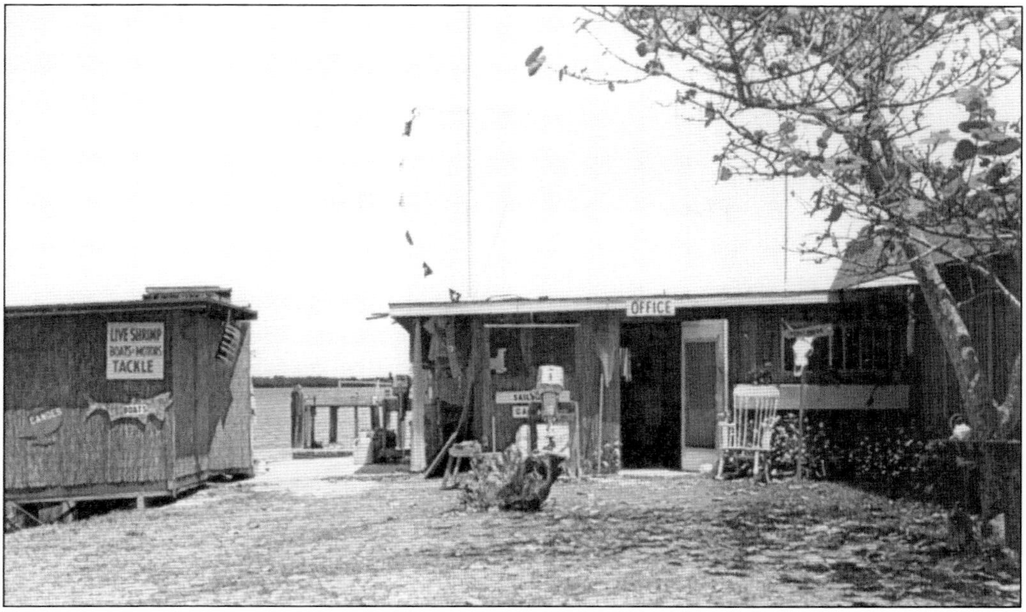

The old Florida look of Tarpon Bay Marina was immortalized on this postcard. This is the Dinkin's Bay Marina, described in the Doc Ford novels created by local author Randy Wayne White. Randy, once a popular guide, chartered fishing trips from this marina, and many of the characters in his books are based on the real people whom he befriended and worked with here. (Courtesy of Deborah Gleason collection.)

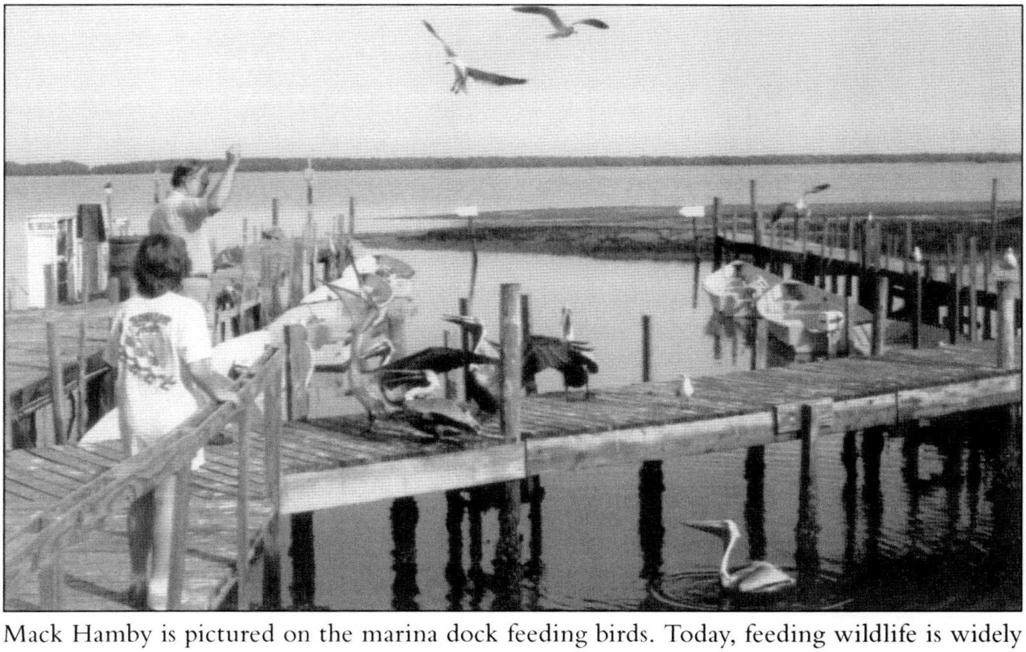

Mack Hamby is pictured on the marina dock feeding birds. Today, feeding wildlife is widely discouraged. Mack leased the marina from the US Fish and Wildlife Service, changing the name from Casa Ybel Marina to Tarpon Bay Marina. Doc Ford's Dinkin's Bay is in the background. Today, this marina is a refuge concession operated by Tarpon Bay Explorers. To kayak on the nearby Commodore Reed Creek Canoe Trail is a must for visitors. (Courtesy of Deborah Gleason collection.)

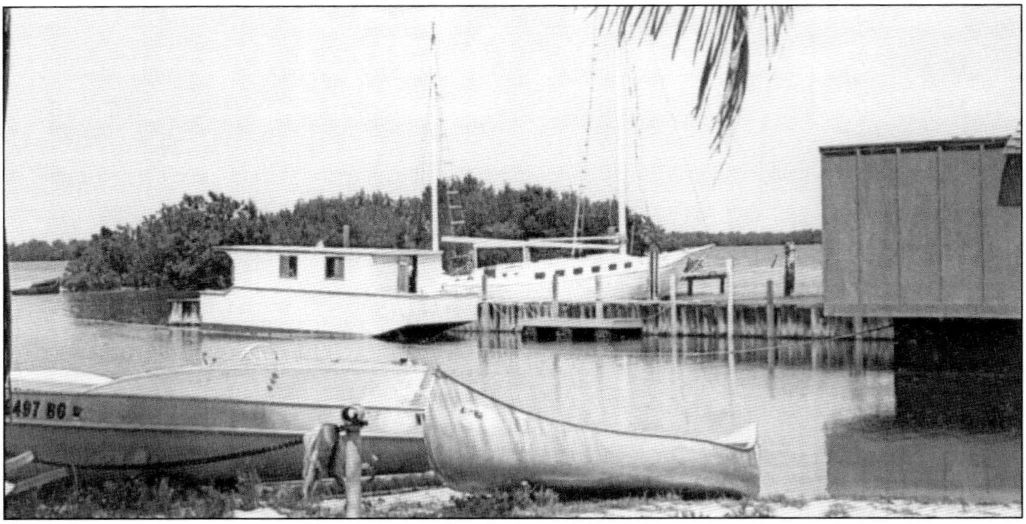

Although deep-draft vessels often had a hard time reaching the marina from Pine Island Sound, Tarpon Bay Marina was once a popular spot for boaters. This late-1960s postcard shows some of the live-aboard boats that berthed at the marina. When Tarpon Bay and Dewey's Marinas left the shore of Tarpon Bay, much of the island's charm went with them and can no longer be appreciated. (Courtesy of Tom Hoopes.)

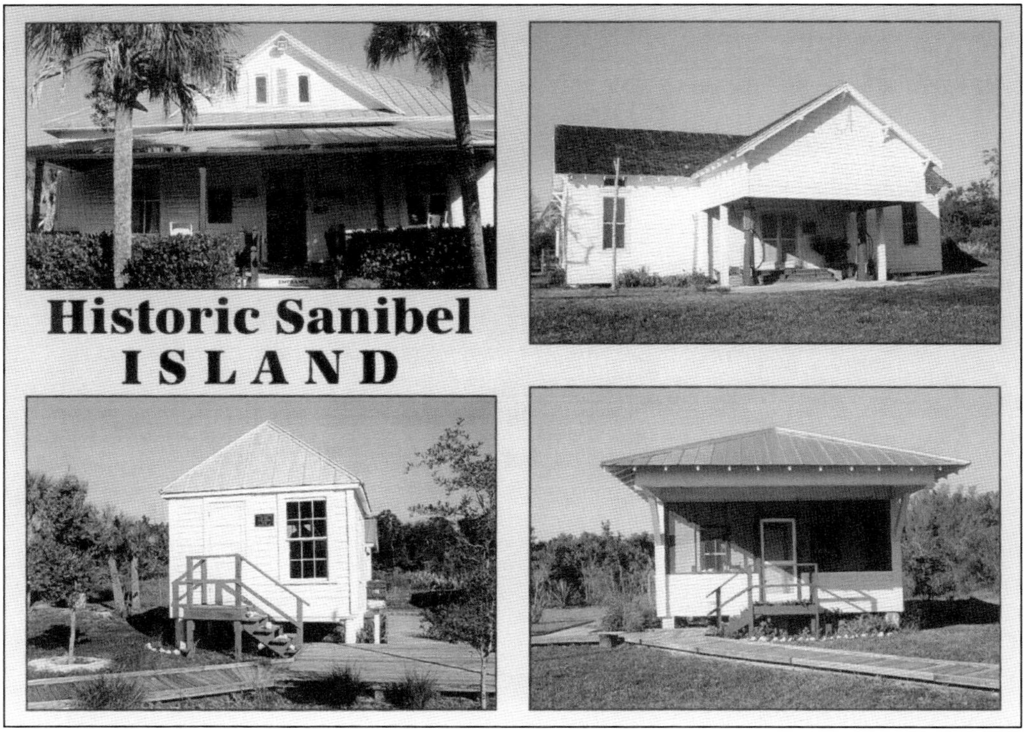

The Sanibel Historical Museum and Village is a must-see stop for all island visitors, and residents should visit the facility regularly. All should support its continued operation through membership. The history of these islands is important to local culture and celebrates the lives and the times of those who lived here before us. This postcard features four of the several historic buildings that have been moved to the village. (Courtesy of Gerri Much.)

Further Reading

Anholt, Betty. *Sanibel's Story: From Calusa to Incorporation.* City of Sanibel, FL, 1998.

Captiva Civic Association. *Voices From the Past . . . True Tales of Old Captiva.* Fort Myers, FL: Sutherland Publishing, 1984.

Doremus, Sharon M. *Shorebirds & Seagrapes.* Exeter, NH: J.N. Townsend Publishing, 1995.

Dormer, Elinore. *The Seashell Islands: A History of Sanibel and Captiva.* New York, NY: Vantage Press, 1975.

Fritz, Florence. *The Unknown Story of Sanibel and Captiva (Ybel y Cautivo).* Parsons, WV: McClain Printing, 1974.

Hill, Yvonne, and Marguerite Jordan, et al. *Sanibel Island.* Charleston, SC: Arcadia Publishing, 2008.

LeBuff, Charles. *Sanybel Light: An Historical Autobiography.* Fort Myers, FL: Amber Publishing, 1998.

———. *The Calusan.* (Kindle and Nook eBook editions available) Fort Myers, FL: Amber Publishing, 2004.

———. *J.N. "Ding" Darling National Wildlife Refuge.* Charleston, SC: Arcadia Publishing, 2011.

Levering, Ted. *The Other Side of the Bridge.* Fort Myers. FL: Willowmead Publishing, 1991

Magg, Jeri. *Historical Sanibel and Captiva Islands: Tales of Paradise.* Charleston, SC: The History Press, 2011

Repko, Marya. *A Brief History of Sanibel Island.* Everglades City, FL: ECity Publishing, 2010.

Sabatino, Robert. *Every Day is Saturday.* Sanibel, FL: Fish-Hawk Publishing, 2008.

Stone, Lynn. *Sanibel Island.* Minneapolis, MN: Voyageur Press, 1991.

Tuttle, Louise Carr. *Homes of Old Captiva.* Captiva, FL: Captiva Memorial Library Board, 2001.